SCIENCE COMICS

SOLAR SYSTEM

Our Place in Space

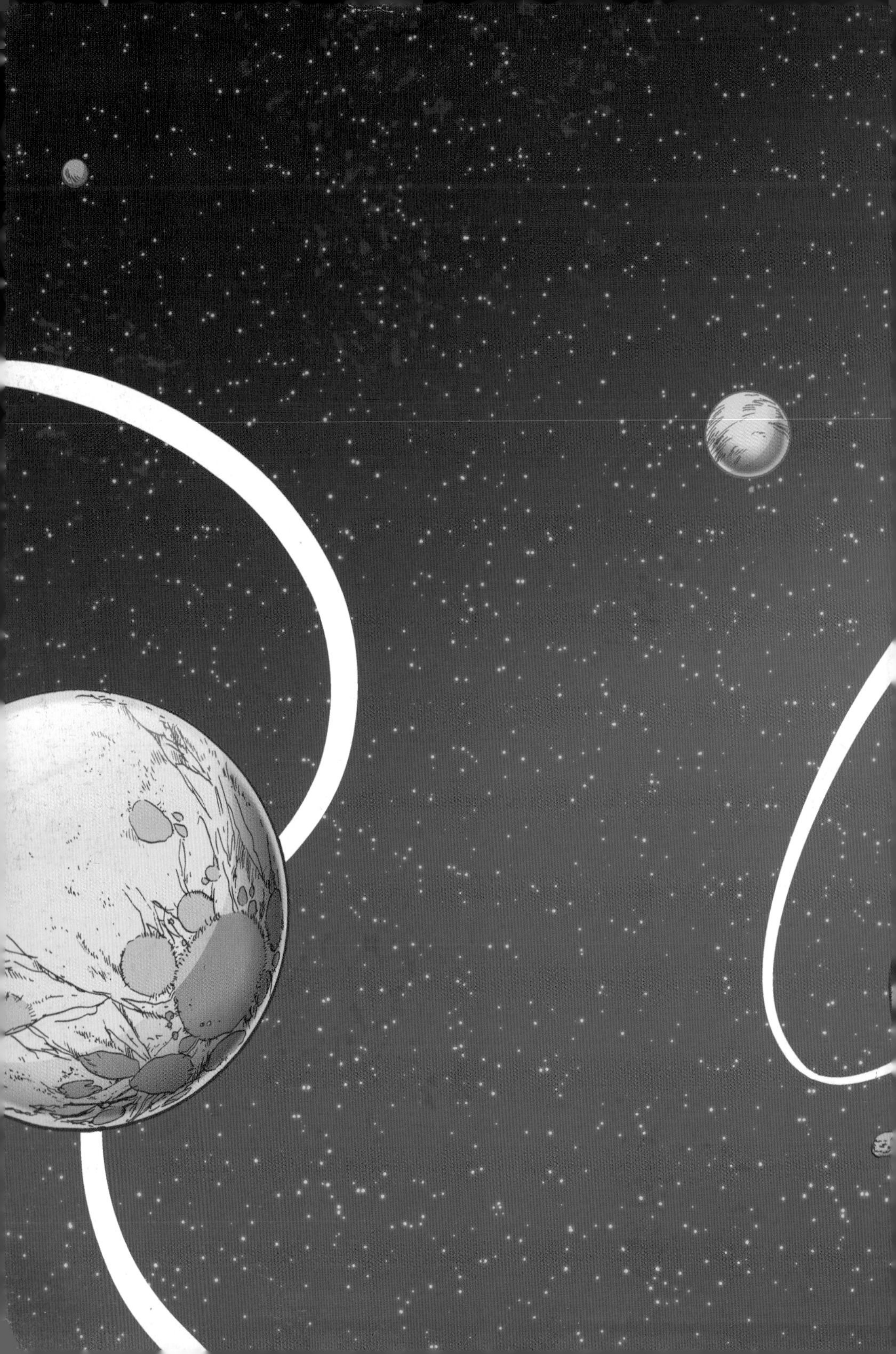

SOLAR SYSTEM

Our Place in Space

ROSEMARY MOSCO
and
JON CHAD

with color by
Luke Healy

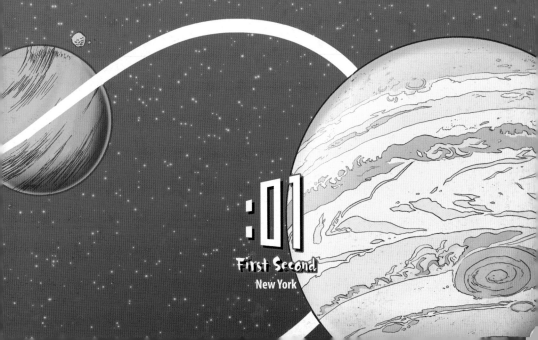

:01
First Second
New York

First Second

Drawn on Strathmore 400-series 2-ply smooth bristol board with a Staedtler 4H pencil. The panel borders were drawn on Clip Studio Pro and the drawings were inked with a combination of Sakura Micron Pens sizes 08, 05, 03, 02, and 005, and an assortment of drawing nibs including the Hunt 102 Crow Quill, the 107 Hawk Quill, the Tachikawa No. 5 School Pen, and the Tachikawa G-Pen, all dipped in Speedball Superblack ink. Colored using Adobe Photoshop.

Published by First Second
First Second is an imprint of Roaring Brook Press,
a division of Holtzbrinck Publishing Holdings Limited Partnership
175 Fifth Avenue, New York, NY 10010

Library of Congress Congress Control Number: 2017957415

Paperback ISBN 978-1-62672-141-8
Hardcover ISBN 978-1-62672-142-5

Our books may be purchased in bulk for promotional, educational, or business use. Please contact your local bookseller or the Macmillan Corporate and Premium Sales Department at (800) 221-7945 ext. 5442 or by e-mail at MacmillanSpecialMarkets@macmillan.com.

First edition, 2018
Edited by Casey Gonzalez
Book design by Jon Chad and John Green
Solar System consultant: Emily Lakdawalla

Printed in China by Toppan Leefung Printing Ltd., Dongguan City, Guangdong Province
Paperback: 10 9 8 7 6 5 4 3 2 1
Hardcover: 10 9 8 7 6 5 4 3 2 1

When I was a kid—back when the Universe was younger, and (GASP) we didn't have the Internet—I used to dream of flying a spaceship to all the objects in our Solar System.

Sometimes in those fantasies I was the captain, and sometimes I was the science officer (I watched a lot of *Star Trek*, which we did have back then), but I always loved to travel in my mind to those weird and wonderful worlds: planets, moons, asteroids, comets . . .

When I think back on that now, I'm not sure if my memories of it are fuzzy or if my imagination was. After all, from Earth, most of those astronomical destinations are hundreds of millions of miles away, and even our best telescopes of the time didn't give us a lot of detail. We could see that Jupiter had stripes, and Saturn had some rings, but the images were blurry. It was hard to tell what was really going on.

But maybe your imagination is better than mine! Can you close your eyes and dream of yourself standing on, say, Venus (with a really good space suit), zooming over the Moon, or whizzing your way through the asteroid belt? What would that be like? How would it feel?

You have a big advantage over me from when I was a kid: our technology is far better now. We have better telescopes and spacecraft to send robots to those distant places in space. When I saw these worlds up close, I found out they're way stranger than what we imagined. Volcanoes on tiny frigid moons spew water instead of lava! Giant chunks of ice orbit the Sun far past Neptune! Mars has dry riverbeds, which means it had flowing water on its surface in the past! Saturn's rings are made of thousands and thousands of narrow ringlets! Did you know that asteroids can have their own moons or that diamonds form inside Uranus?

These are fantastic discoveries, and they're nothing at all like what I imagined or what I dreamed of back then.

So, do you think you can outimagine nature? I'll warn you: it's not easy. Nature is clever, and has all of science at its disposal. It's had billions of years and a million, million places to test out ideas. That means there are lots of things out in space that will seem strange, even bizarre to us. And that's just what we find! Everywhere we go in space, everything we see . . . it's all wonderful and so different from what we thought it would be. The Solar System isn't just weirder than we imagined, but (to borrow a phrase from the scientist J. B. S. Haldane), it's weirder than we *could* imagine. Whenever we go somewhere new, we find things we didn't expect.

That's why I like this book by my friend Rosemary Mosco. Her imagination is better than mine, and she loves science and space. The travels her characters go on are a lot like the ones I dreamed of, but now we know so much more about the Solar System, so they can really have fun experiencing those journeys. And Jon Chad's artwork makes it feel even more real.

And let me tell you a secret, something scientists know very well, but maybe other people don't understand: we'll never run out of adventures. It's true! We've learned a bunch of cool things about all these worlds since I was a kid, but we're not running out of things to know. We can't! That's the wonderful nature of science: there's always more to learn, more to find out.

The Universe is like a puzzle spread out across the sky, and who could ever face a puzzle like that and not want to try to get the pieces to fit? That's what scientists do, and when we do it, we find that there are more pieces to play with, more places to discover, and more ideas to understand. The universal puzzle is one that never ends. The more you explore, the more there is to explore.

But you have to start somewhere, right?

So here's how you start: turn the page.

—Dr. Phil Plait,
Astronomer and Founder of Bad Astronomy

PART 1: INTRODUCTION

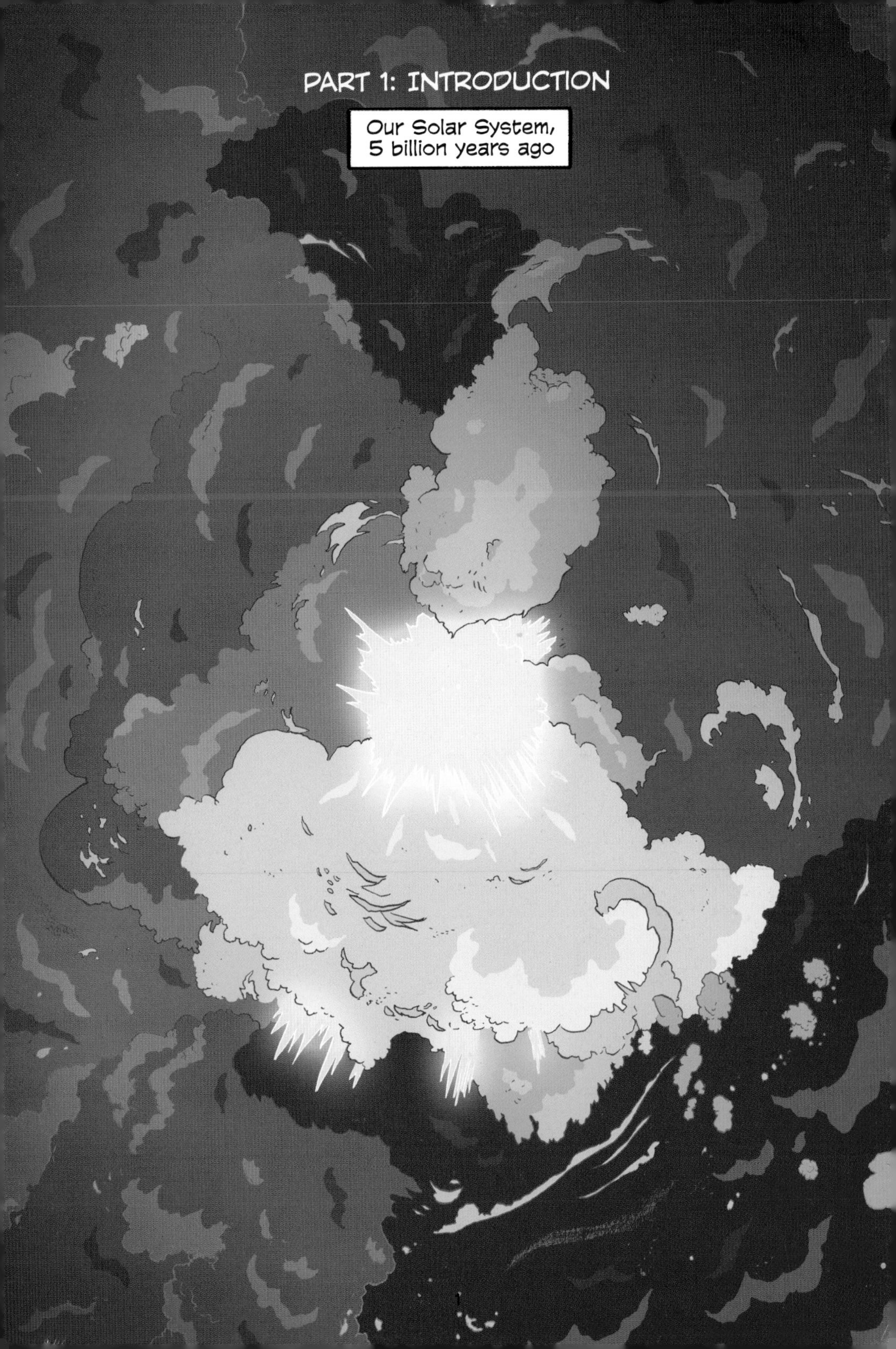
Our Solar System,
5 billion years ago

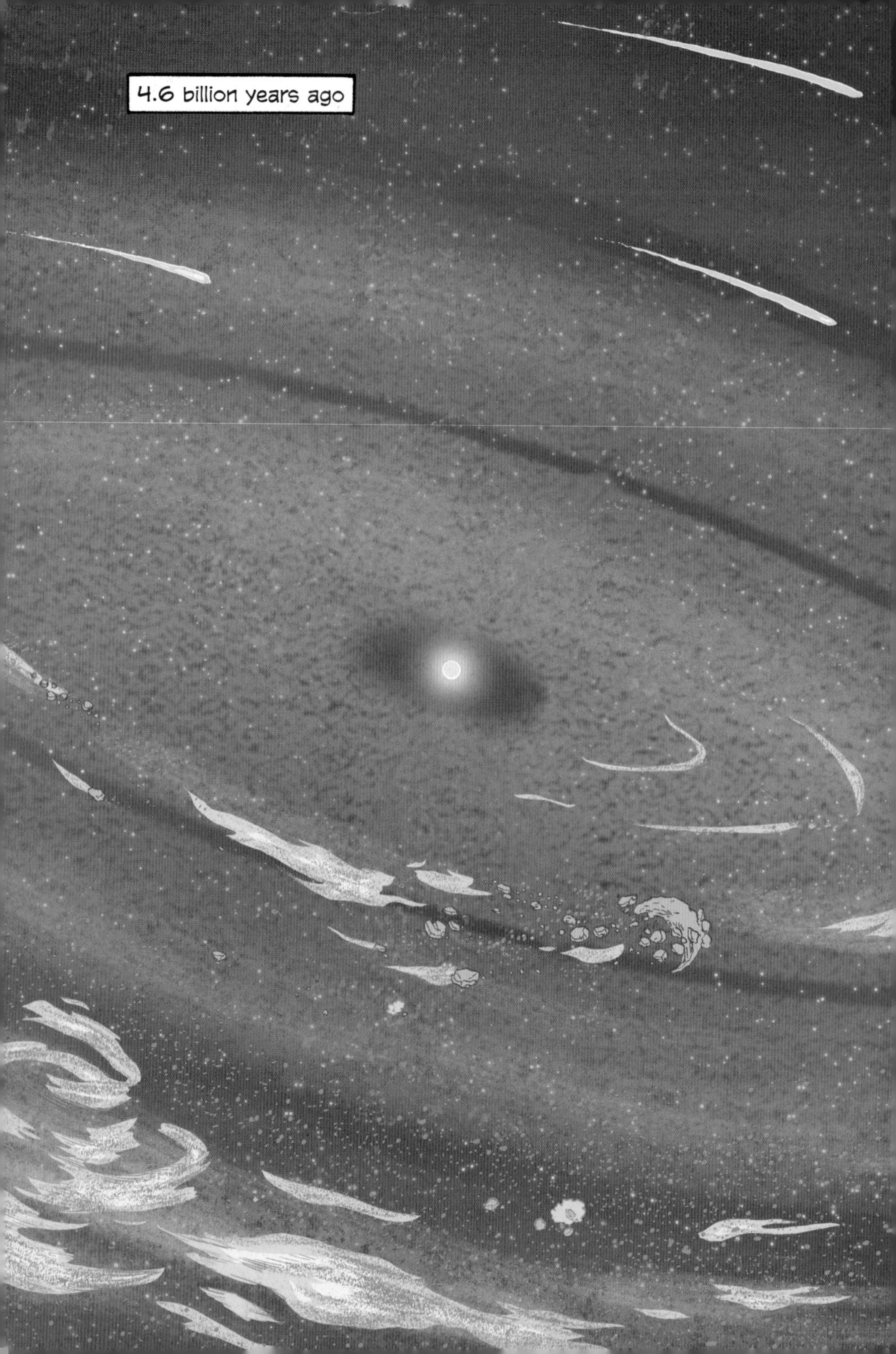
4.6 billion years ago

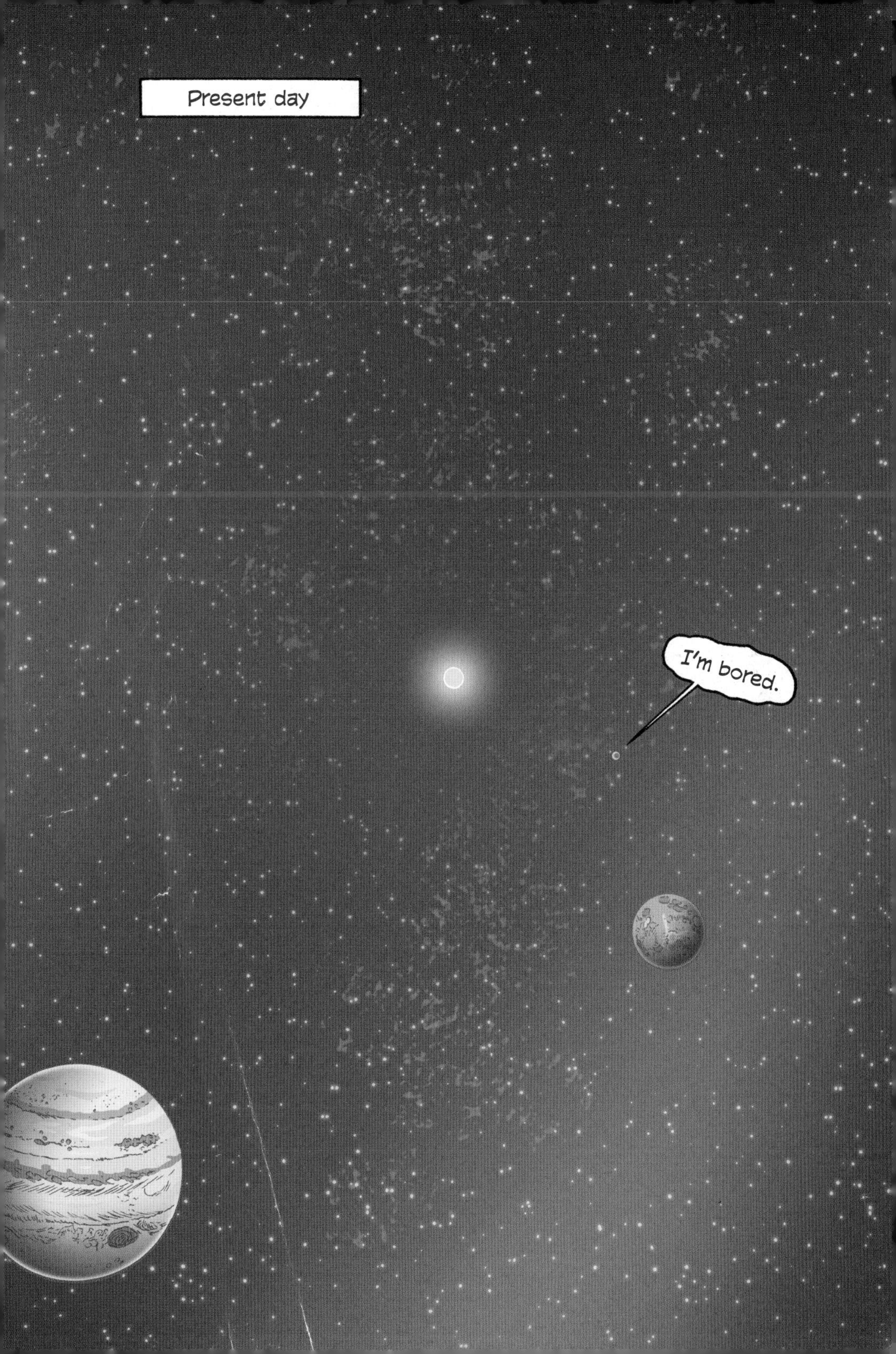
Present day
I'm bored.

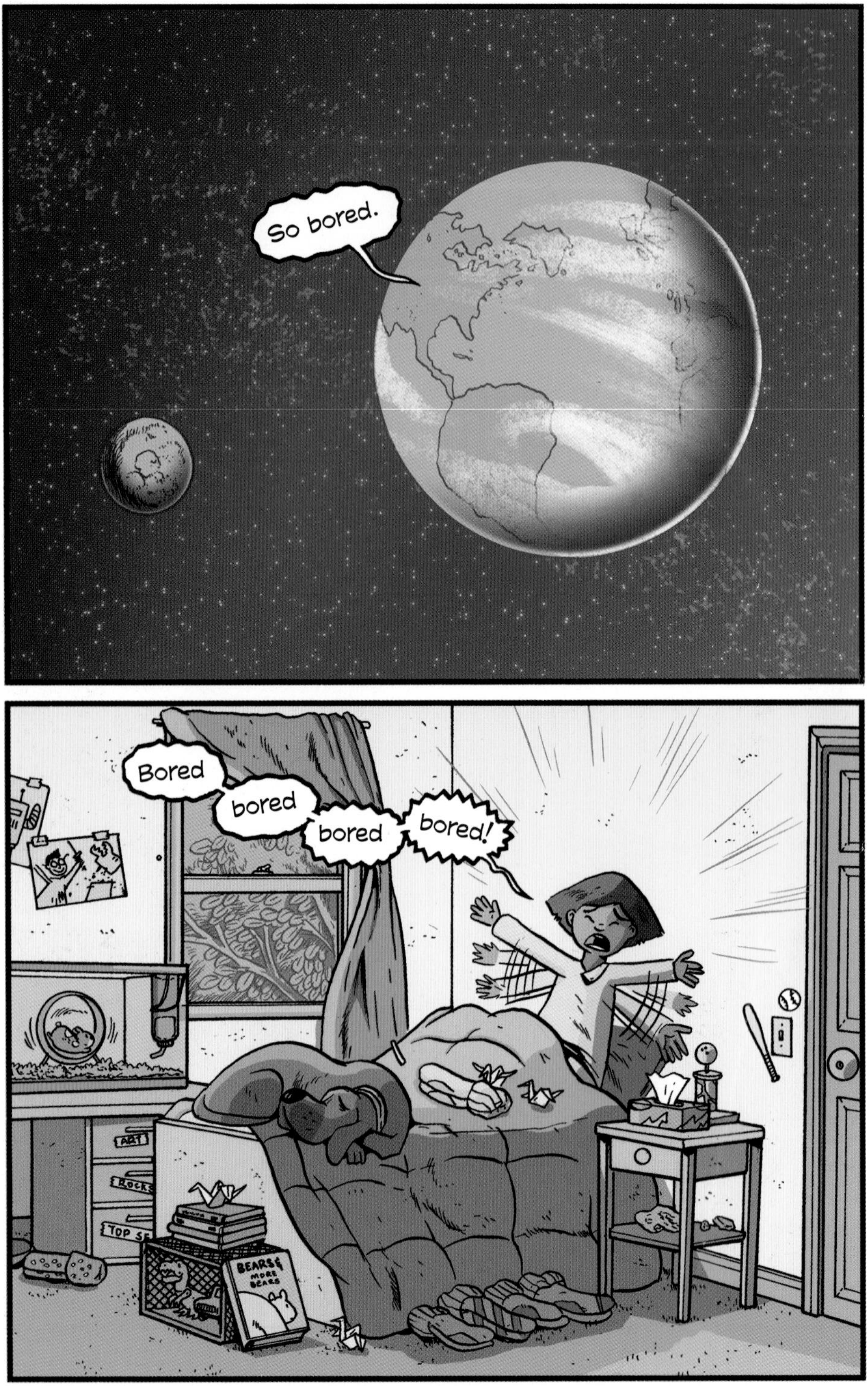
So bored.
Bored
bored
bored
bored!
ART
ROCKS
TOP SE
BEARS & MORE BEARS

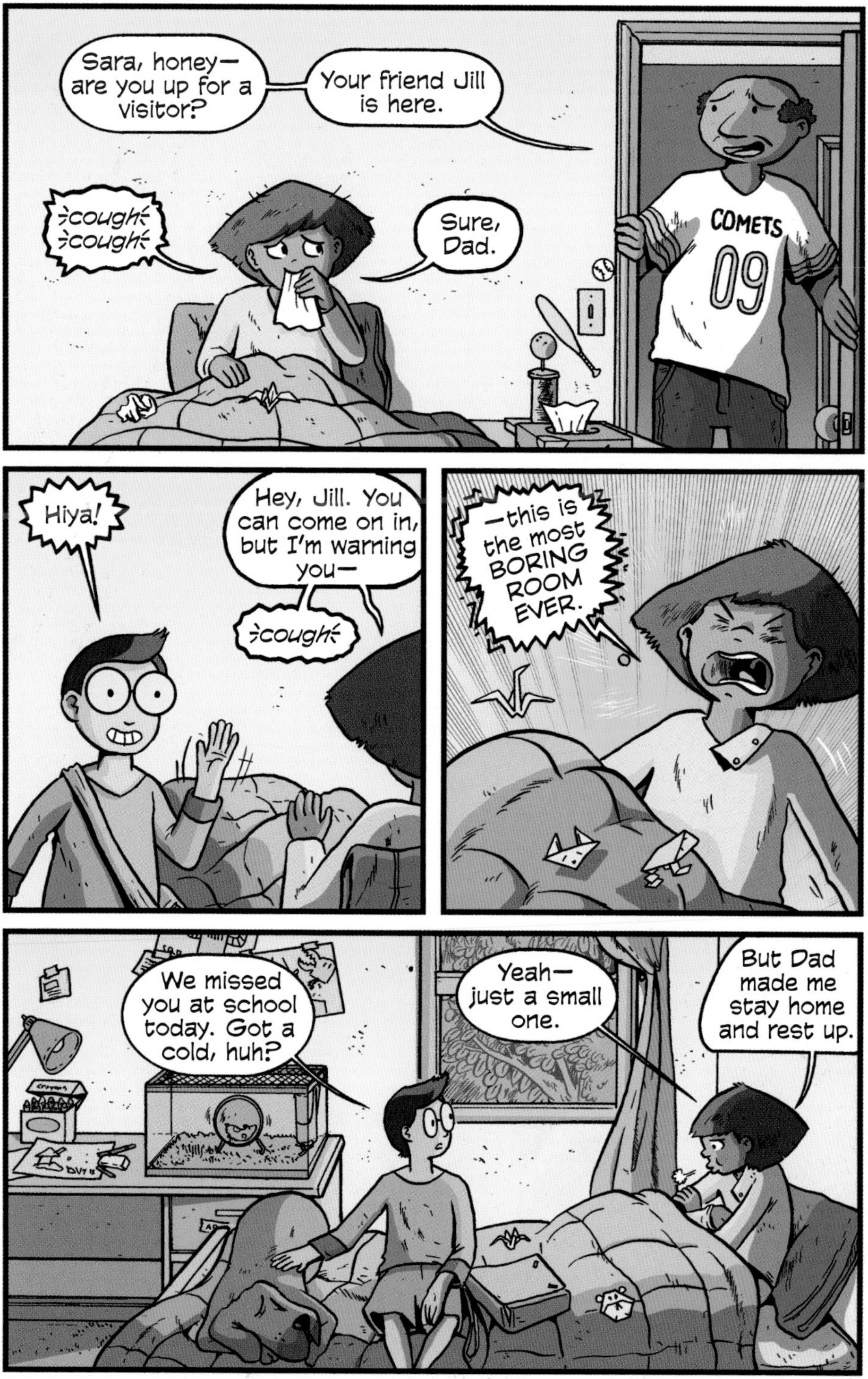
Sara, honey— are you up for a visitor?
Your friend Jill is here.
COMETS 09
⋮cough⋮ ⋮cough⋮
Sure, Dad.
Hiya!
Hey, Jill. You can come on in, but I'm warning you—
⋮cough⋮
—this is the most BORING ROOM EVER.
We missed you at school today. Got a cold, huh?
Yeah— just a small one.
But Dad made me stay home and rest up.

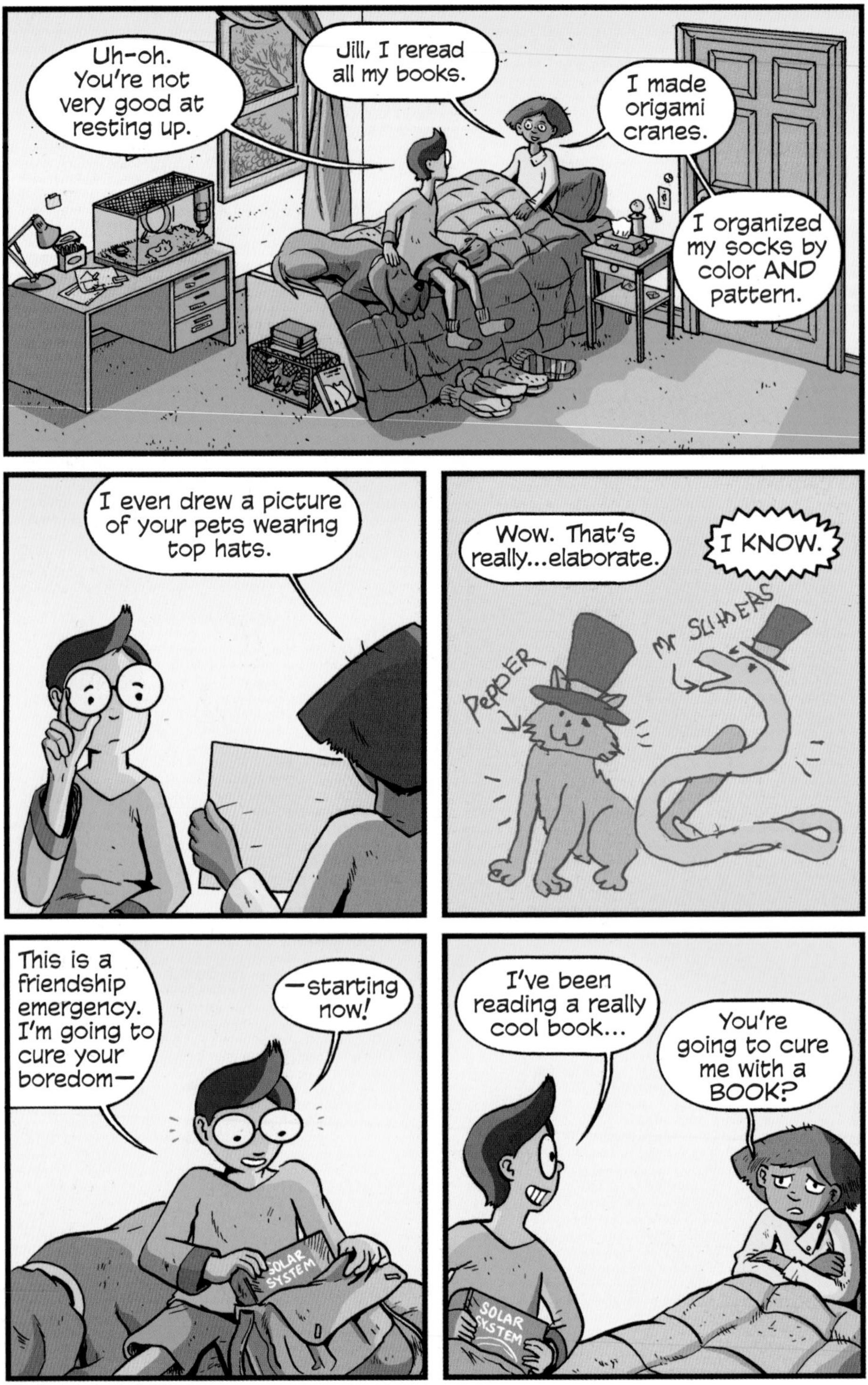
Uh-oh. You're not very good at resting up.
Jill, I reread all my books.
I made origami cranes.
I organized my socks by color AND pattern.
I even drew a picture of your pets wearing top hats.
Wow. That's really...elaborate.
I KNOW.
PEPPER
Mr SLITHERS
This is a friendship emergency. I'm going to cure your boredom—
—starting now!
SOLAR SYSTEM
I've been reading a really cool book...
You're going to cure me with a BOOK?
SOLAR SYSTEM

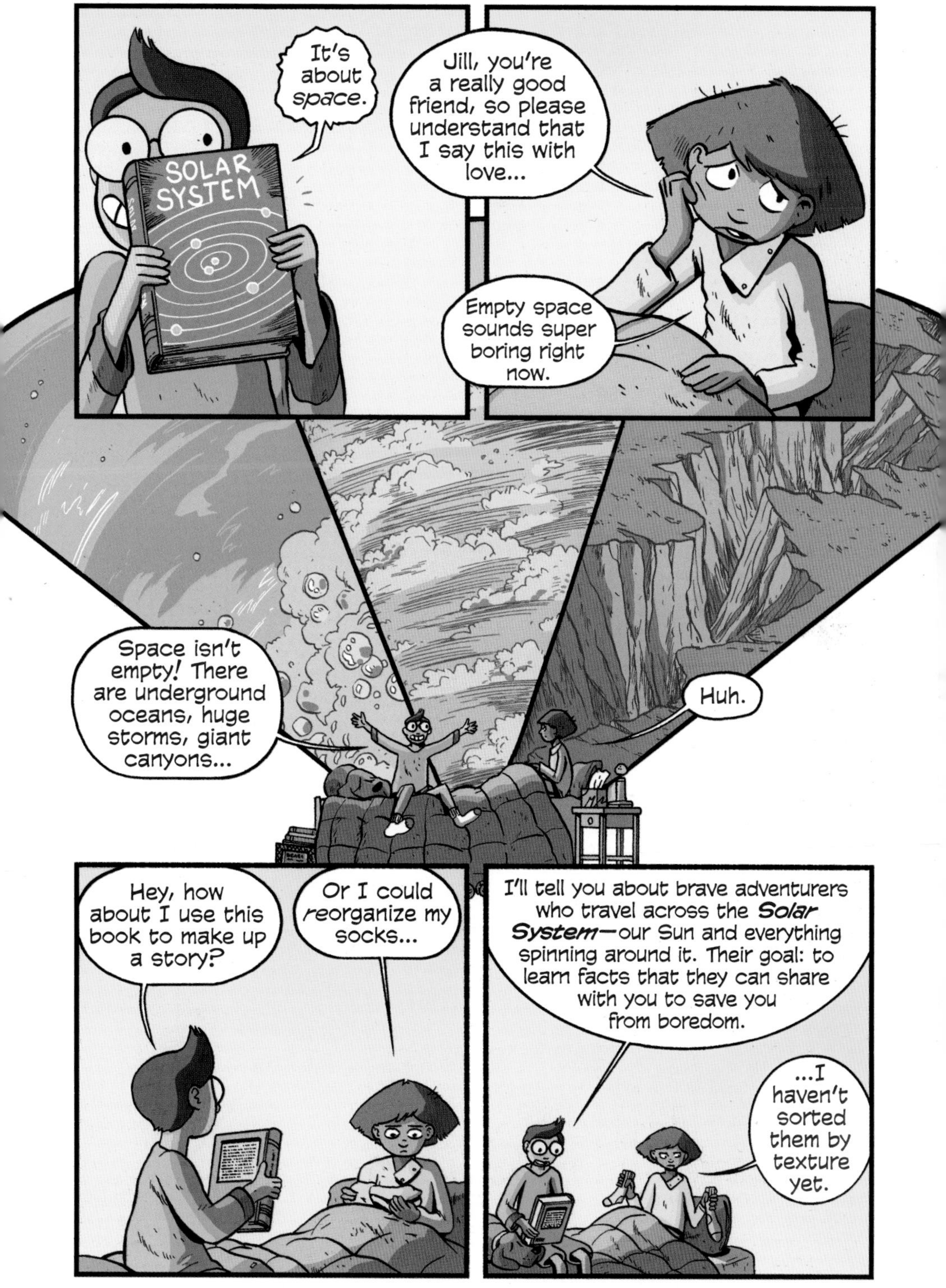
It's about *space*.
SOLAR SYSTEM
Jill, you're a really good friend, so please understand that I say this with love...
Empty space sounds super boring right now.
Space isn't empty! There are underground oceans, huge storms, giant canyons...
Huh.
Hey, how about I use this book to make up a story?
Or I could *re*organize my socks...
I'll tell you about brave adventurers who travel across the ***Solar System***—our Sun and everything spinning around it. Their goal: to learn facts that they can share with you to save you from boredom.
...I haven't sorted them by texture yet.

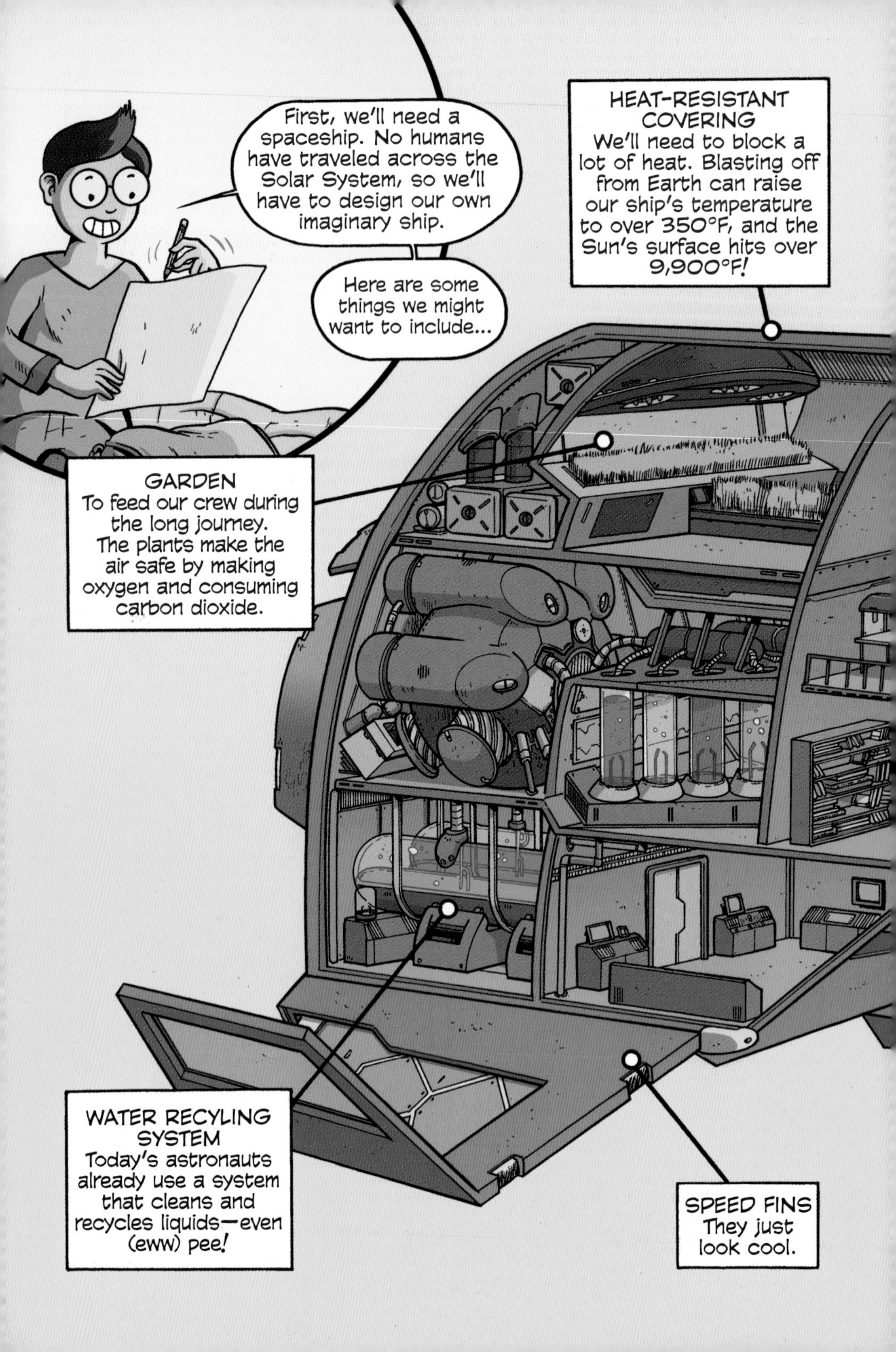
First, we'll need a spaceship. No humans have traveled across the Solar System, so we'll have to design our own imaginary ship.
Here are some things we might want to include...
HEAT-RESISTANT COVERING
We'll need to block a lot of heat. Blasting off from Earth can raise our ship's temperature to over 350°F, and the Sun's surface hits over 9,900°F!
GARDEN
To feed our crew during the long journey. The plants make the air safe by making oxygen and consuming carbon dioxide.
WATER RECYLING SYSTEM
Today's astronauts already use a system that cleans and recycles liquids—even (eww) pee!
SPEED FINS
They just look cool.

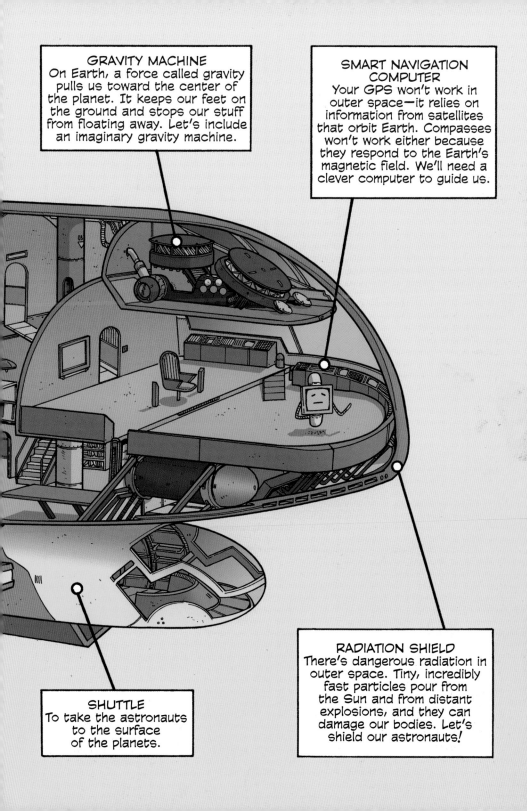

GRAVITY MACHINE
On Earth, a force called gravity pulls us toward the center of the planet. It keeps our feet on the ground and stops our stuff from floating away. Let's include an imaginary gravity machine.

SMART NAVIGATION COMPUTER
Your GPS won't work in outer space—it relies on information from satellites that orbit Earth. Compasses won't work either because they respond to the Earth's magnetic field. We'll need a clever computer to guide us.

RADIATION SHIELD
There's dangerous radiation in outer space. Tiny, incredibly fast particles pour from the Sun and from distant explosions, and they can damage our bodies. Let's shield our astronauts!

SHUTTLE
To take the astronauts to the surface of the planets.

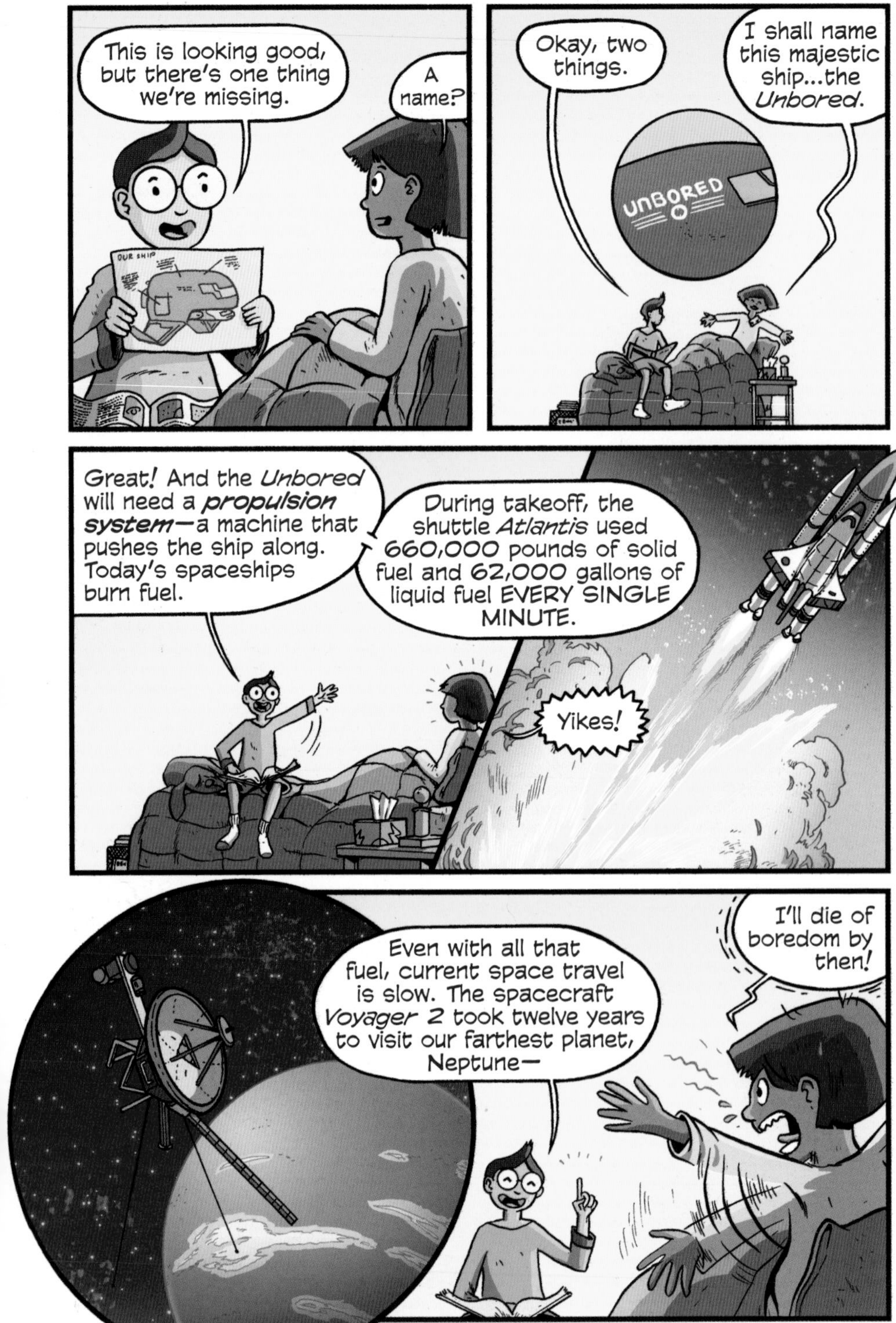
This is looking good, but there's one thing we're missing.
A name?
OUR SHIP
Okay, two things.
I shall name this majestic ship...the *Unbored*.
UNBORED
Great! And the *Unbored* will need a ***propulsion system***—a machine that pushes the ship along. Today's spaceships burn fuel.
During takeoff, the shuttle *Atlantis* used 660,000 pounds of solid fuel and 62,000 gallons of liquid fuel EVERY SINGLE MINUTE.
Yikes!
Even with all that fuel, current space travel is slow. The spacecraft *Voyager 2* took twelve years to visit our farthest planet, Neptune—
I'll die of boredom by then!

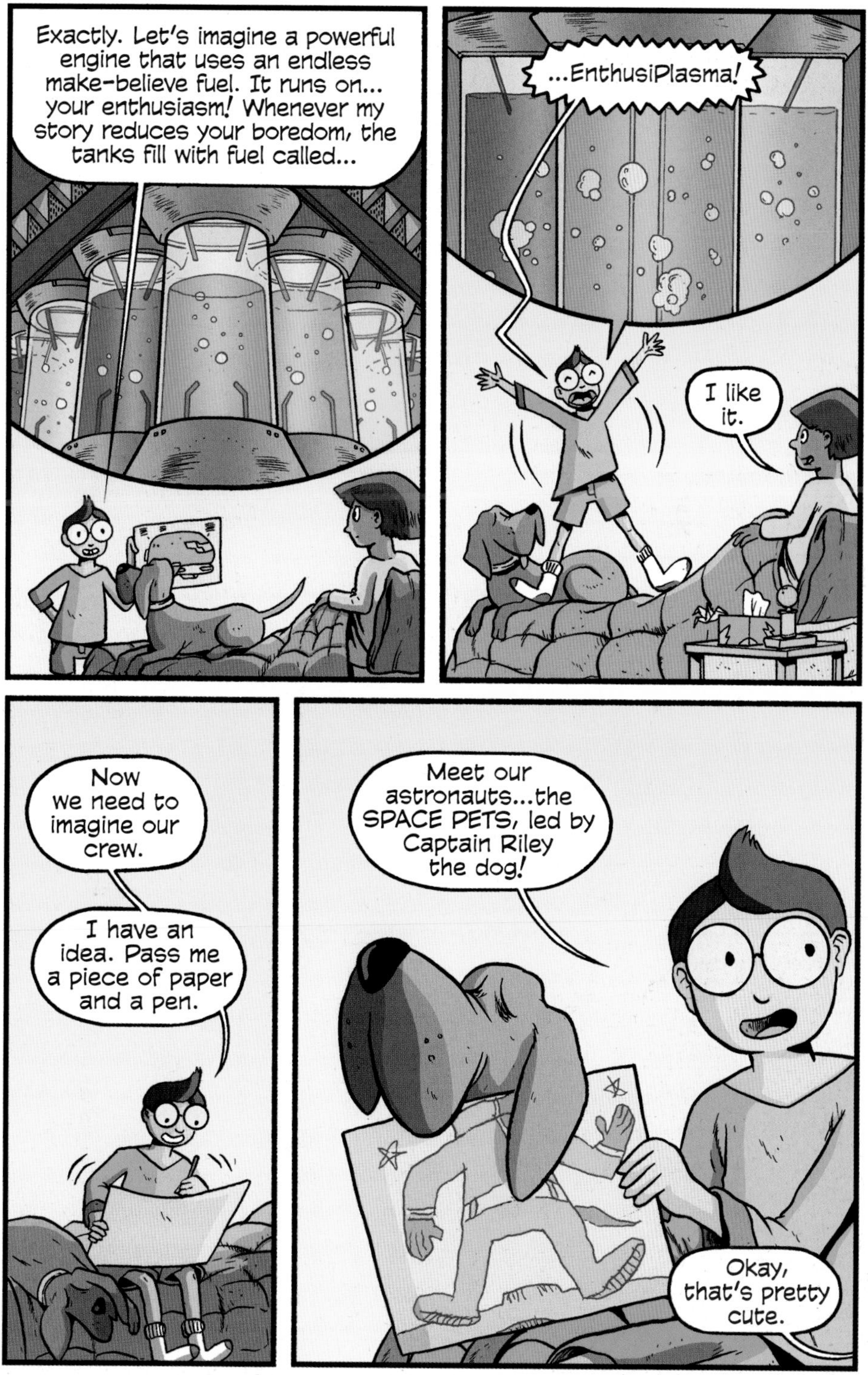
Exactly. Let's imagine a powerful engine that uses an endless make-believe fuel. It runs on... your enthusiasm! Whenever my story reduces your boredom, the tanks fill with fuel called...
...EnthusiPlasma!
I like it.
Now we need to imagine our crew.
I have an idea. Pass me a piece of paper and a pen.
Meet our astronauts...the SPACE PETS, led by Captain Riley the dog!
Okay, that's pretty cute.

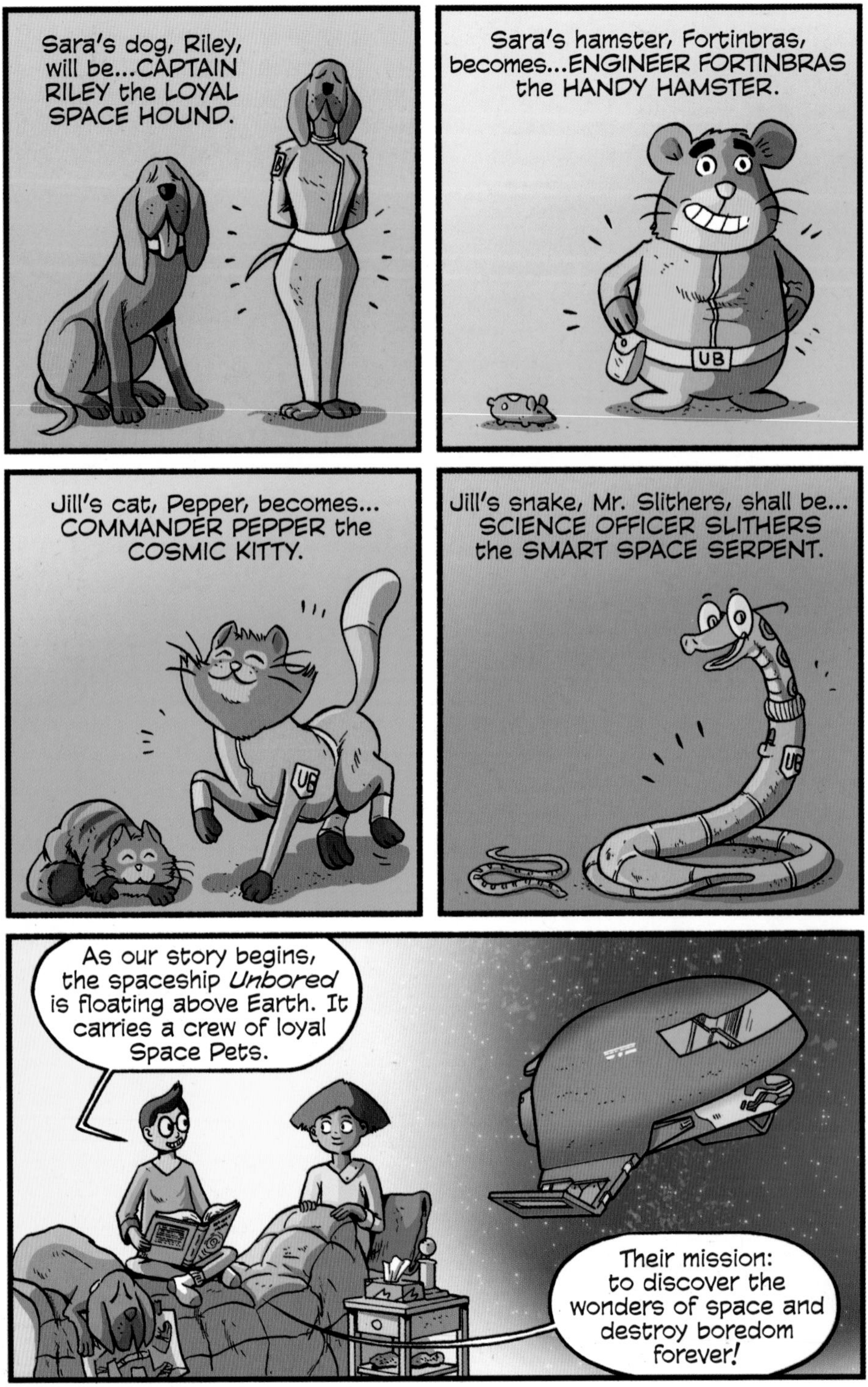
Sara's dog, Riley, will be...CAPTAIN RILEY the LOYAL SPACE HOUND.
Sara's hamster, Fortinbras, becomes...ENGINEER FORTINBRAS the HANDY HAMSTER.
UB
Jill's cat, Pepper, becomes... COMMANDER PEPPER the COSMIC KITTY.
UB
Jill's snake, Mr. Slithers, shall be... SCIENCE OFFICER SLITHERS the SMART SPACE SERPENT.
UB
As our story begins, the spaceship *Unbored* is floating above Earth. It carries a crew of loyal Space Pets.
Their mission: to discover the wonders of space and destroy boredom forever!

Your attention, crew: we have left Earth, and we're about to em*bark* on an important mission.

Our human friend Sara is home sick and super bored.

To cheer her up, we will travel across the Solar System and share amazing facts that—

Pepper, stop that!

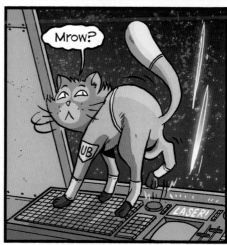

Mrow?

LASER!

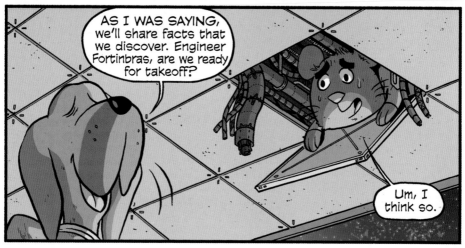

AS I WAS SAYING, we'll share facts that we discover. Engineer Fortinbras, are we ready for takeoff?

Um, I think so.

Sara isn't very excited about this mission, but we have enough EnthusiPlasma to get us to the Sun. After that, we may be DOOMED.

Roger that.

Precise Astronomical Locator, are you ready to navigate?

P.A.L. here. Logically speaking, I am always ready to navigate, because I am a futuristic navigational computer.

‡snort‡

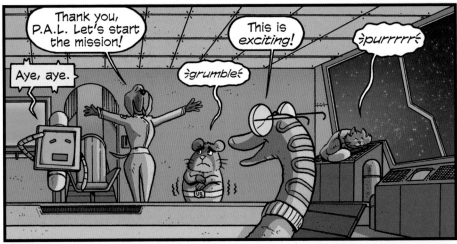

Thank you, P.A.L. Let's start the mission!

Aye, aye.

This is exciting!

‡grumble‡

‡purrrrr‡

I am commencing the approximately 93-million-mile journey to the Sun.

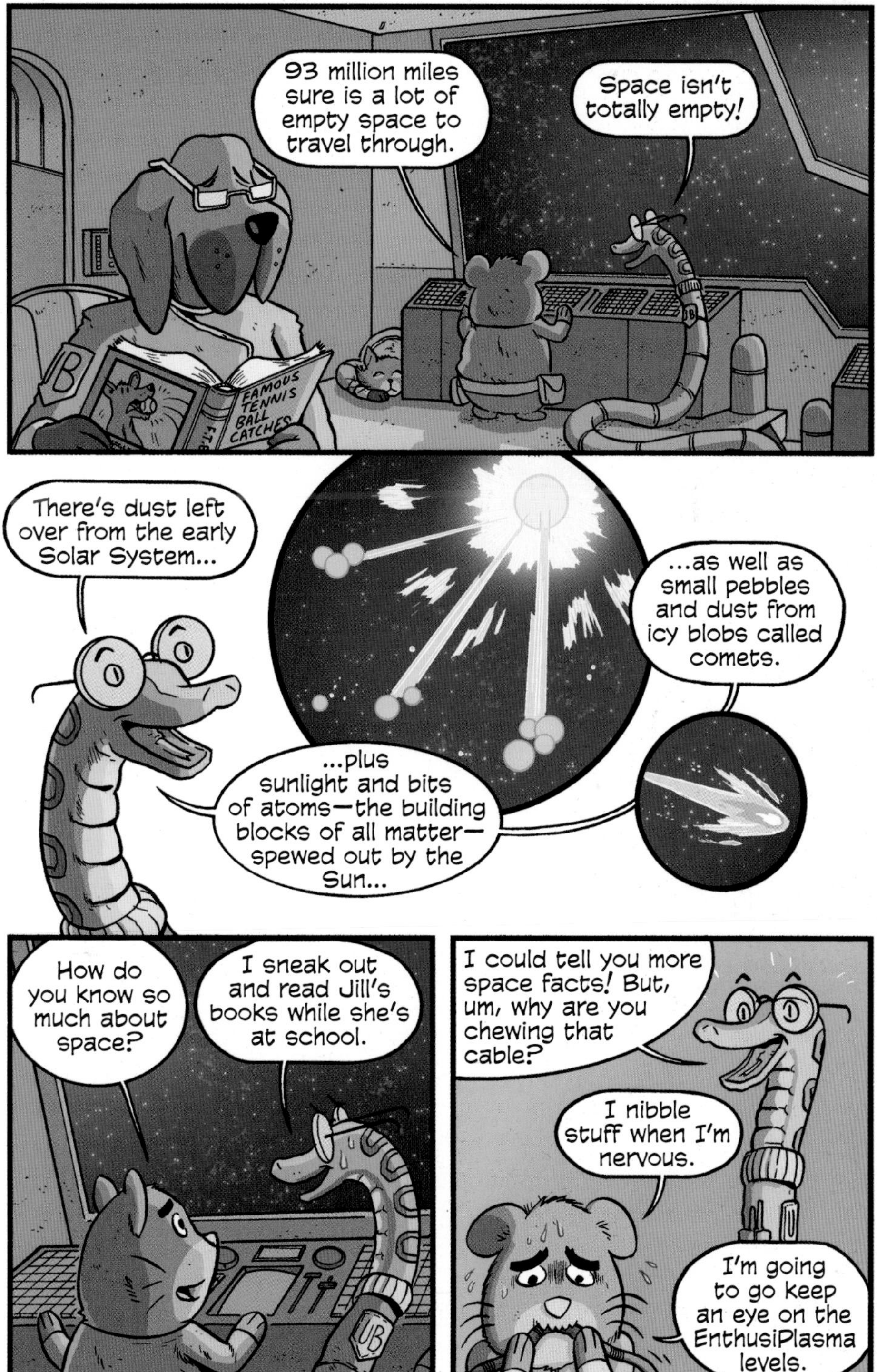
93 million miles sure is a lot of empty space to travel through.
Space isn't totally empty!
FAMOUS TENNIS BALL CATCHES
There's dust left over from the early Solar System...
...as well as small pebbles and dust from icy blobs called comets.
...plus sunlight and bits of atoms—the building blocks of all matter—spewed out by the Sun...
How do you know so much about space?
I sneak out and read Jill's books while she's at school.
I could tell you more space facts! But, um, why are you chewing that cable?
I nibble stuff when I'm nervous.
I'm going to go keep an eye on the EnthusiPlasma levels.

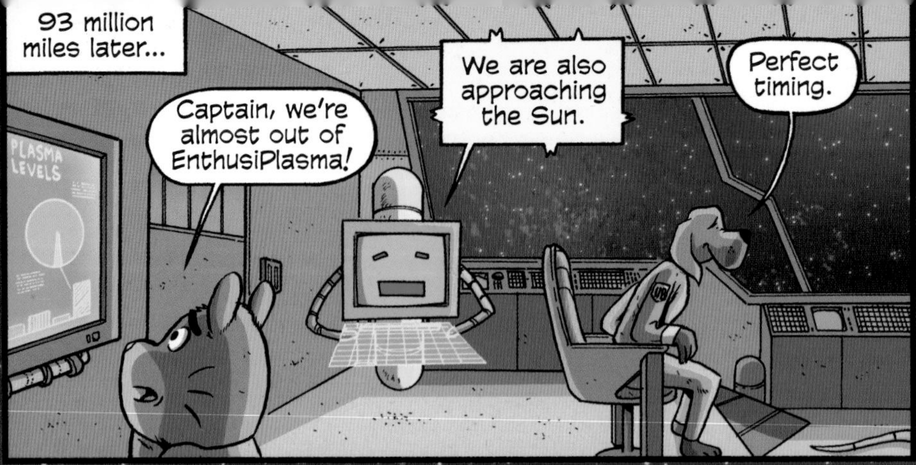
93 million miles later...
Captain, we're almost out of EnthusiPlasma!
We are also approaching the Sun.
Perfect timing.
PLASMA LEVELS

PART 3: THE SUN

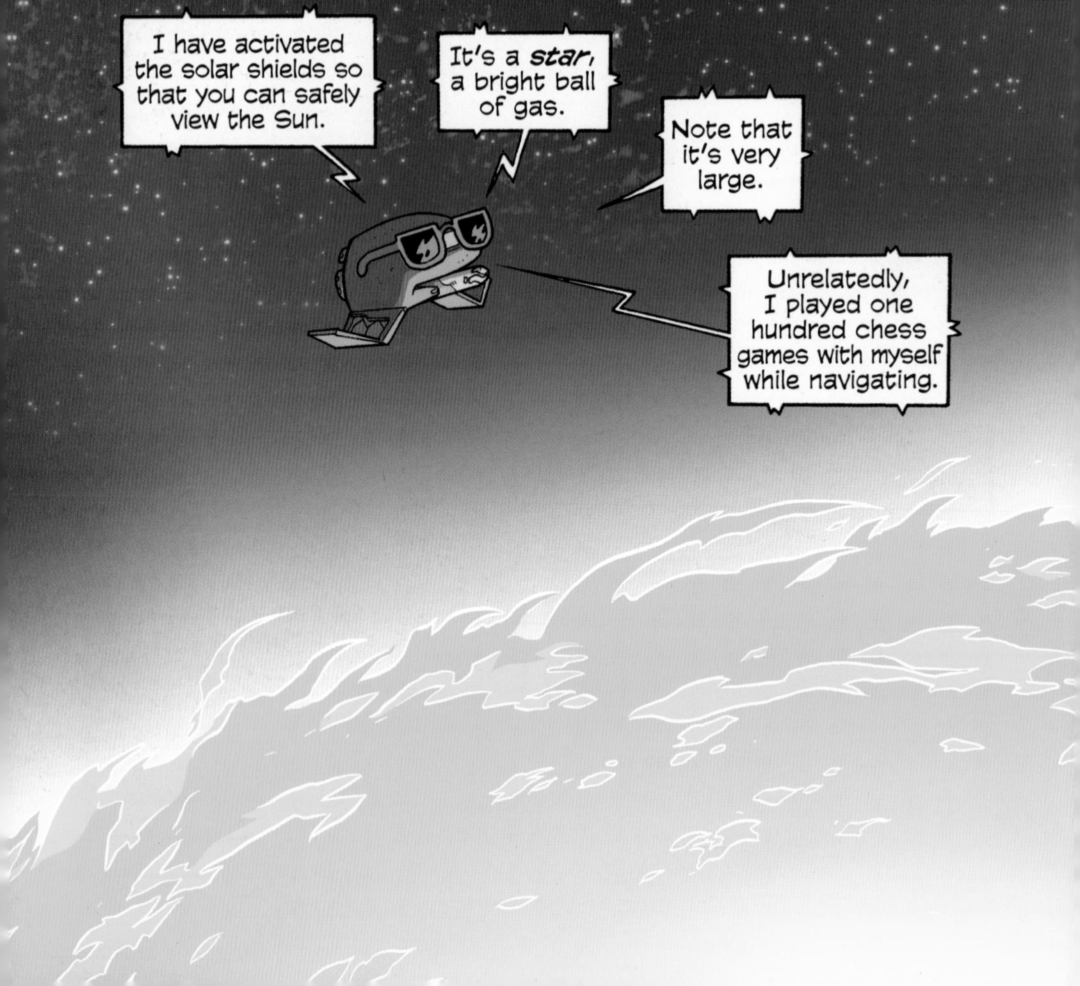
I have activated the solar shields so that you can safely view the Sun.
It's a *star*, a bright ball of gas.
Note that it's very large.
Unrelatedly, I played one hundred chess games with myself while navigating.

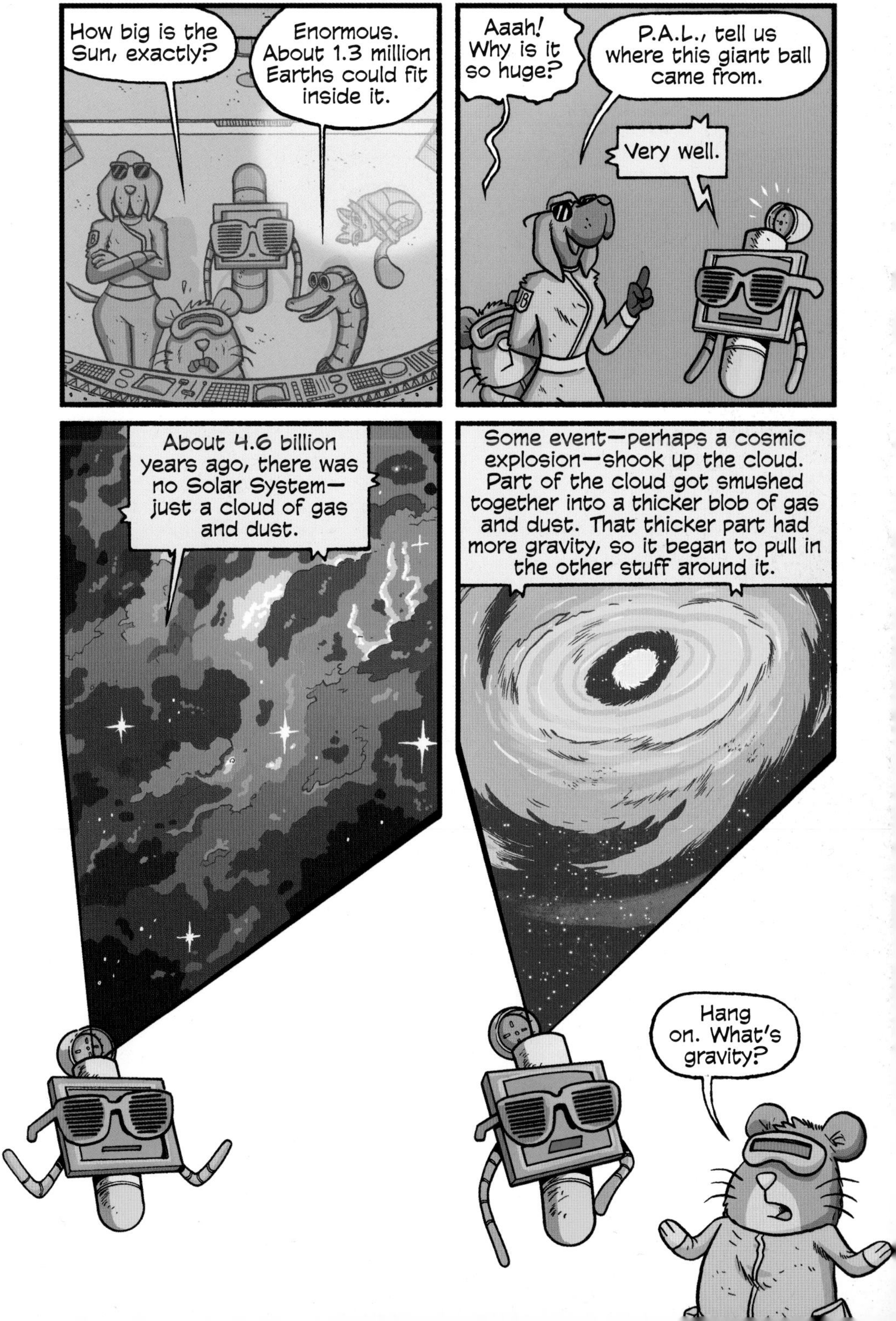
How big is the Sun, exactly?
Enormous. About 1.3 million Earths could fit inside it.
Aaah! Why is it so huge?
P.A.L., tell us where this giant ball came from.
Very well.
About 4.6 billion years ago, there was no Solar System—just a cloud of gas and dust.
Some event—perhaps a cosmic explosion—shook up the cloud. Part of the cloud got smushed together into a thicker blob of gas and dust. That thicker part had more gravity, so it began to pull in the other stuff around it.
Hang on. What's gravity?

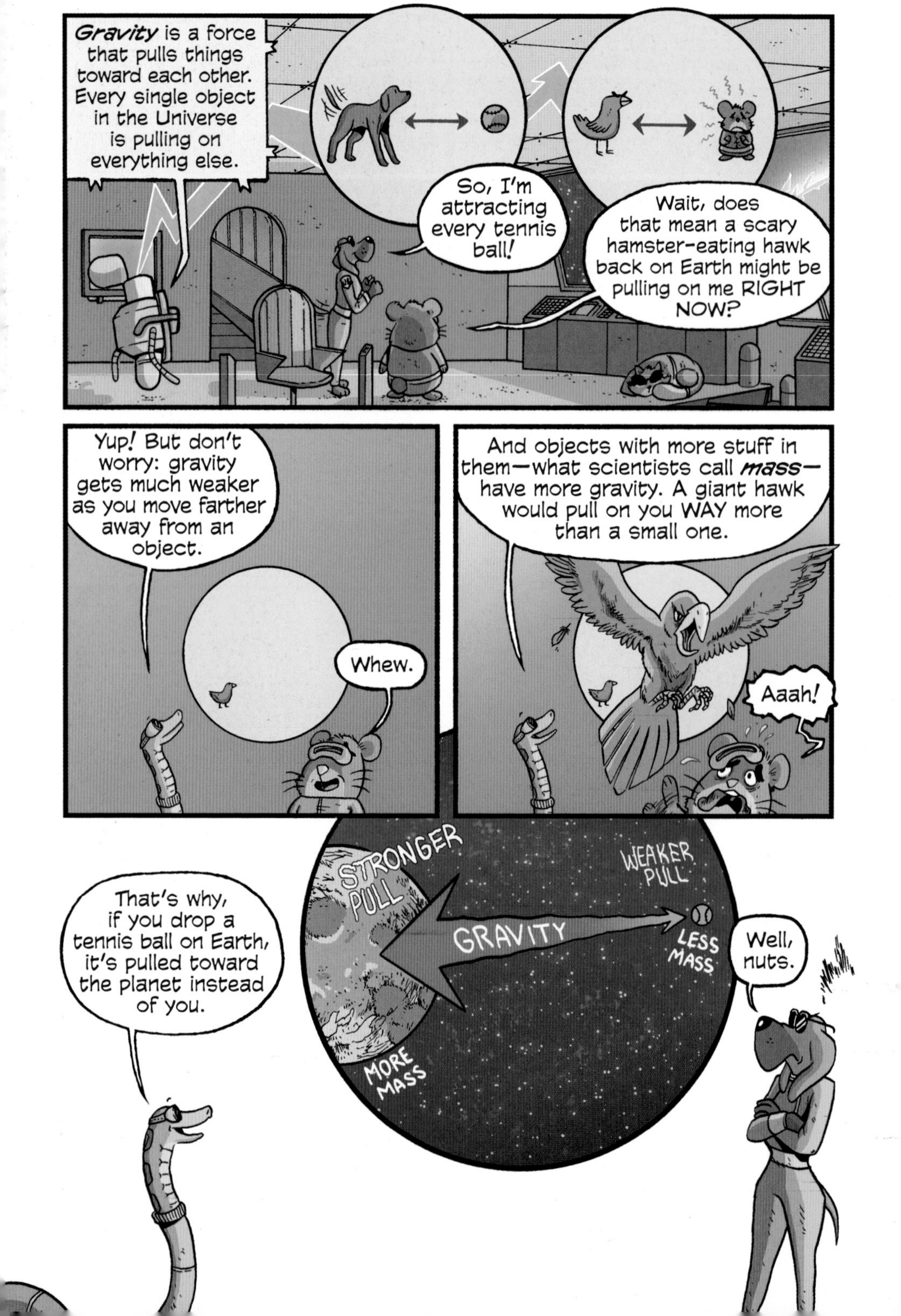
Gravity is a force that pulls things toward each other. Every single object in the Universe is pulling on everything else.
So, I'm attracting every tennis ball!
Wait, does that mean a scary hamster-eating hawk back on Earth might be pulling on me RIGHT NOW?
Yup! But don't worry: gravity gets much weaker as you move farther away from an object.
Whew.
And objects with more stuff in them—what scientists call mass—have more gravity. A giant hawk would pull on you WAY more than a small one.
Aaah!
That's why, if you drop a tennis ball on Earth, it's pulled toward the planet instead of you.
STRONGER PULL
WEAKER PULL
GRAVITY
LESS MASS
MORE MASS
Well, nuts.

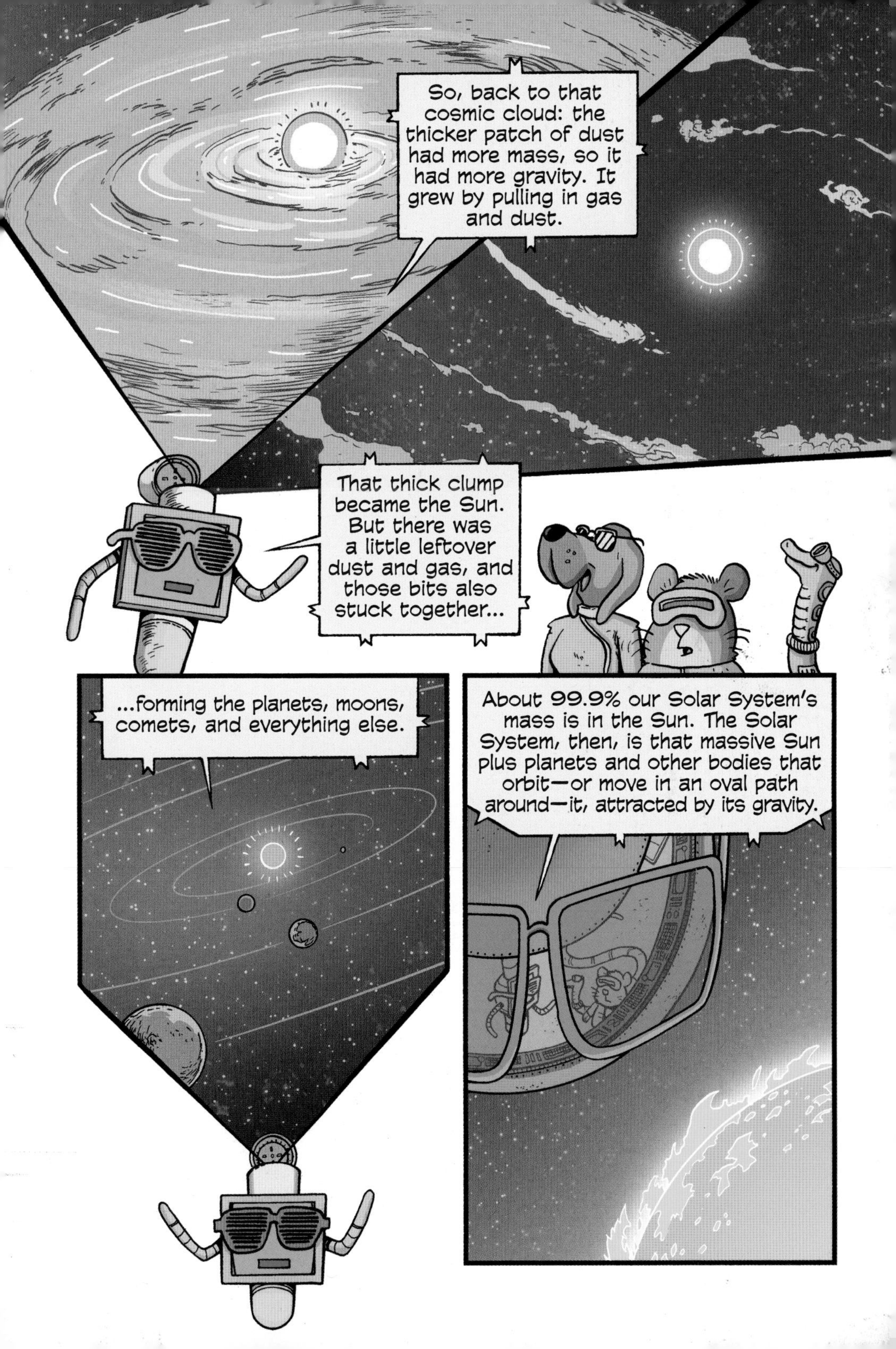
So, back to that cosmic cloud: the thicker patch of dust had more mass, so it had more gravity. It grew by pulling in gas and dust.
That thick clump became the Sun. But there was a little leftover dust and gas, and those bits also stuck together...
...forming the planets, moons, comets, and everything else.
About 99.9% our Solar System's mass is in the Sun. The Solar System, then, is that massive Sun plus planets and other bodies that orbit—or move in an oval path around—it, attracted by its gravity.

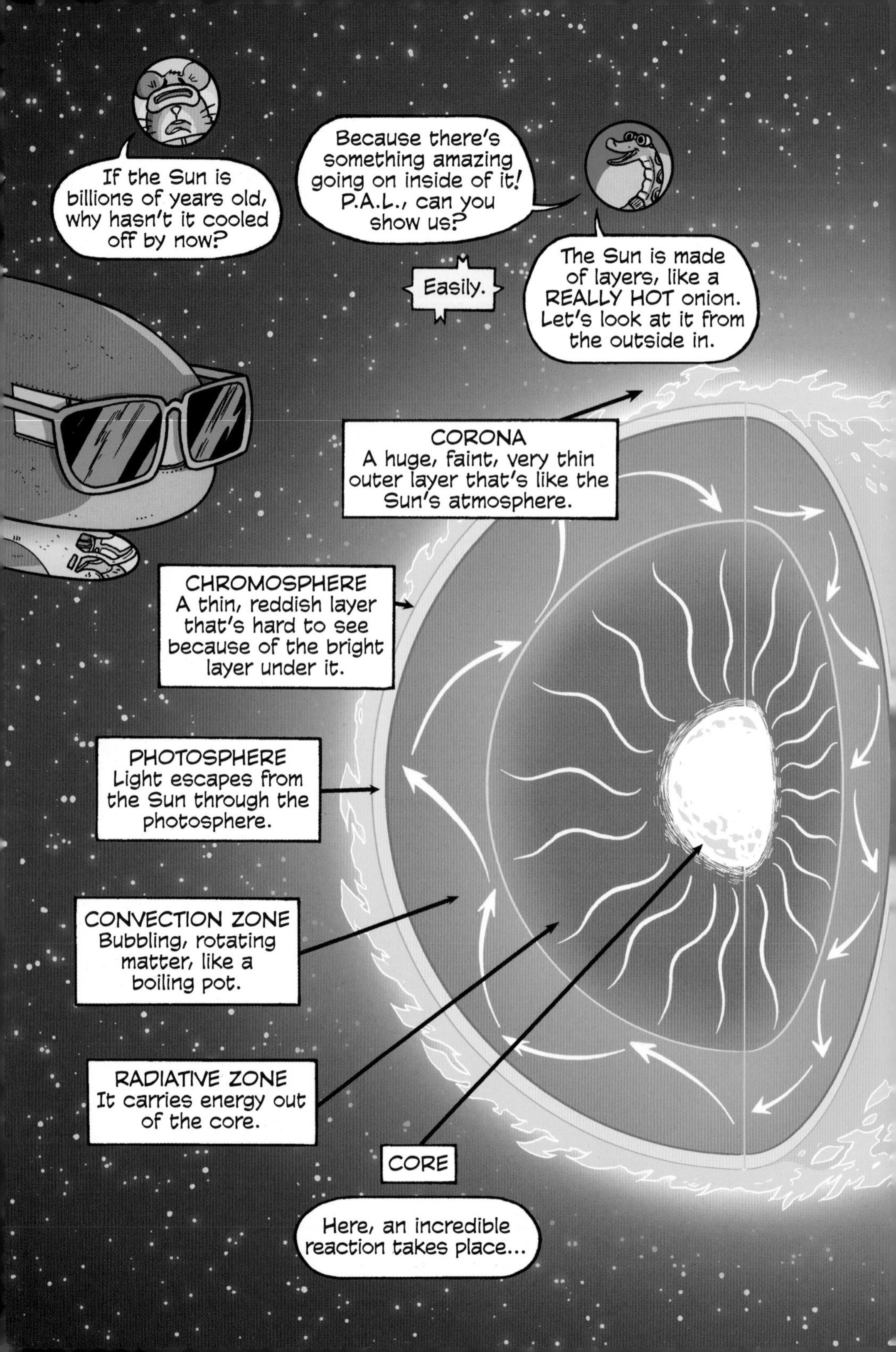

If the Sun is billions of years old, why hasn't it cooled off by now?
Because there's something amazing going on inside of it! P.A.L., can you show us?
Easily.
The Sun is made of layers, like a REALLY HOT onion. Let's look at it from the outside in.
CORONA
A huge, faint, very thin outer layer that's like the Sun's atmosphere.
CHROMOSPHERE
A thin, reddish layer that's hard to see because of the bright layer under it.
PHOTOSPHERE
Light escapes from the Sun through the photosphere.
CONVECTION ZONE
Bubbling, rotating matter, like a boiling pot.
RADIATIVE ZONE
It carries energy out of the core.
CORE
Here, an incredible reaction takes place...

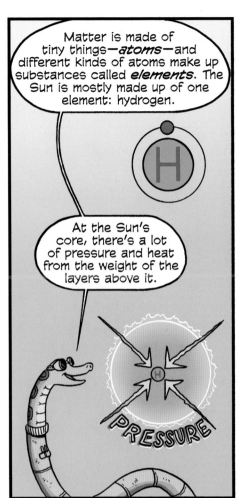

Matter is made of tiny things—*atoms*—and different kinds of atoms make up substances called *elements*. The Sun is mostly made up of one element: hydrogen.
H
At the Sun's core, there's a lot of pressure and heat from the weight of the layers above it.
H
PRESSURE
The hydrogen atoms get squeezed so hard that they break apart and re-form, becoming a whole other element: helium. Called *fusion*, this reaction releases a LOT of light and heat.
H
H
H
H
v
v
²H
H
H
²H
y
y
³He
³He
H
H
⁴He
y = gamma ray
v = neutrino
How much heat are we talking about?
The core is approximately 27 million °F.
Though the photosphere's just 10,000°F!
Aaah! We'll melt into little puddles!
Your fear is illogical. I possess the latest in imaginary shield technology. I could protect us while winning ten games of chess.

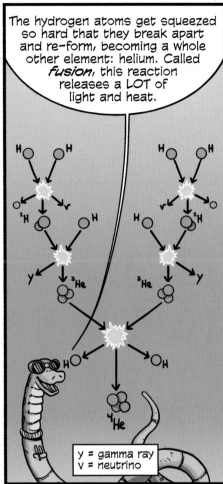

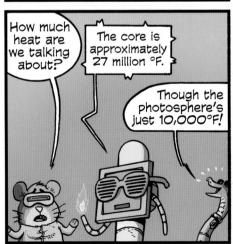

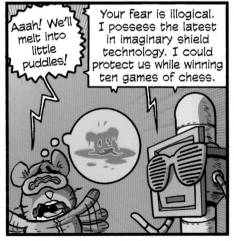

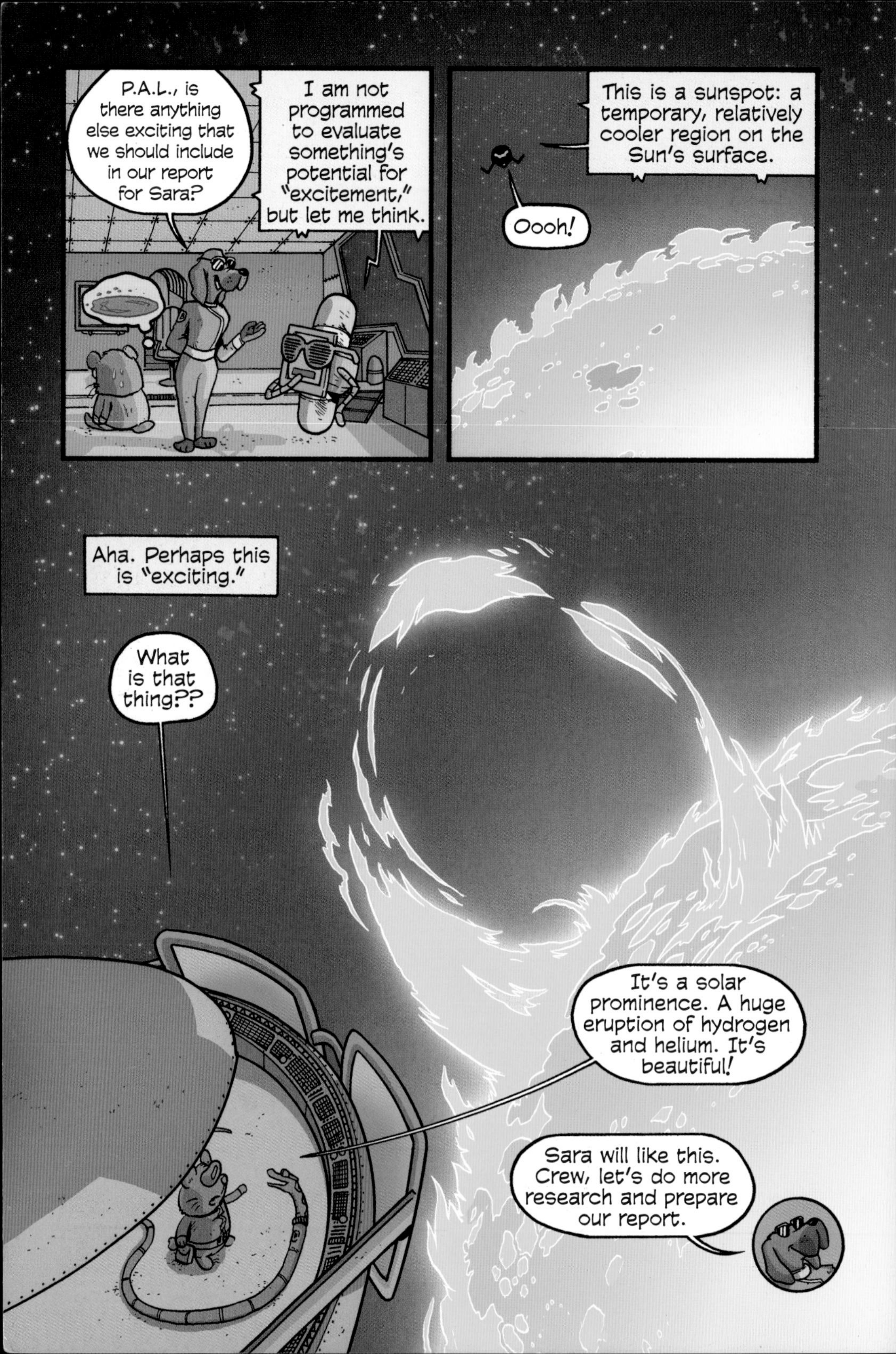
P.A.L., is there anything else exciting that we should include in our report for Sara?
I am not programmed to evaluate something's potential for "excitement," but let me think.
This is a sunspot: a temporary, relatively cooler region on the Sun's surface.
Oooh!
Aha. Perhaps this is "exciting."
What is that thing??
It's a solar prominence. A huge eruption of hydrogen and helium. It's beautiful!
Sara will like this. Crew, let's do more research and prepare our report.

THE SUN: A REPORT

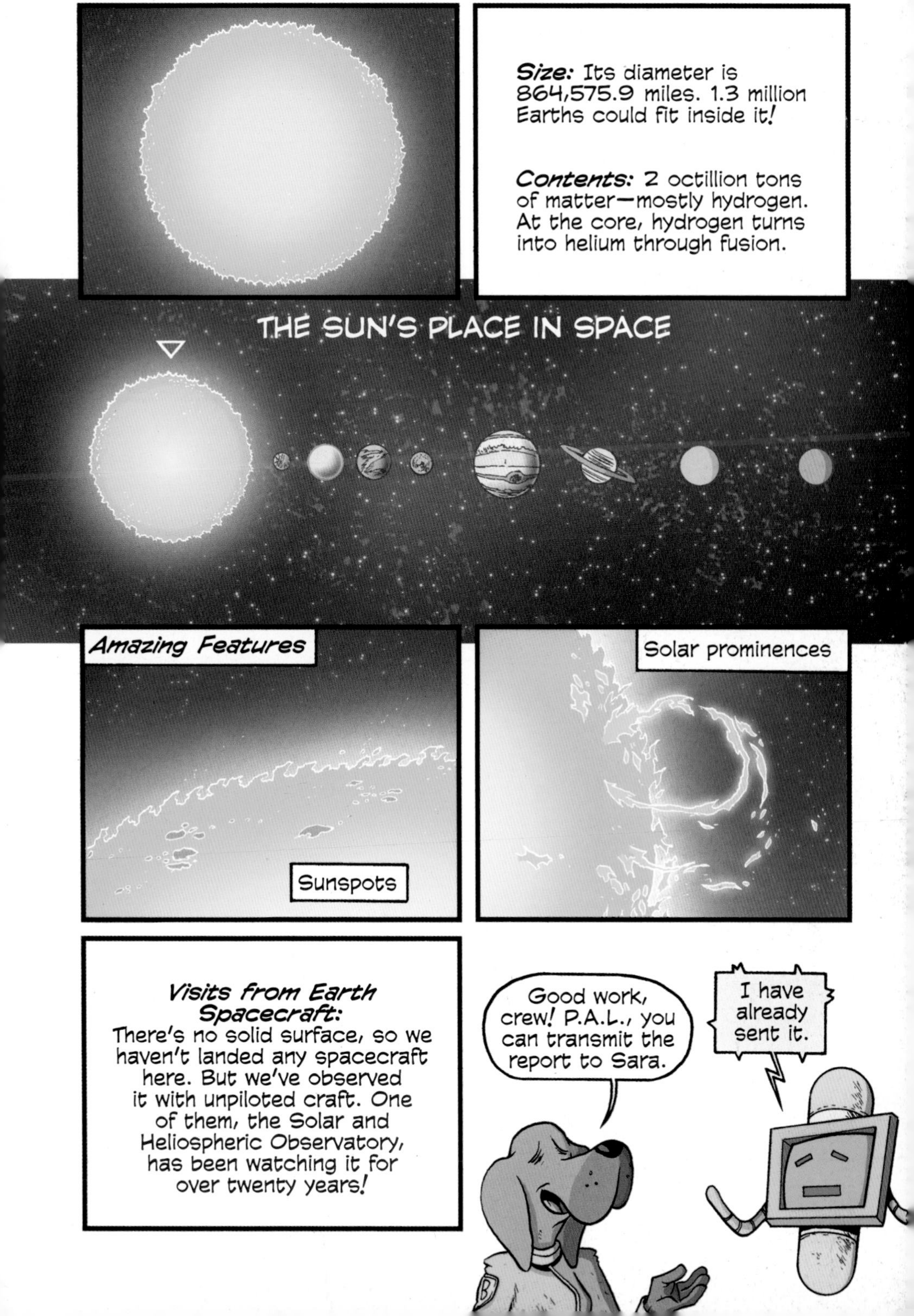

Size: Its diameter is 864,575.9 miles. 1.3 million Earths could fit inside it!
Contents: 2 octillion tons of matter—mostly hydrogen. At the core, hydrogen turns into helium through fusion.
THE SUN'S PLACE IN SPACE
Amazing Features
Sunspots
Solar prominences
Visits from Earth Spacecraft: There's no solid surface, so we haven't landed any spacecraft here. But we've observed it with unpiloted craft. One of them, the Solar and Heliospheric Observatory, has been watching it for over twenty years!
Good work, crew! P.A.L., you can transmit the report to Sara.
I have already sent it.

Well? Was the Sun interesting?

It was *achooť* pretty okay.

Uh-oh.

ENTHUSIPLASMA %

LOW

Captain Riley, we've got just enough fuel to get to the nearest planet—

—but that's all.

Hmm. Sara sees the Sun every day.

ENTHUSIPLASMA %

LOW

Maybe landing on a planet would give us an extra boost? P.A.L., take us to the nearest planet.

Don't worry, Fort. I'm sure we'll find tons of interesting stuff there. Plus, it probably won't be as hot!

Humph.

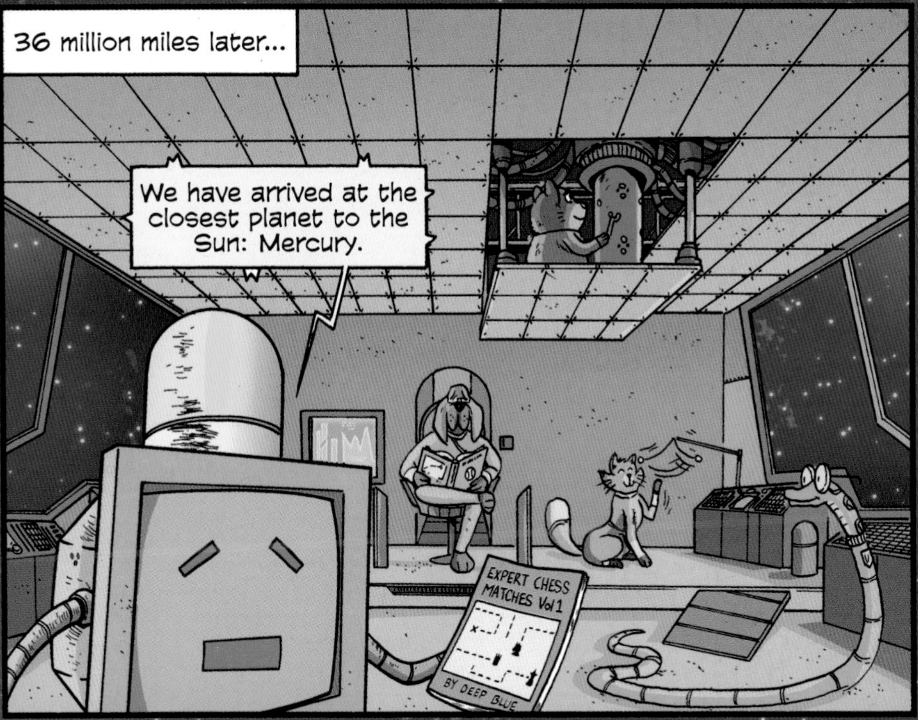
36 million miles later...
We have arrived at the closest planet to the Sun: Mercury.
EXPERT CHESS MATCHES Vol 1
BY DEEP BLUE

PART 4: MERCURY

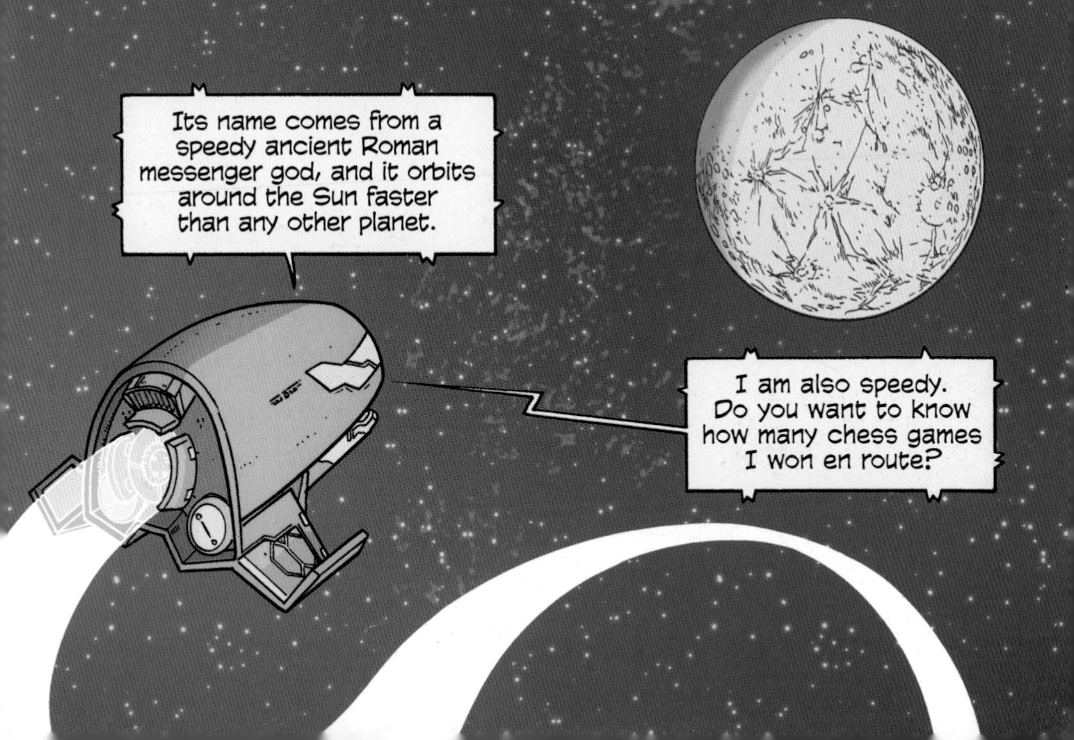
Its name comes from a speedy ancient Roman messenger god, and it orbits around the Sun faster than any other planet.
I am also speedy. Do you want to know how many chess games I won en route?

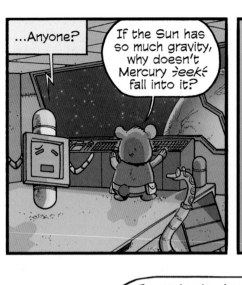

...Anyone?

If the Sun has so much gravity, why doesn't Mercury *eek!* fall into it?

Well, most of the stuff in the early Solar System fell into the Sun. But a few planets stayed safe because they were moving at just the right speed.

Here, let me show you!

The string is always pulling on the mouse, but the mouse never hits my tail. In a somewhat similar way, the planets are attracted to the Sun but they're moving around it at just the right speed so that they don't crash into it.

SUN

OOF!

I *guess* that makes me feel a little better.

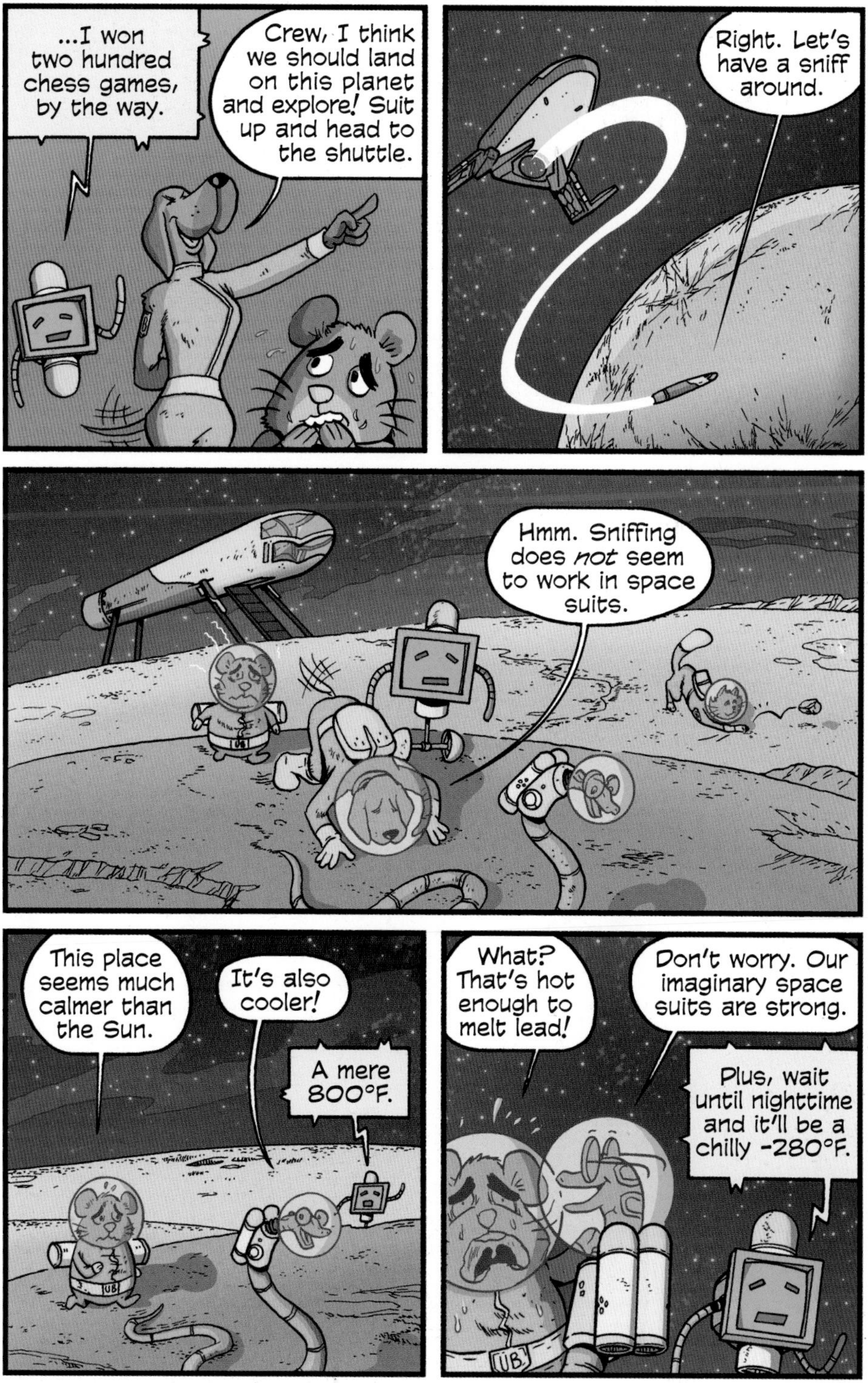
...I won two hundred chess games, by the way.
Crew, I think we should land on this planet and explore! Suit up and head to the shuttle.
Right. Let's have a sniff around.
Hmm. Sniffing does *not* seem to work in space suits.
This place seems much calmer than the Sun.
It's also cooler!
A mere 800°F.
What? That's hot enough to melt lead!
Don't worry. Our imaginary space suits are strong.
Plus, wait until nighttime and it'll be a chilly -280°F.

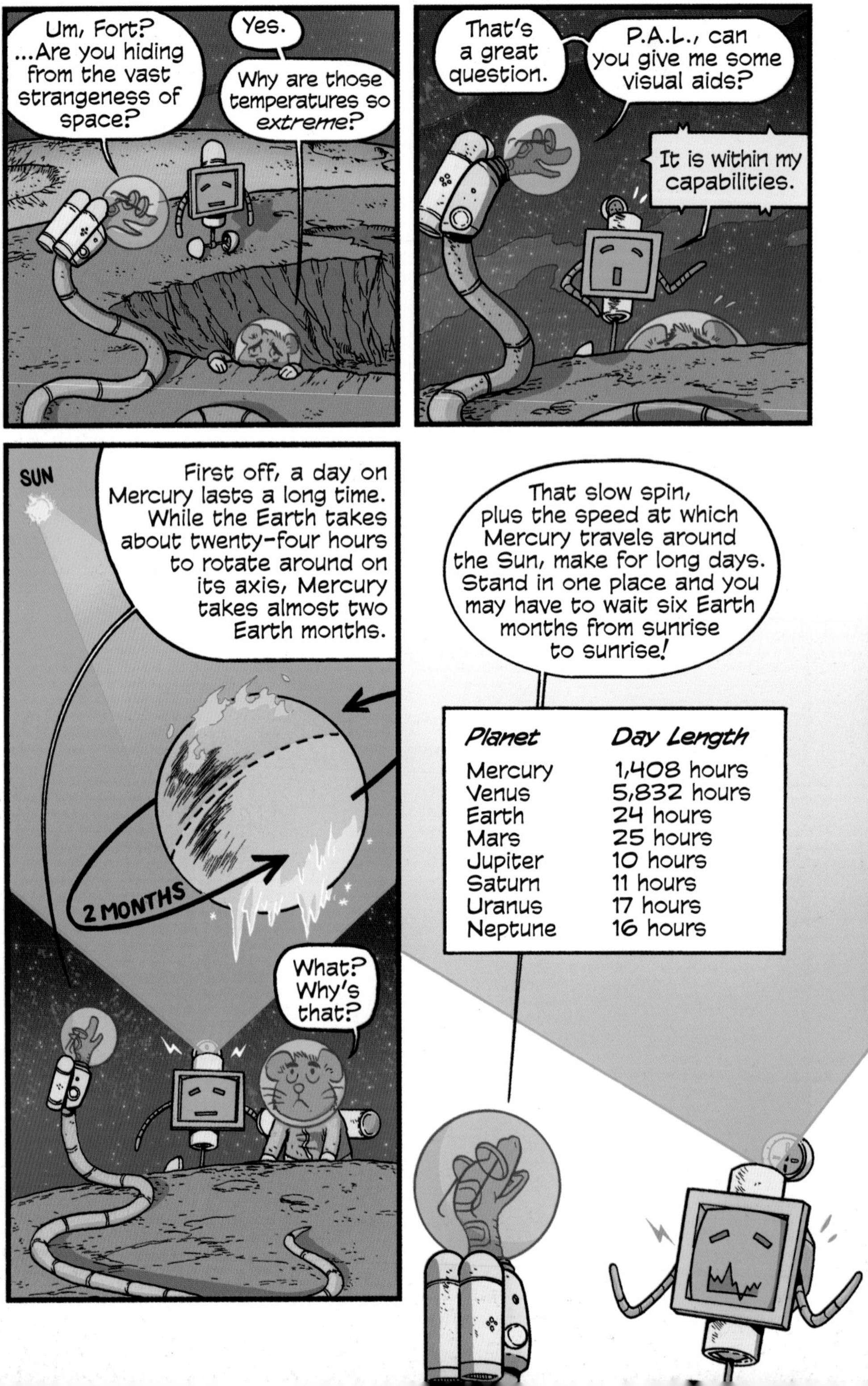
Um, Fort? ...Are you hiding from the vast strangeness of space?
Yes.
Why are those temperatures so *extreme*?
That's a great question.
P.A.L., can you give me some visual aids?
It is within my capabilities.
SUN
First off, a day on Mercury lasts a long time. While the Earth takes about twenty-four hours to rotate around on its axis, Mercury takes almost two Earth months.
2 MONTHS
What? Why's that?
That slow spin, plus the speed at which Mercury travels around the Sun, make for long days. Stand in one place and you may have to wait six Earth months from sunrise to sunrise!
Planet *Day Length*
Mercury 1,408 hours
Venus 5,832 hours
Earth 24 hours
Mars 25 hours
Jupiter 10 hours
Saturn 11 hours
Uranus 17 hours
Neptune 16 hours

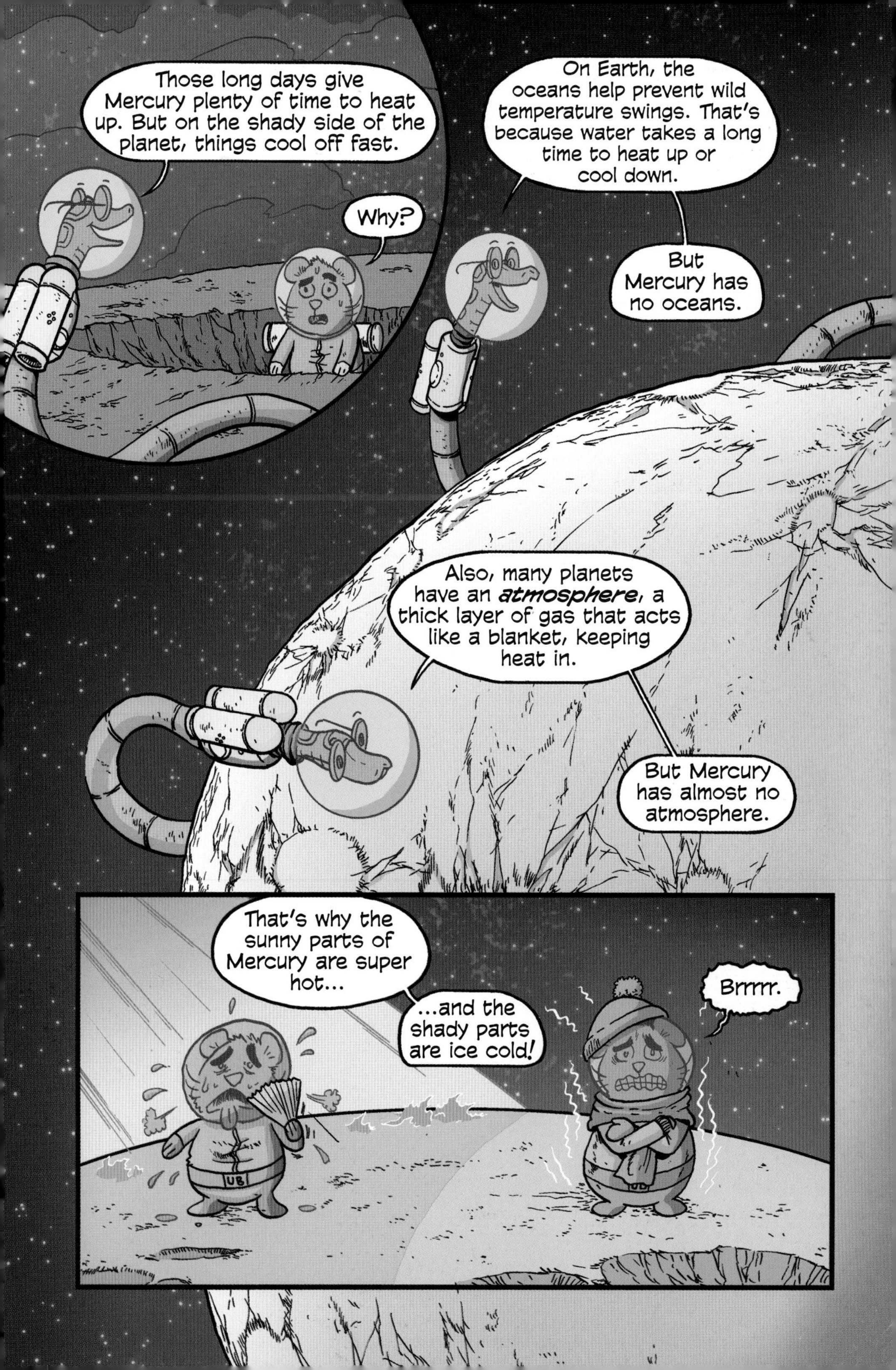
Those long days give Mercury plenty of time to heat up. But on the shady side of the planet, things cool off fast.
Why?
On Earth, the oceans help prevent wild temperature swings. That's because water takes a long time to heat up or cool down.
But Mercury has no oceans.
Also, many planets have an *atmosphere*, a thick layer of gas that acts like a blanket, keeping heat in.
But Mercury has almost no atmosphere.
That's why the sunny parts of Mercury are super hot...
...and the shady parts are ice cold!
Brrrrr.
UB
UB

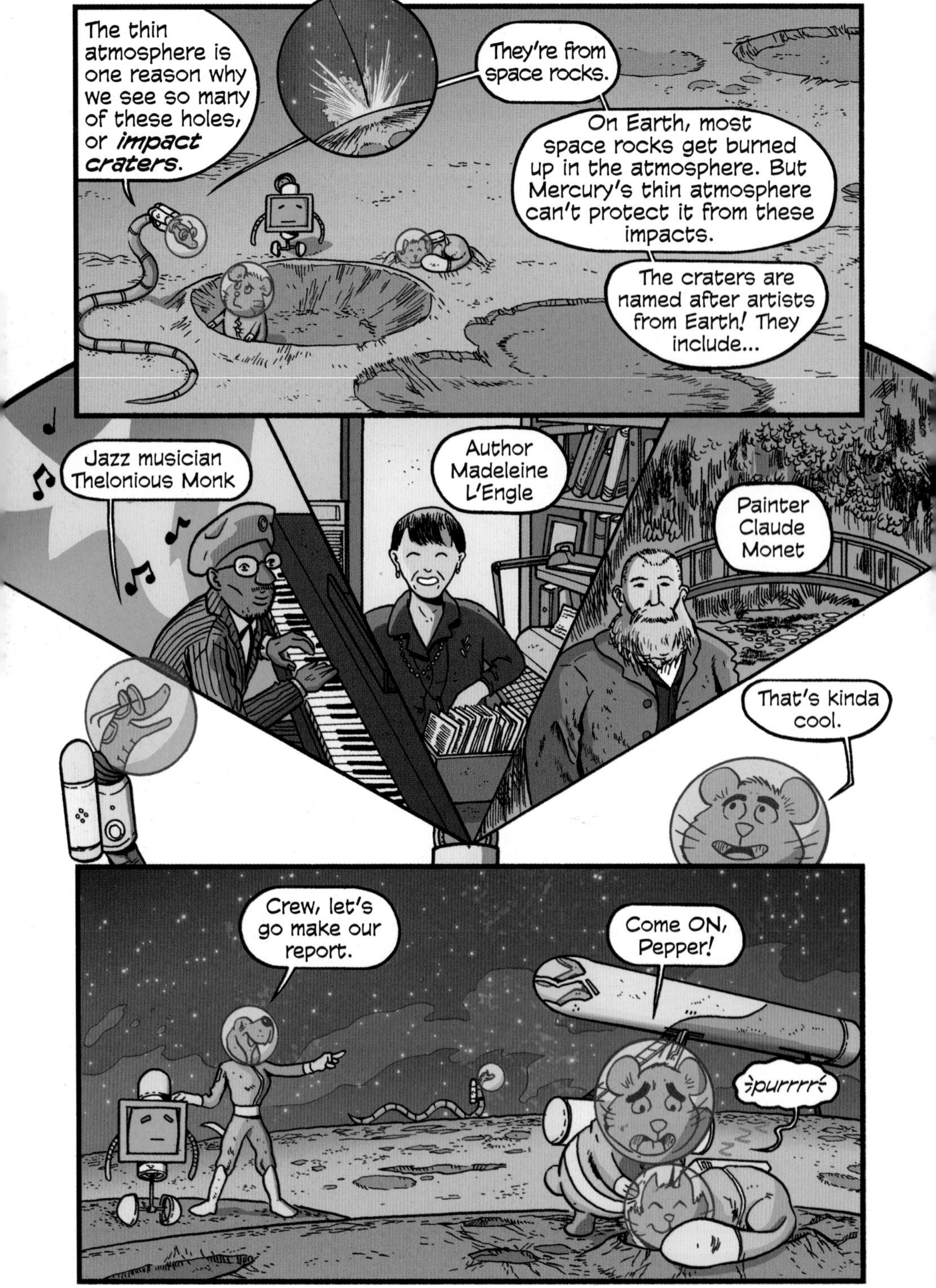

The thin atmosphere is one reason why we see so many of these holes, or *impact craters*.
They're from space rocks.
On Earth, most space rocks get burned up in the atmosphere. But Mercury's thin atmosphere can't protect it from these impacts.
The craters are named after artists from Earth! They include...
Jazz musician Thelonious Monk
Author Madeleine L'Engle
Painter Claude Monet
That's kinda cool.
Crew, let's go make our report.
Come ON, Pepper!
purrrr

MERCURY: A REPORT

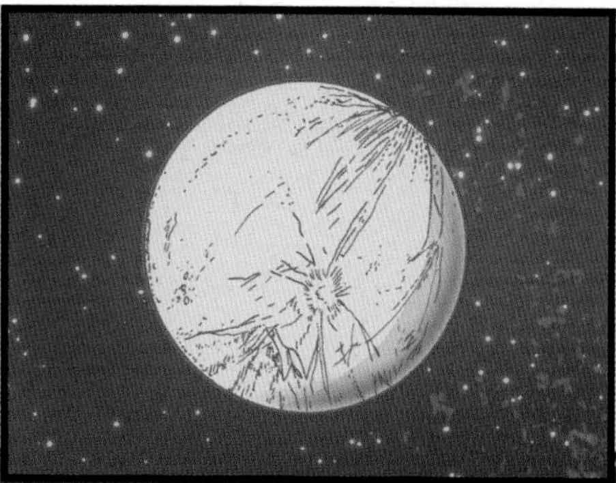

Origin of Name: The ancient Roman messenger god.

Size: 3,031.7 miles in diameter, just 1/3 the width of Earth.

Contents: Like the other planets, it has layers. During Mercury's formation, gravity pulled the heaviest stuff (mostly metal) to the core, which is now liquid iron. The lighter stuff (mostly rock) floated to the surface.

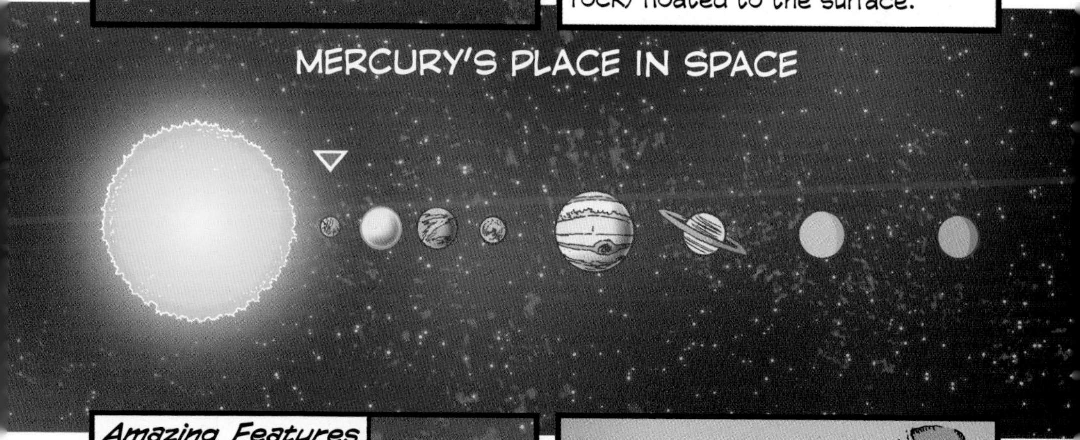
MERCURY'S PLACE IN SPACE

Amazing Features

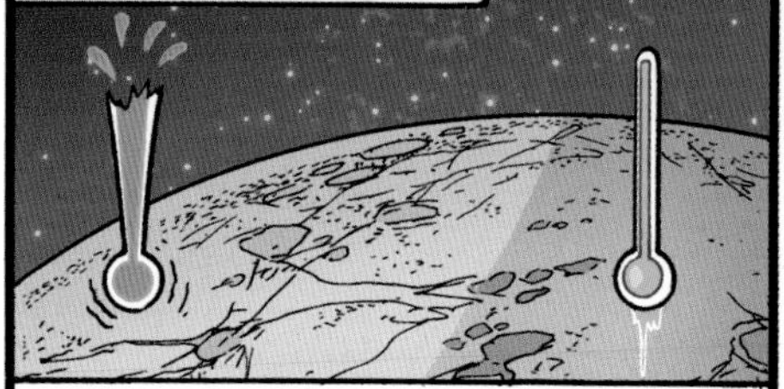

Its sunny side is 800°F, and its shady side is -280°F!

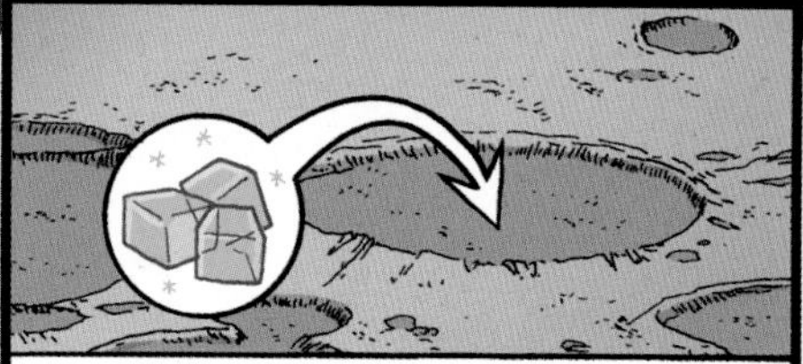

There's even frozen water deep in craters at the poles, where sunlight never reaches! The water may have come from comets smashing into the planet.

Visits from Earth Spacecraft:
Mercury is hard to visit because of the extreme temperatures and the strength of the Sun's gravity at that distance. *Mariner 10* flew by 1974–75. *MESSENGER* orbited 2008–2015. Europe's *BepiColombo* arrives in 2025!!

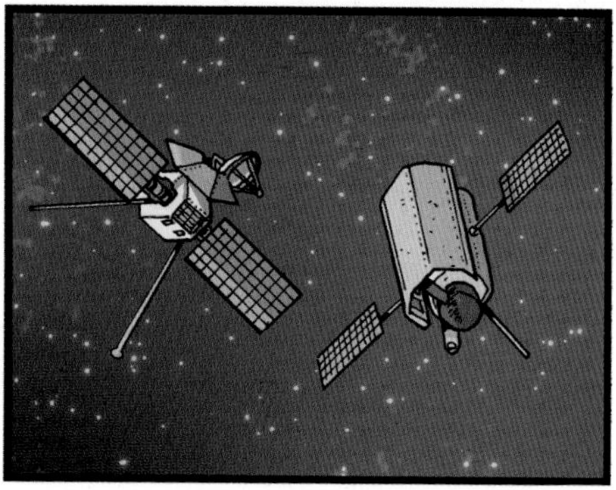

Well, what did you think?

It's neat how Mercury is so hot and cold, like when my dad tries to reheat frozen chili.

I'll take it!

SOLAR SYSTEM

C'mon, c'mon... I guess that'll have to do.

Captain, we have just enough EnthusiPlasma to reach the next planet.

ENTHUSIPLASMA %

STILL PRETTY

LOL

That's not bad, but we need to show Sara something even more extreme. Onward!

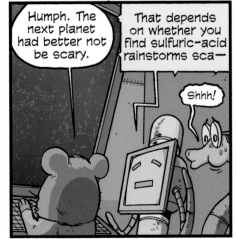

Humph. The next planet had better not be scary.

That depends on whether you find sulfuric-acid rainstorms sca—

Shhh!

Wait, WHAT?!

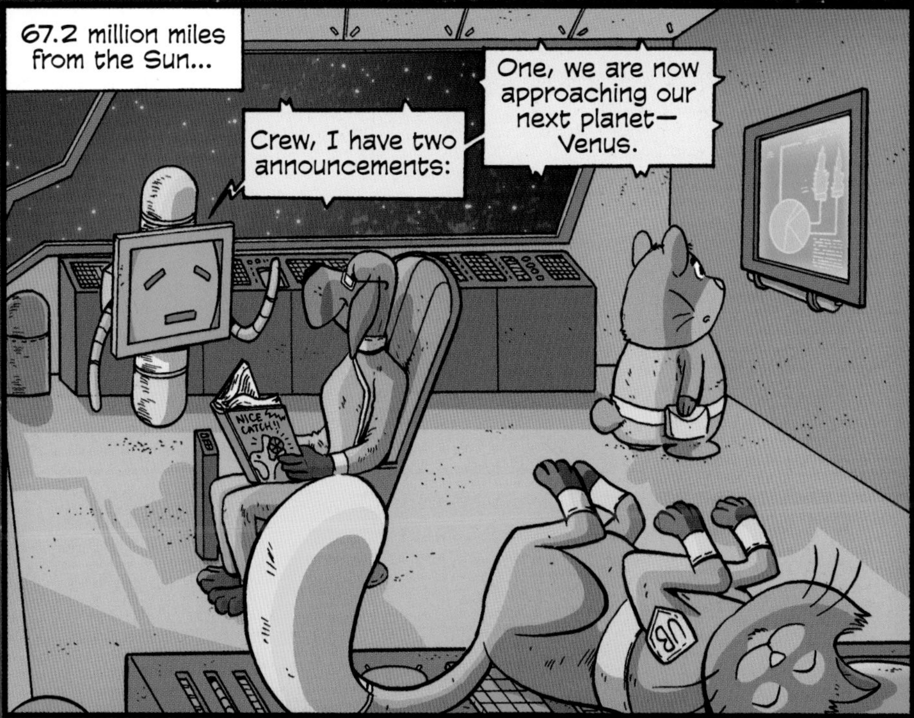
67.2 million miles from the Sun...
Crew, I have two announcements:
One, we are now approaching our next planet—Venus.
NICE CATCH!!

PART 5: VENUS

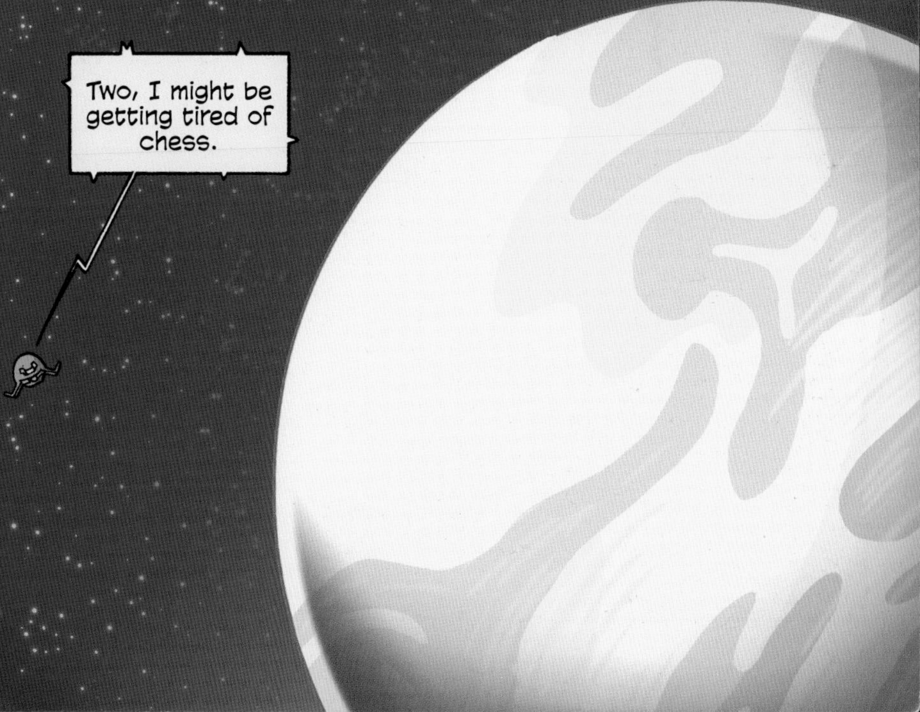
Two, I might be getting tired of chess.

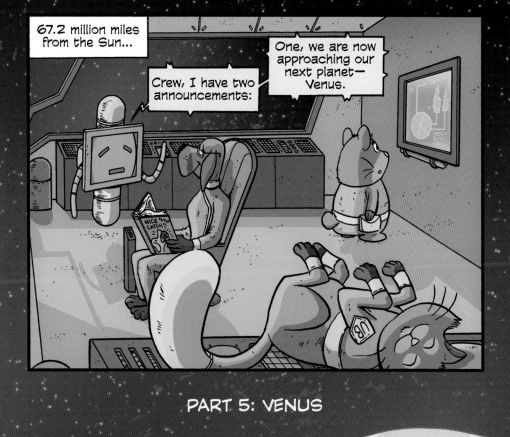

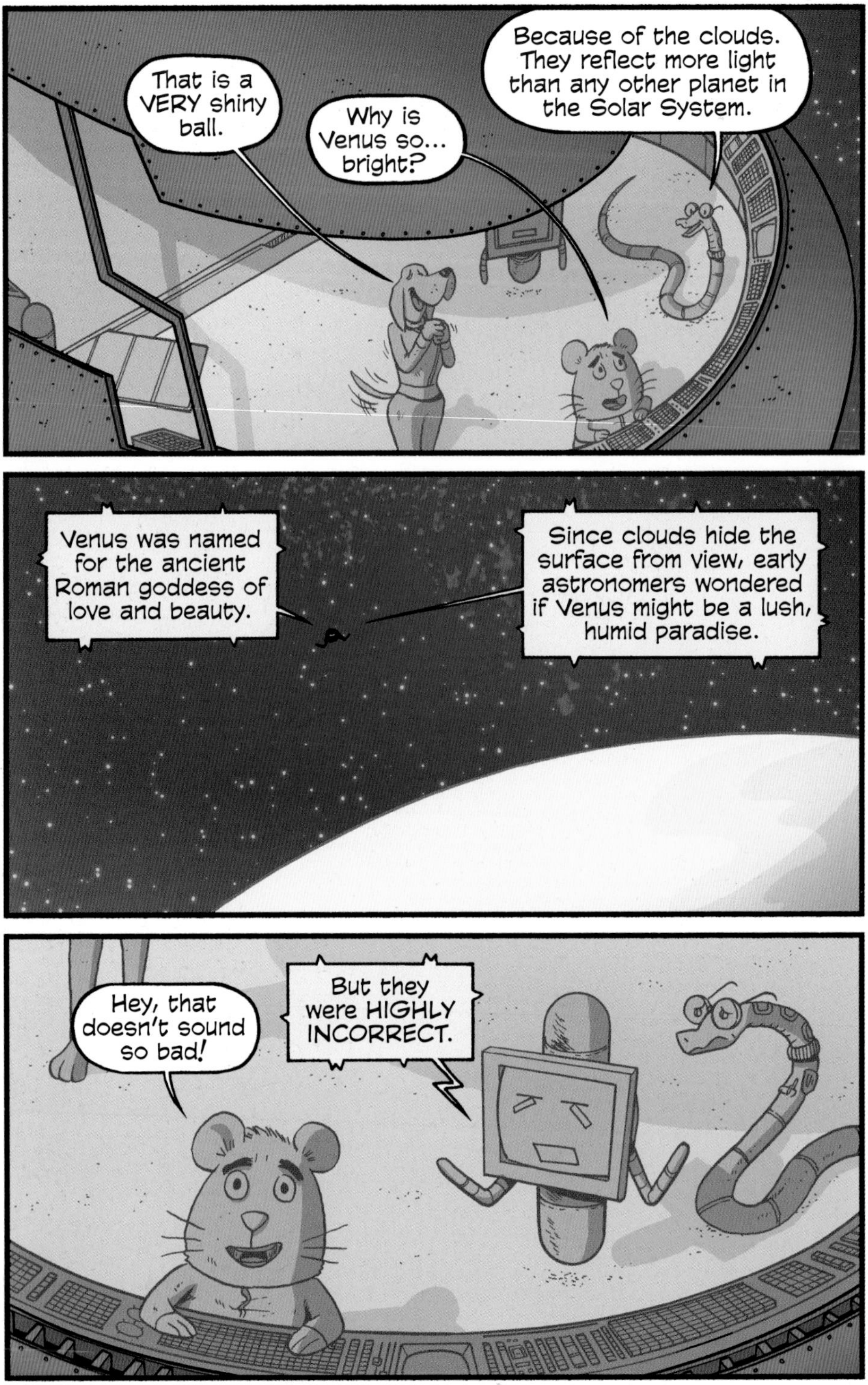
That is a VERY shiny ball.
Why is Venus so... bright?
Because of the clouds. They reflect more light than any other planet in the Solar System.
Venus was named for the ancient Roman goddess of love and beauty.
Since clouds hide the surface from view, early astronomers wondered if Venus might be a lush, humid paradise.
Hey, that doesn't sound so bad!
But they were HIGHLY INCORRECT.

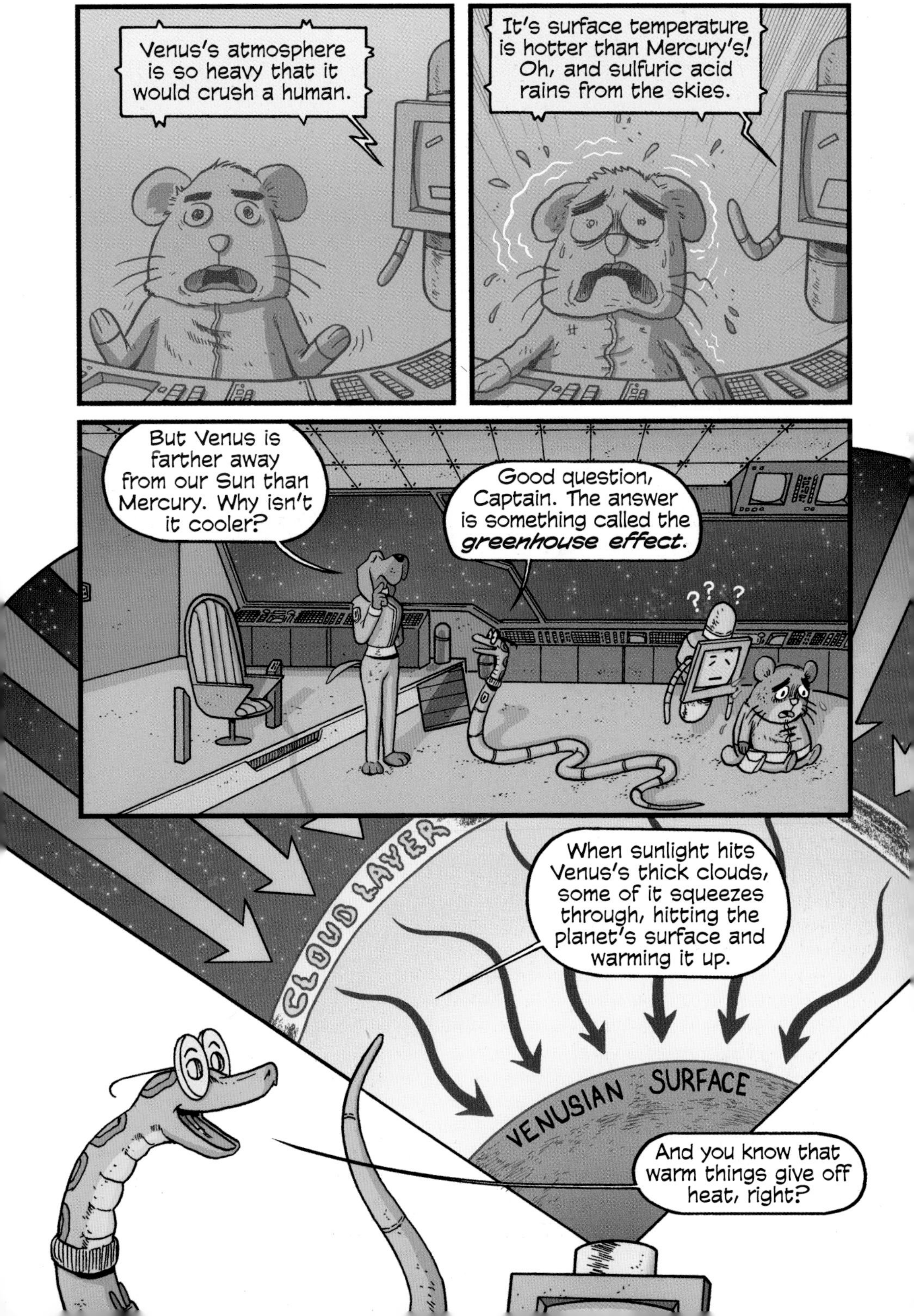
Venus's atmosphere is so heavy that it would crush a human.
It's surface temperature is hotter than Mercury's! Oh, and sulfuric acid rains from the skies.
But Venus is farther away from our Sun than Mercury. Why isn't it cooler?
Good question, Captain. The answer is something called the *greenhouse effect*.
? ? ?
CLOUD LAYER
When sunlight hits Venus's thick clouds, some of it squeezes through, hitting the planet's surface and warming it up.
VENUSIAN SURFACE
And you know that warm things give off heat, right?

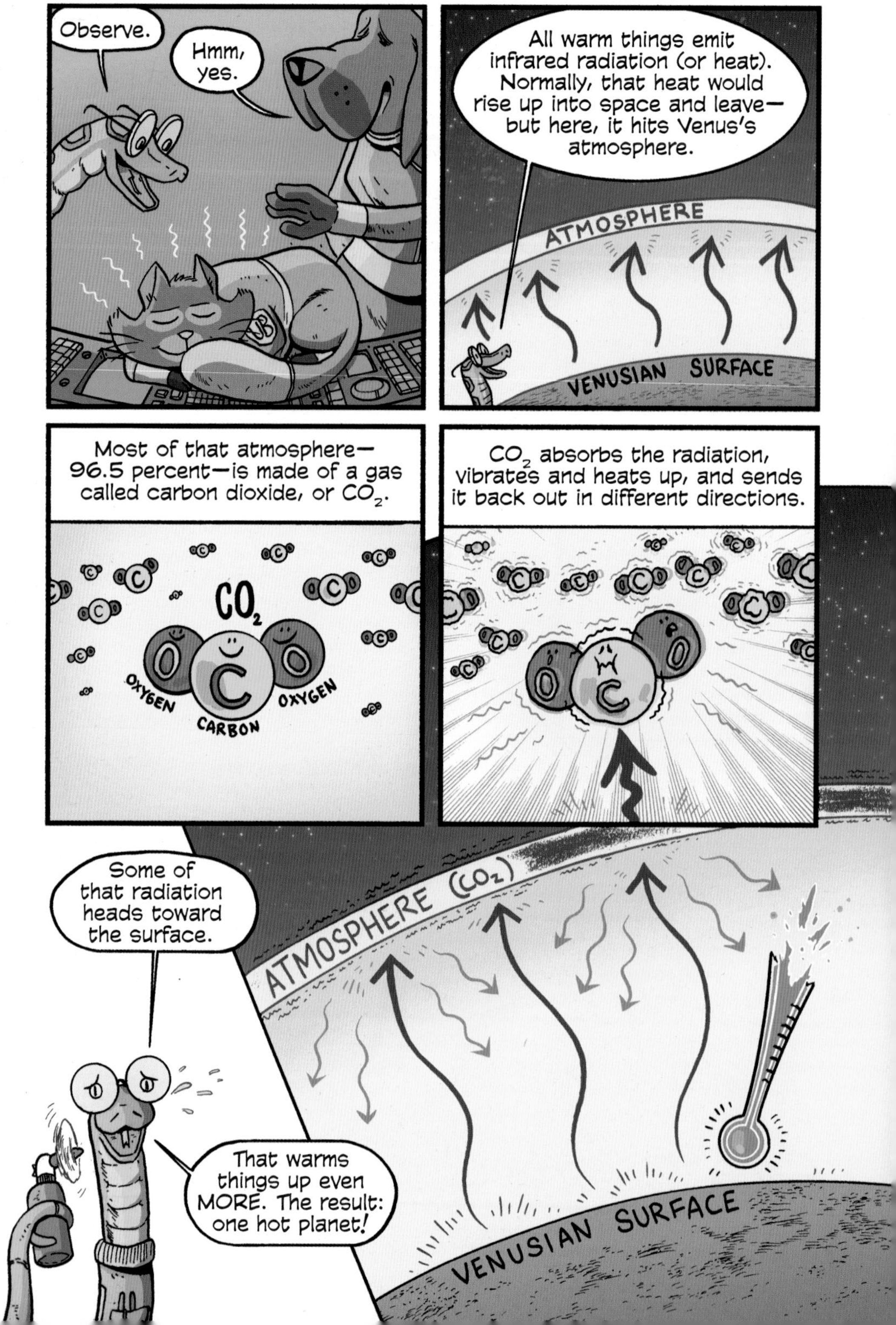
Observe.
Hmm, yes.
All warm things emit infrared radiation (or heat). Normally, that heat would rise up into space and leave—but here, it hits Venus's atmosphere.
ATMOSPHERE
VENUSIAN SURFACE
Most of that atmosphere—96.5 percent—is made of a gas called carbon dioxide, or CO_2.
CO_2
OXYGEN
CARBON
OXYGEN
CO_2 absorbs the radiation, vibrates and heats up, and sends it back out in different directions.
Some of that radiation heads toward the surface.
ATMOSPHERE (CO_2)
VENUSIAN SURFACE
That warms things up even MORE. The result: one hot planet!

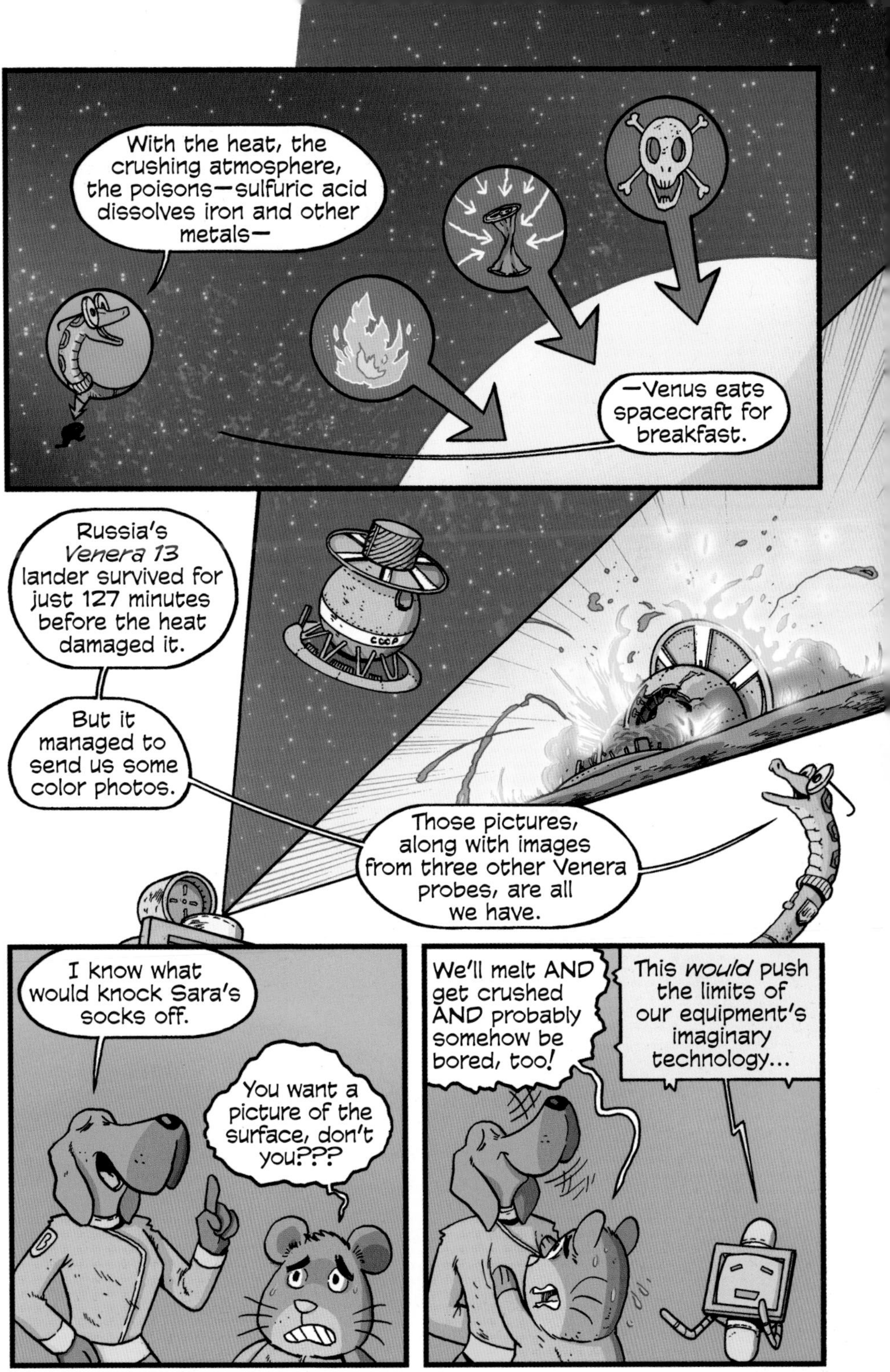
With the heat, the crushing atmosphere, the poisons—sulfuric acid dissolves iron and other metals—
—Venus eats spacecraft for breakfast.
Russia's *Venera 13* lander survived for just 127 minutes before the heat damaged it.
But it managed to send us some color photos.
CCCP
Those pictures, along with images from three other Venera probes, are all we have.
I know what would knock Sara's socks off.
You want a picture of the surface, don't you???
We'll melt AND get crushed AND probably somehow be bored, too!
This *would* push the limits of our equipment's imaginary technology...

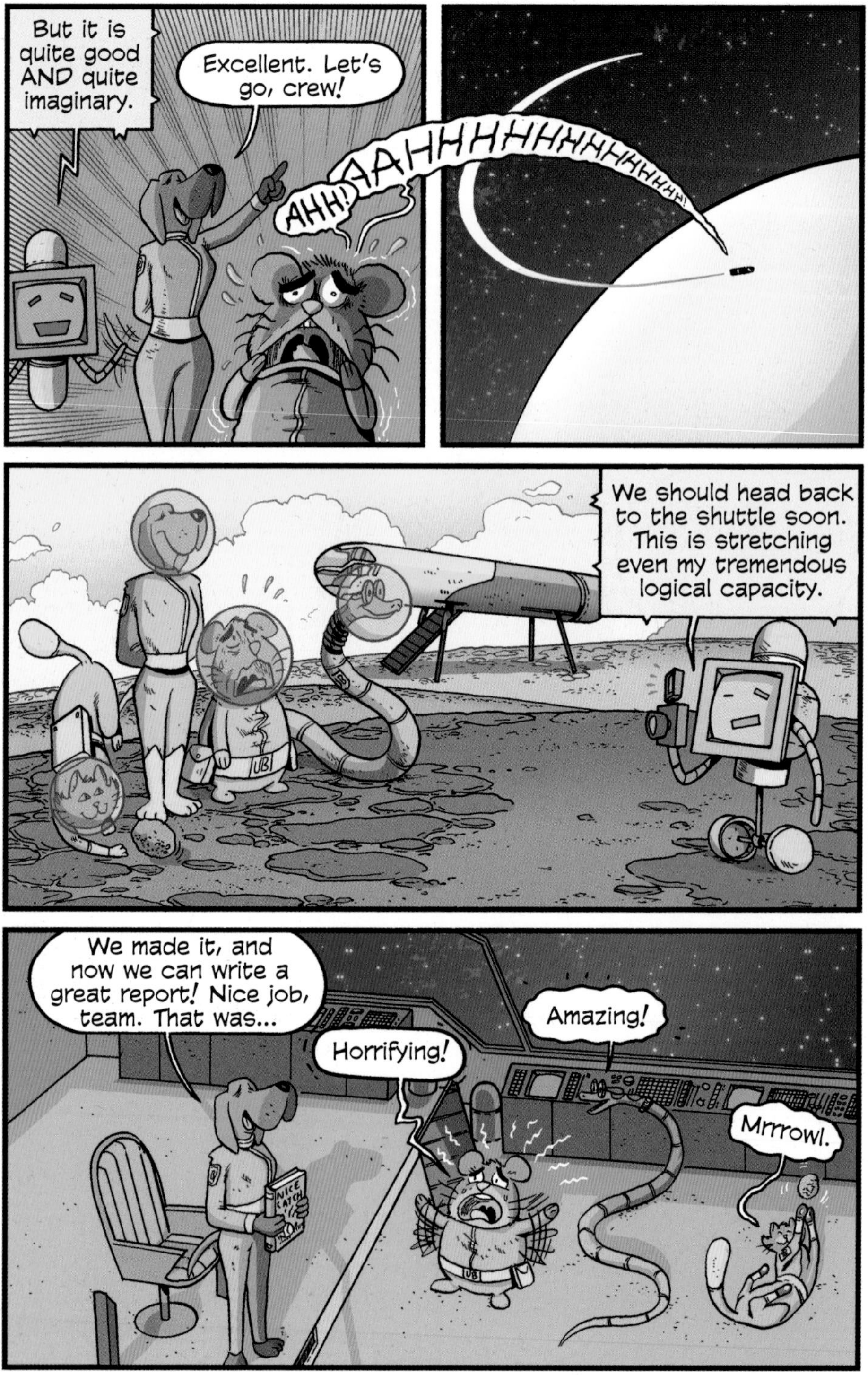
But it is quite good AND quite imaginary.
Excellent. Let's go, crew!
AHH!
AAHHHHHHHHHHHHHHHH!
We should head back to the shuttle soon. This is stretching even my tremendous logical capacity.
We made it, and now we can write a great report! Nice job, team. That was...
Horrifying!
Amazing!
Mrrrowl.
NICE CATCH

VENUS: A REPORT

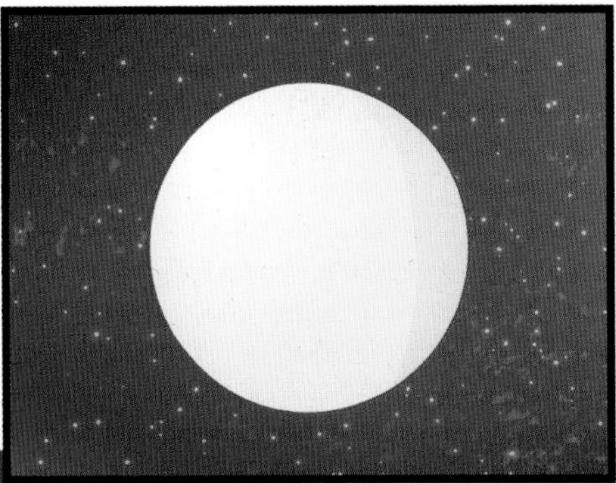

Origin of Name: The ancient Roman goddess of love and beauty.

Size: 7,520.8 miles across—just a little smaller than the Earth.

Contents: An iron core, a rocky mantle, and a rocky crust, plus a thick atmosphere.

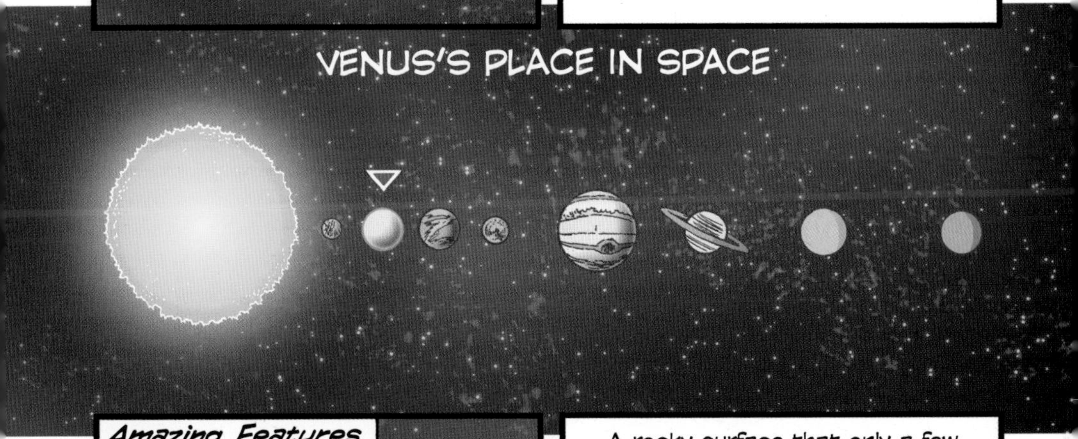
VENUS'S PLACE IN SPACE

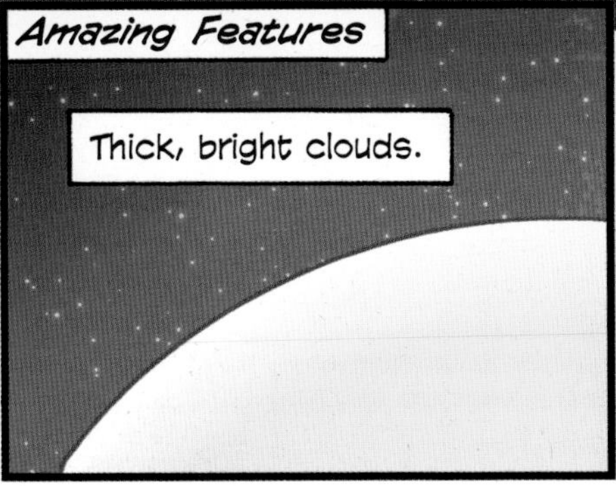
Amazing Features
Thick, bright clouds.

A rocky surface that only a few unpiloted spacecraft—and now a few brave Space Pets—have touched.

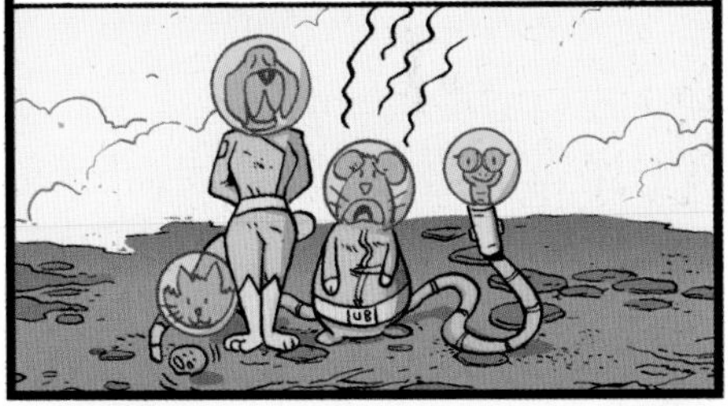

Visits from Earth Spacecraft:
We've made many unpiloted flybys, orbits, and landings. In 1966, *Venera 3* was the first spacecraft to (crash) land on another planet. Most of our info comes from orbiters such as *Magellan* that peek through the clouds with radar.

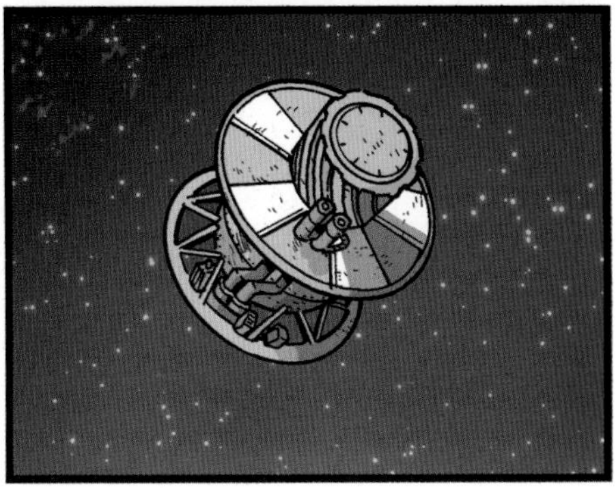

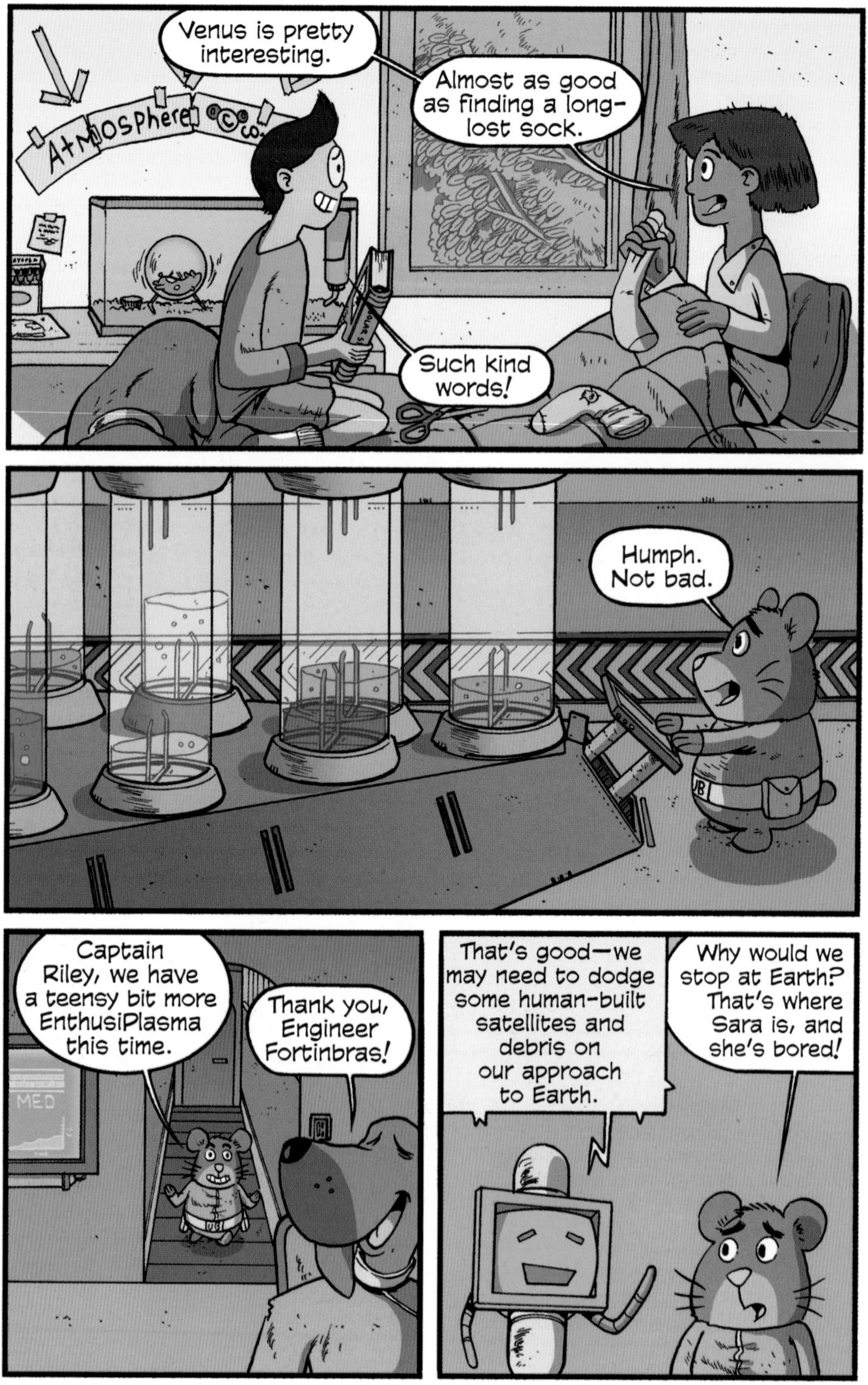
Atmosphere
Venus is pretty interesting.
Almost as good as finding a long-lost sock.
Such kind words!
Humph. Not bad.
Captain Riley, we have a teensy bit more EnthusiPlasma this time.
Thank you, Engineer Fortinbras!
MED
That's good—we may need to dodge some human-built satellites and debris on our approach to Earth.
Why would we stop at Earth? That's where Sara is, and she's bored!

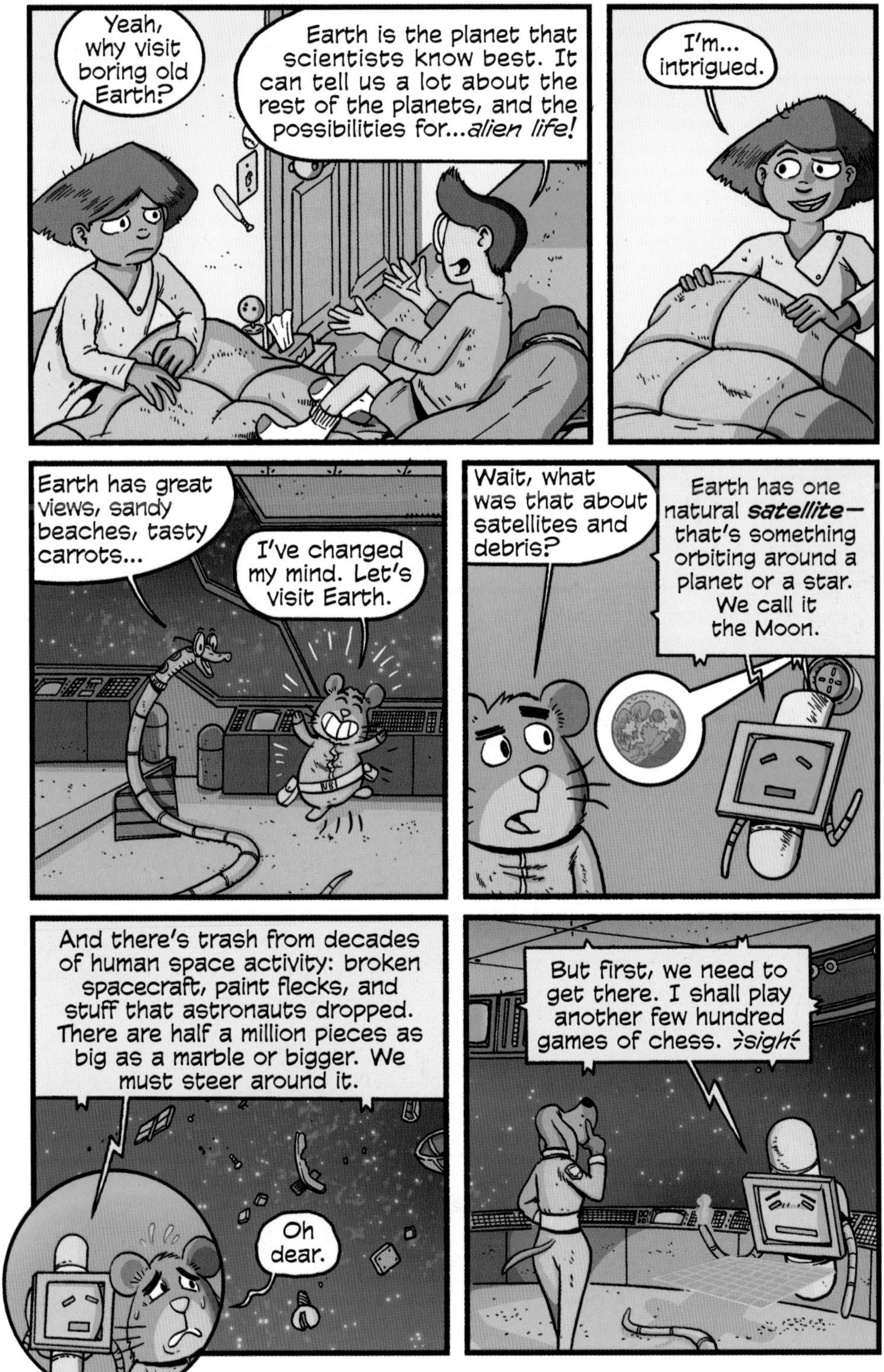

Yeah, why visit boring old Earth?
Earth is the planet that scientists know best. It can tell us a lot about the rest of the planets, and the possibilities for...*alien life!*
I'm... intrigued.
Earth has great views, sandy beaches, tasty carrots...
I've changed my mind. Let's visit Earth.
UB
Wait, what was that about satellites and debris?
Earth has one natural ***satellite***—that's something orbiting around a planet or a star. We call it the Moon.
And there's trash from decades of human space activity: broken spacecraft, paint flecks, and stuff that astronauts dropped. There are half a million pieces as big as a marble or bigger. We must steer around it.
Oh dear.
But first, we need to get there. I shall play another few hundred games of chess. *sigh*

PART 6: EARTH

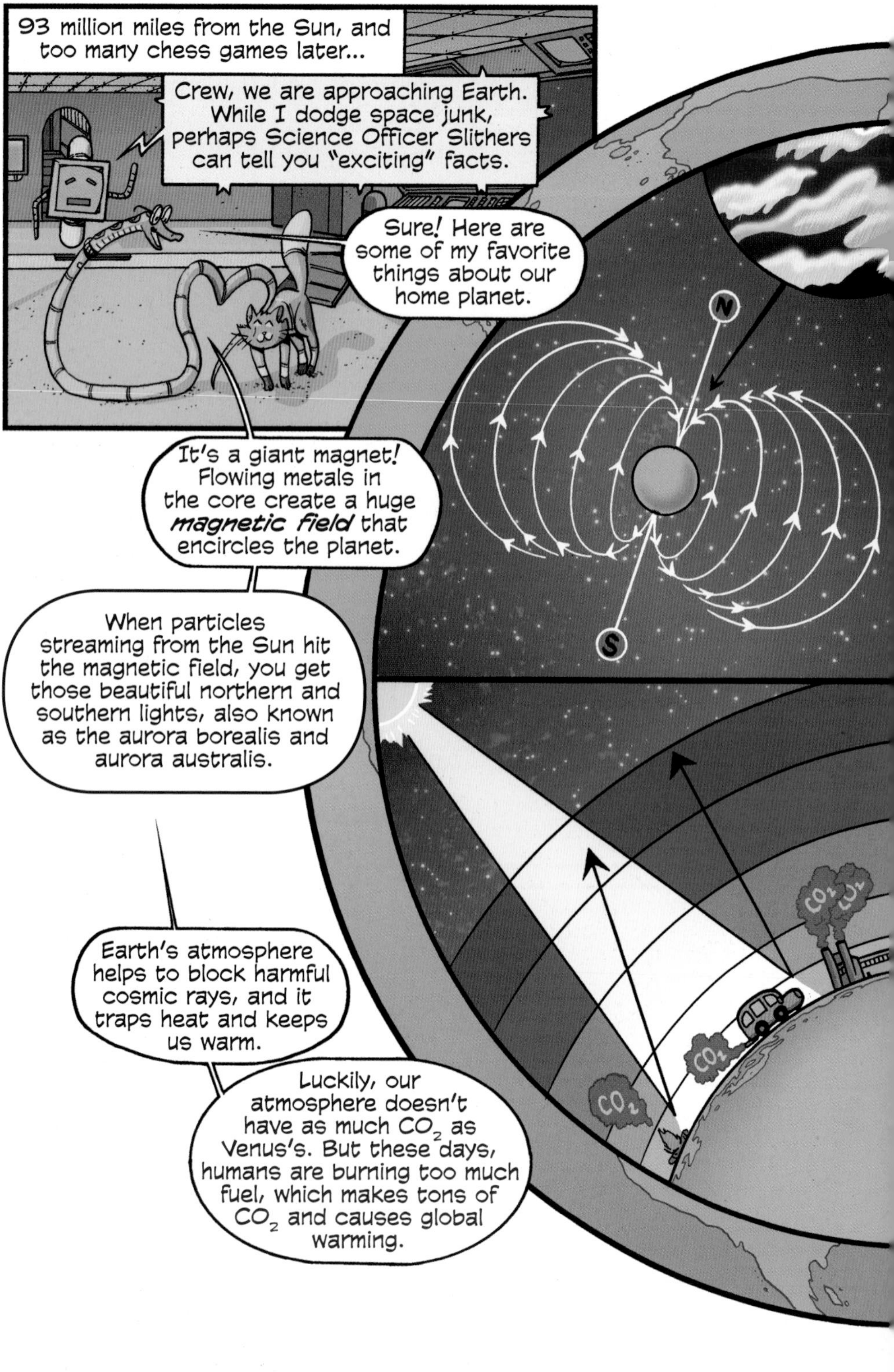

93 million miles from the Sun, and too many chess games later...
Crew, we are approaching Earth. While I dodge space junk, perhaps Science Officer Slithers can tell you "exciting" facts.
Sure! Here are some of my favorite things about our home planet.
It's a giant magnet! Flowing metals in the core create a huge *magnetic field* that encircles the planet.
N
S
When particles streaming from the Sun hit the magnetic field, you get those beautiful northern and southern lights, also known as the aurora borealis and aurora australis.
Earth's atmosphere helps to block harmful cosmic rays, and it traps heat and keeps us warm.
Luckily, our atmosphere doesn't have as much CO_2 as Venus's. But these days, humans are burning too much fuel, which makes tons of CO_2 and causes global warming.
CO_2
CO_2
CO_2
CO_2

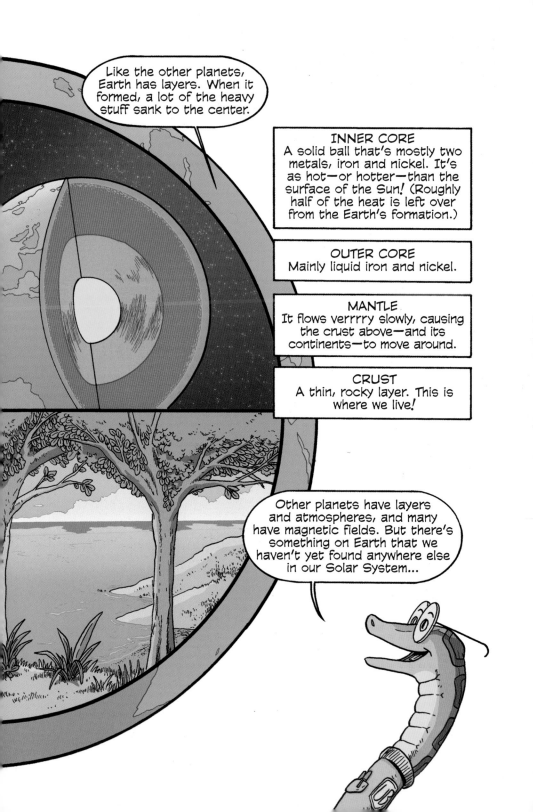

Like the other planets, Earth has layers. When it formed, a lot of the heavy stuff sank to the center.

INNER CORE
A solid ball that's mostly two metals, iron and nickel. It's as hot—or hotter—than the surface of the Sun! (Roughly half of the heat is left over from the Earth's formation.)

OUTER CORE
Mainly liquid iron and nickel.

MANTLE
It flows verrrry slowly, causing the crust above—and its continents—to move around.

CRUST
A thin, rocky layer. This is where we live!

Other planets have layers and atmospheres, and many have magnetic fields. But there's something on Earth that we haven't yet found anywhere else in our Solar System...

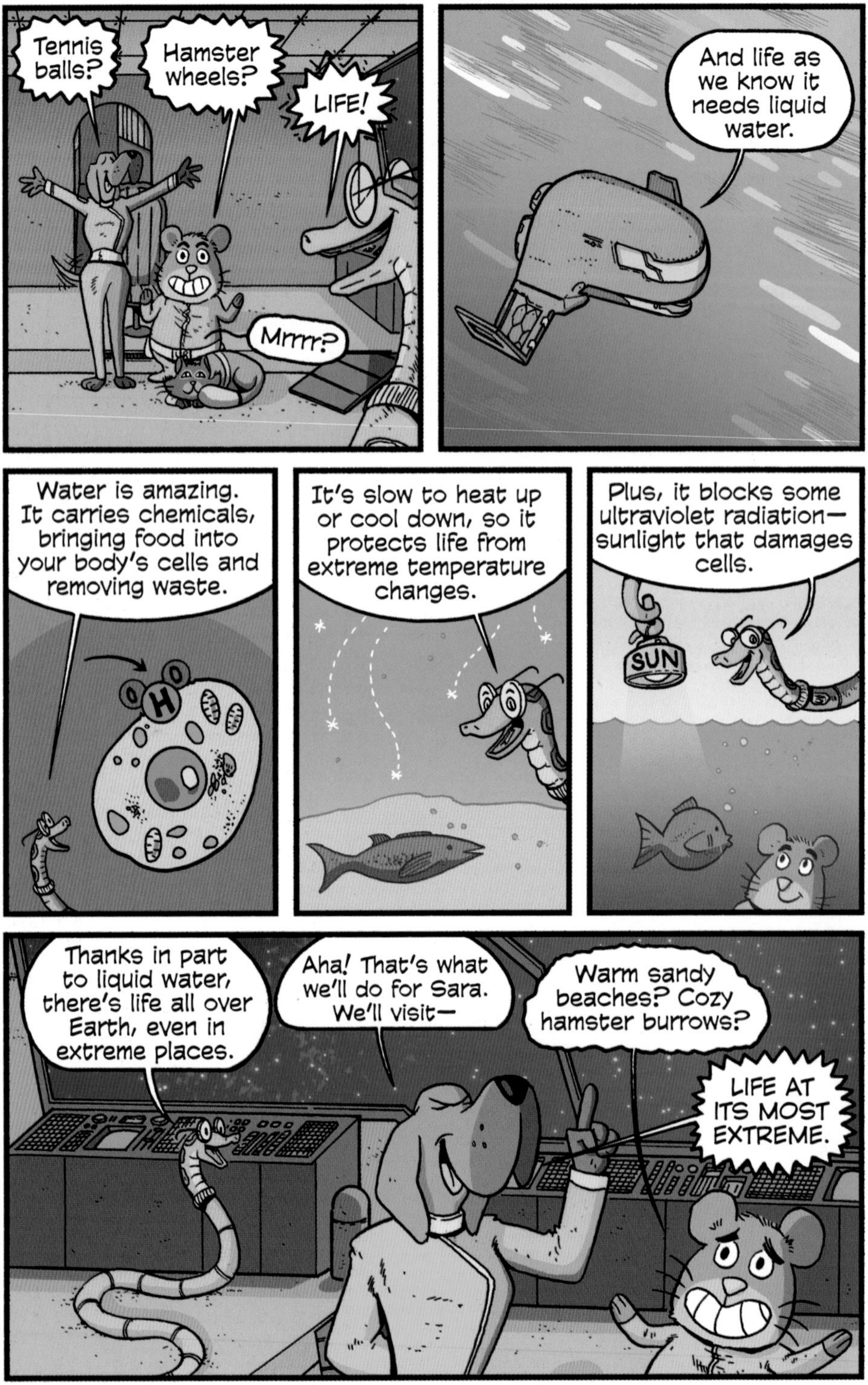
Tennis balls?
Hamster wheels?
LIFE!
Mrrrr?
And life as we know it needs liquid water.
Water is amazing. It carries chemicals, bringing food into your body's cells and removing waste.
H
It's slow to heat up or cool down, so it protects life from extreme temperature changes.
Plus, it blocks some ultraviolet radiation—sunlight that damages cells.
SUN
Thanks in part to liquid water, there's life all over Earth, even in extreme places.
Aha! That's what we'll do for Sara. We'll visit—
Warm sandy beaches? Cozy hamster burrows?
LIFE AT ITS MOST EXTREME.

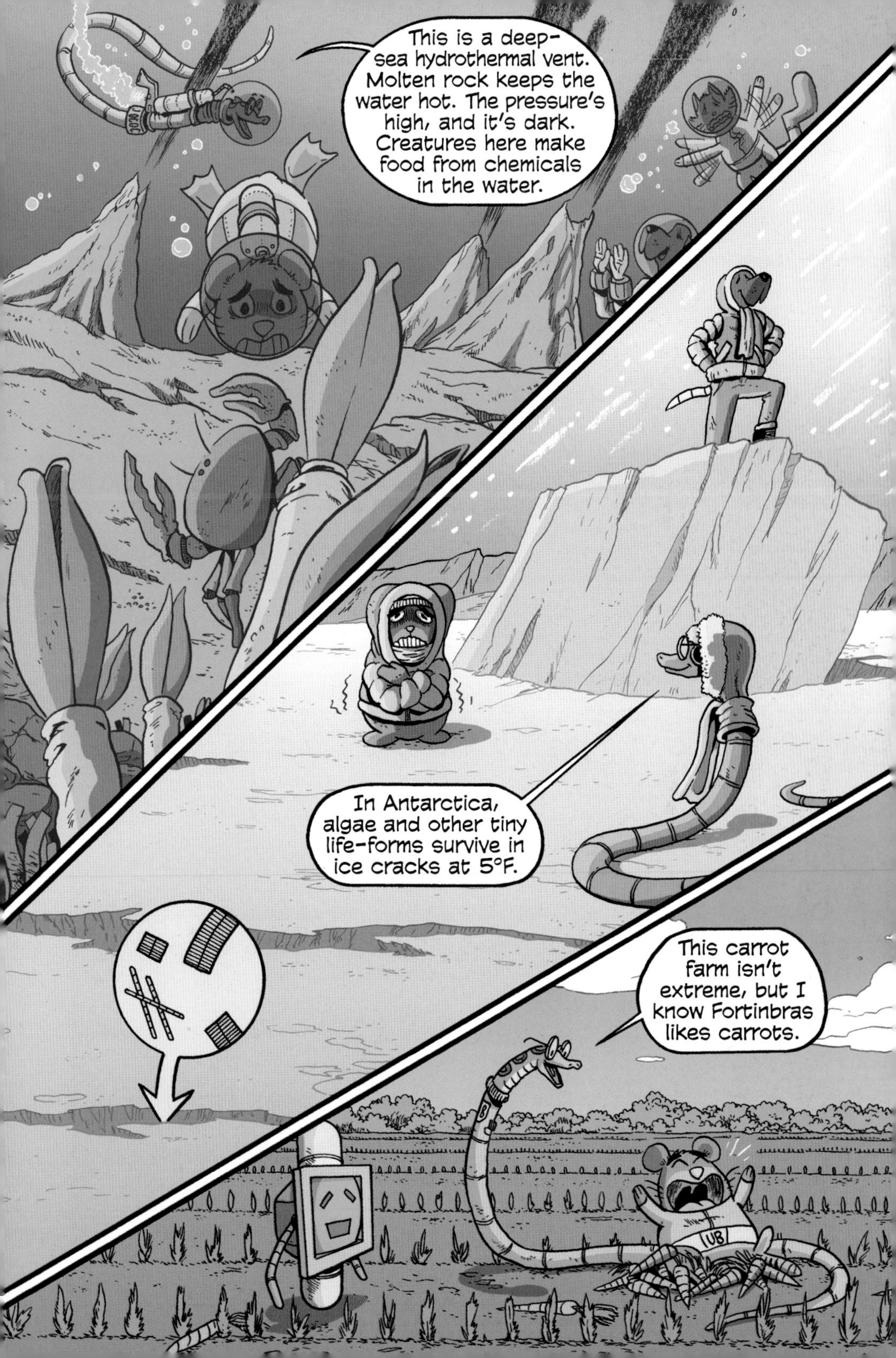
This is a deep-sea hydrothermal vent. Molten rock keeps the water hot. The pressure's high, and it's dark. Creatures here make food from chemicals in the water.
In Antarctica, algae and other tiny life-forms survive in ice cracks at 5°F.
This carrot farm isn't extreme, but I know Fortinbras likes carrots.
UB

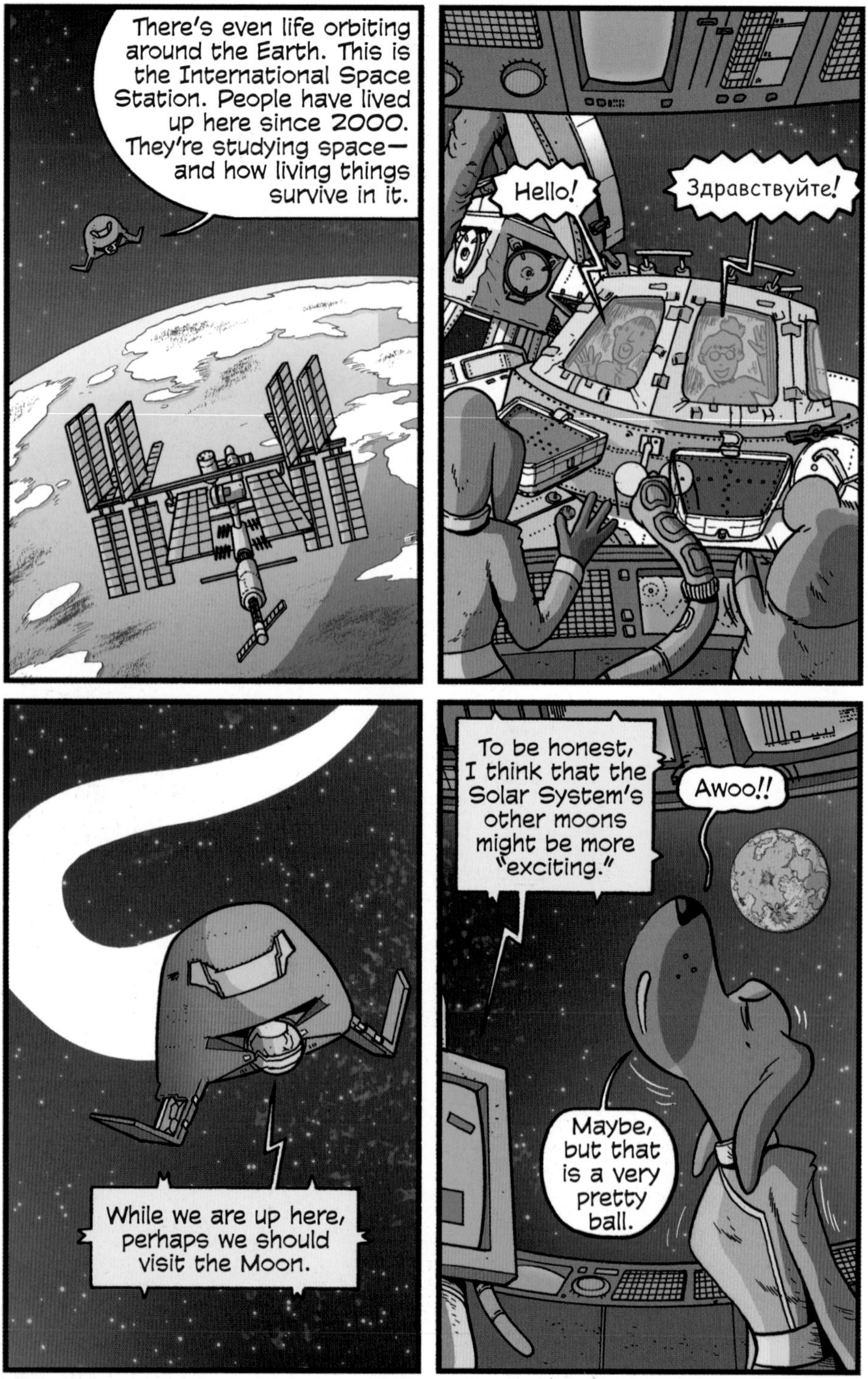
There's even life orbiting around the Earth. This is the International Space Station. People have lived up here since 2000. They're studying space—and how living things survive in it.
Hello!
Здравствуйте!
While we are up here, perhaps we should visit the Moon.
To be honest, I think that the Solar System's other moons might be more "exciting."
Awoo!!
Maybe, but that is a very pretty ball.

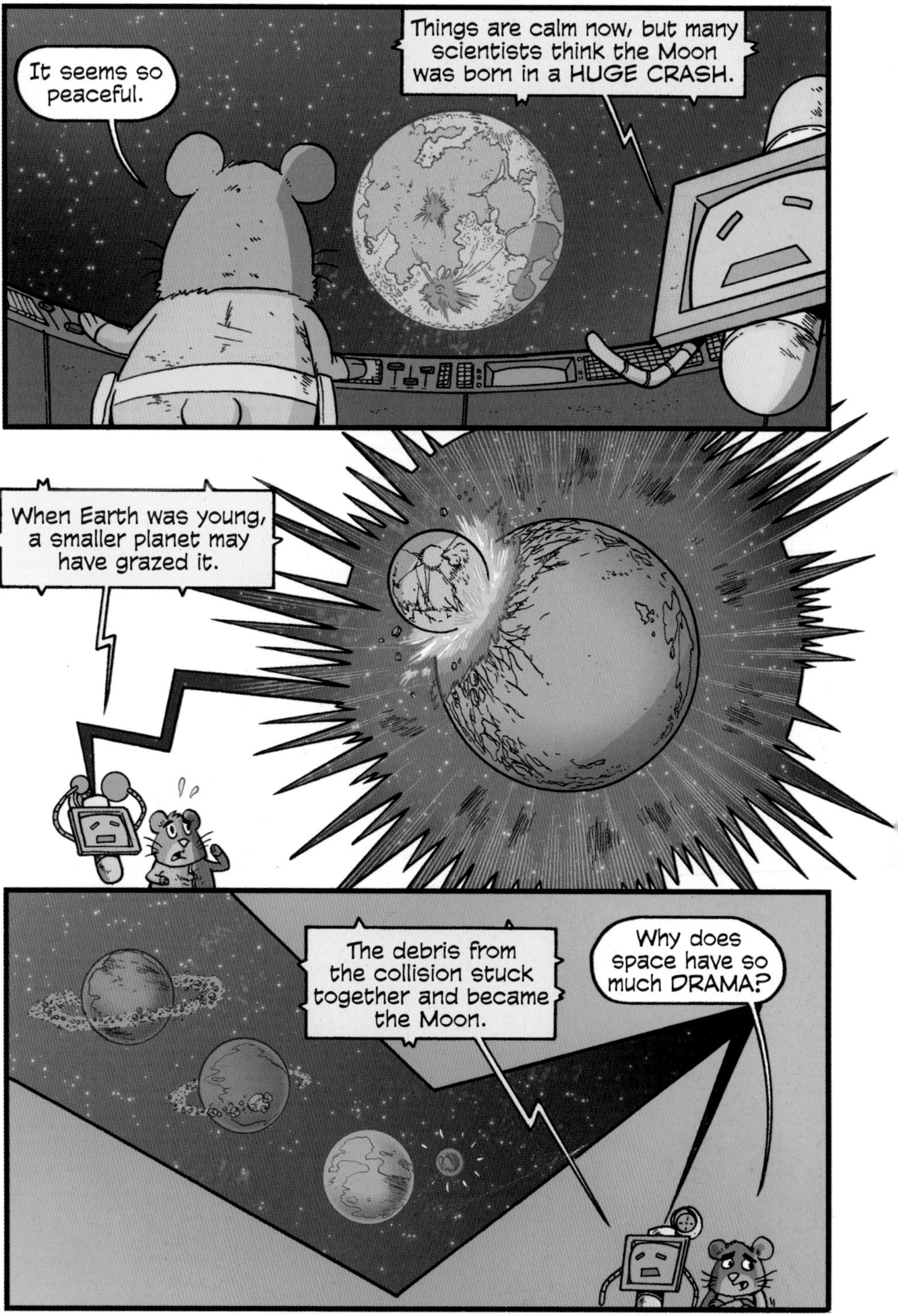
It seems so peaceful.
Things are calm now, but many scientists think the Moon was born in a HUGE CRASH.
When Earth was young, a smaller planet may have grazed it.
The debris from the collision stuck together and became the Moon.
Why does space have so much DRAMA?

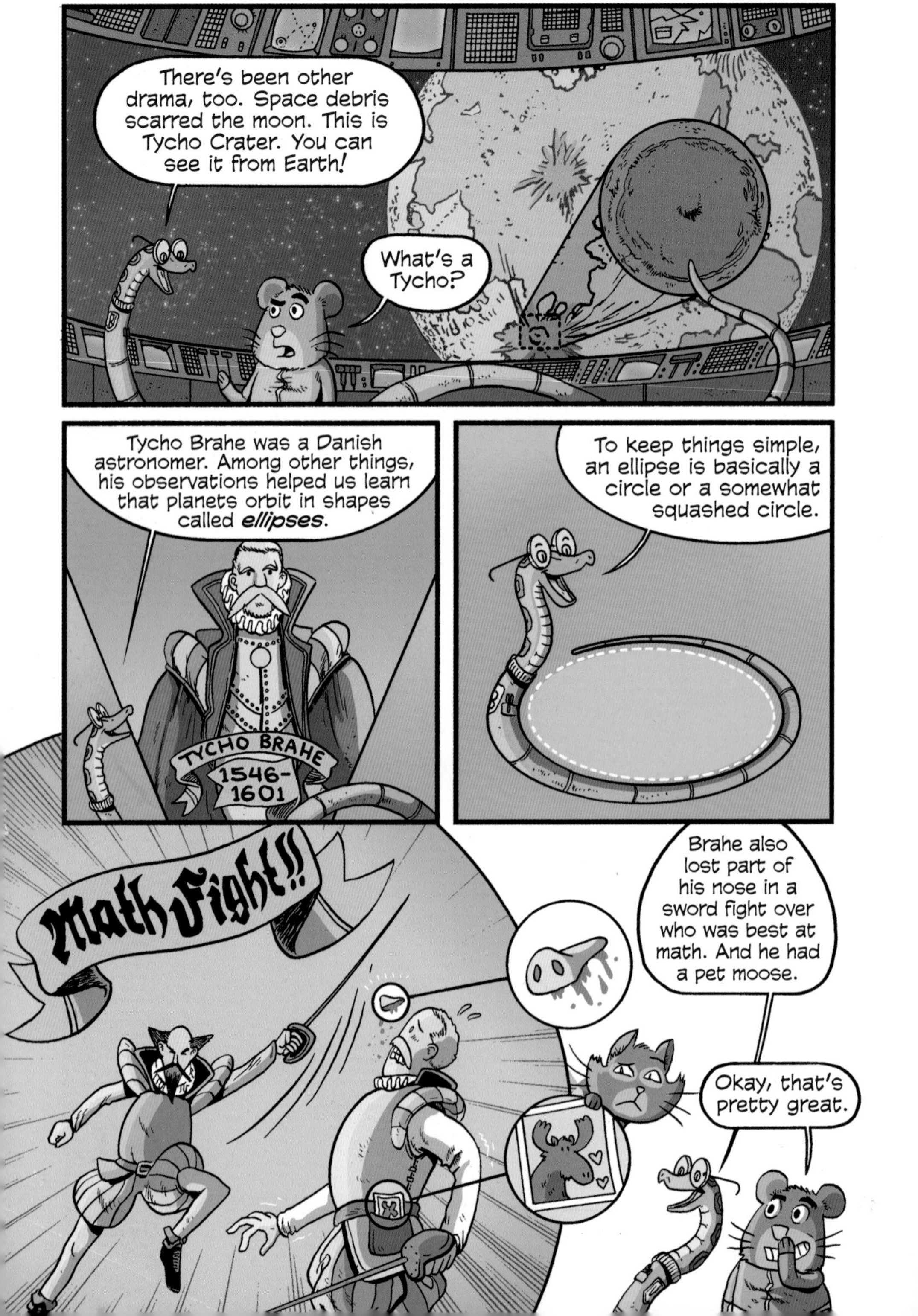
There's been other drama, too. Space debris scarred the moon. This is Tycho Crater. You can see it from Earth!
What's a Tycho?
Tycho Brahe was a Danish astronomer. Among other things, his observations helped us learn that planets orbit in shapes called *ellipses*.
TYCHO BRAHE
1546-1601
To keep things simple, an ellipse is basically a circle or a somewhat squashed circle.
Math Fight!!
Brahe also lost part of his nose in a sword fight over who was best at math. And he had a pet moose.
Okay, that's pretty great.

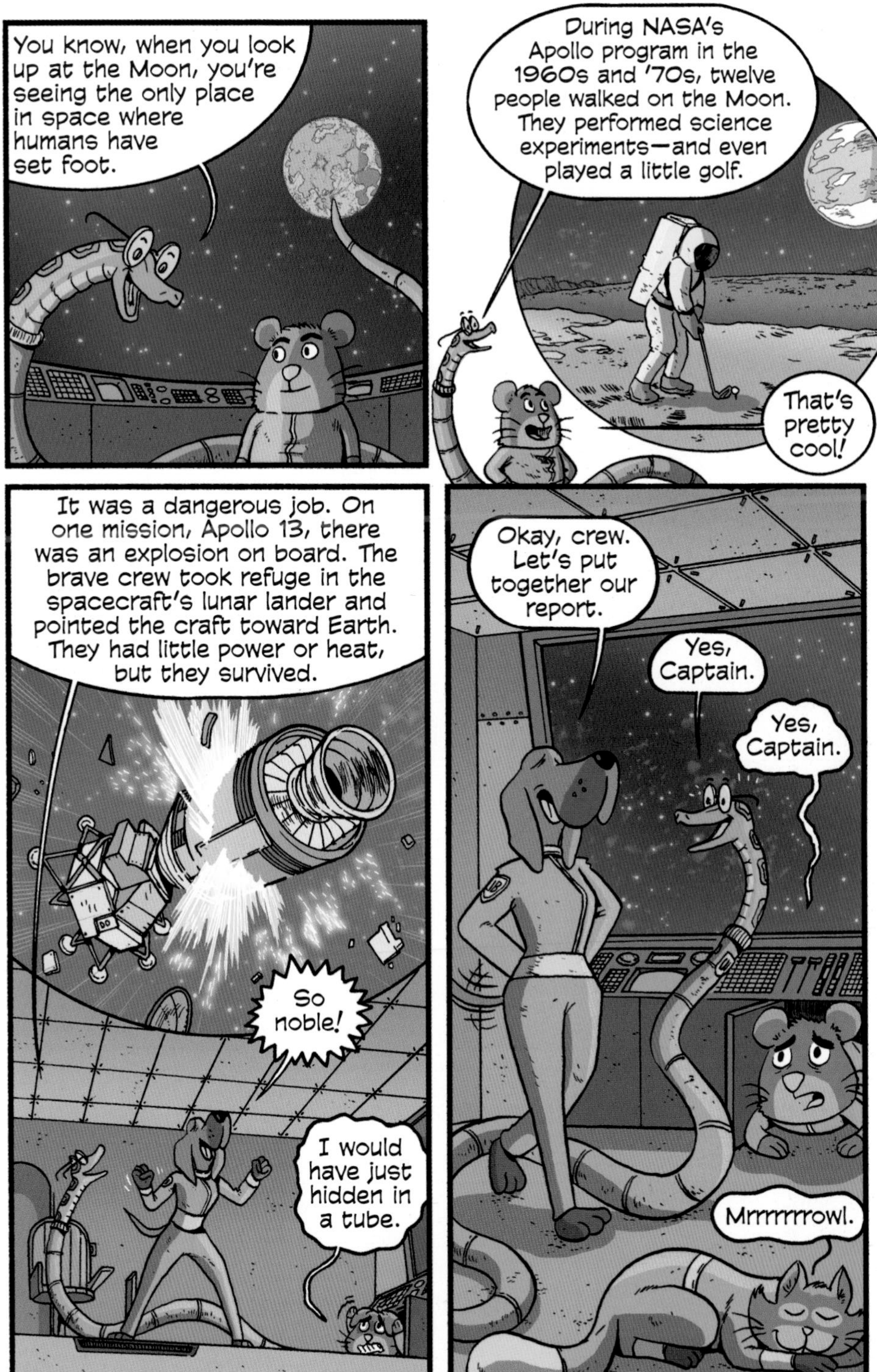
You know, when you look up at the Moon, you're seeing the only place in space where humans have set foot.
During NASA's Apollo program in the 1960s and '70s, twelve people walked on the Moon. They performed science experiments—and even played a little golf.
That's pretty cool!
It was a dangerous job. On one mission, Apollo 13, there was an explosion on board. The brave crew took refuge in the spacecraft's lunar lander and pointed the craft toward Earth. They had little power or heat, but they survived.
So noble!
I would have just hidden in a tube.
Okay, crew. Let's put together our report.
Yes, Captain.
Yes, Captain.
Mrrrrrrowl.

EARTH: A REPORT

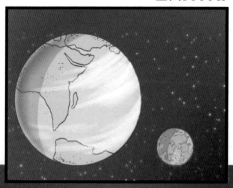

Size: 7,917.5 miles in diameter—more than 3 times wider than the Moon (2,159.2 miles).

Contents: A solid-metal inner core, a liquid-metal outer core, a rocky flowing mantle, and a thin stiff crust, plus an atmosphere that keeps us nice and toasty.

EARTH'S PLACE IN SPACE

Amazing Features

Liquid water, which is important for life.

The Moon, plus all sorts of satellites built by people, including the International Space Station!

Important Note:

Earth is the only place in the Solar System where we've found life. It exists in many extreme places, such as deep-sea hydrothermal vents, ice cracks in Antarctica, and tasty carrot farms.

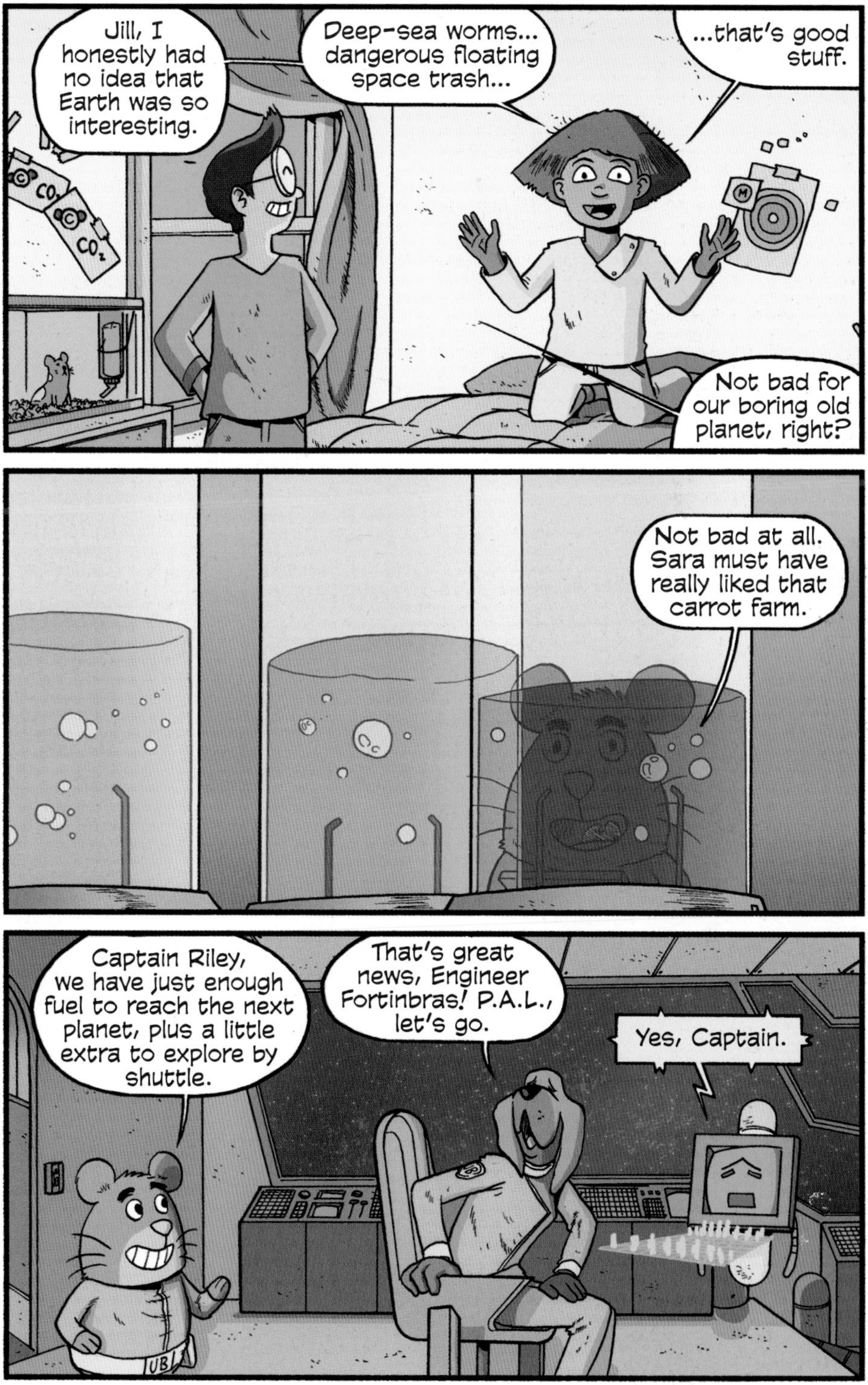
Jill, I honestly had no idea that Earth was so interesting.
Deep-sea worms... dangerous floating space trash...
...that's good stuff.
Not bad for our boring old planet, right?
Not bad at all. Sara must have really liked that carrot farm.
Captain Riley, we have just enough fuel to reach the next planet, plus a little extra to explore by shuttle.
That's great news, Engineer Fortinbras! P.A.L., let's go.
Yes, Captain.

PART 7: MARS

141.6 million miles from the Sun...

Crew, we are approaching the planet Mars. It's named for the ancient Roman god of war, perhaps because it is red and reminded people of blood.

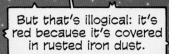

But that's illogical: it's red because it's covered in rusted iron dust.

sigh

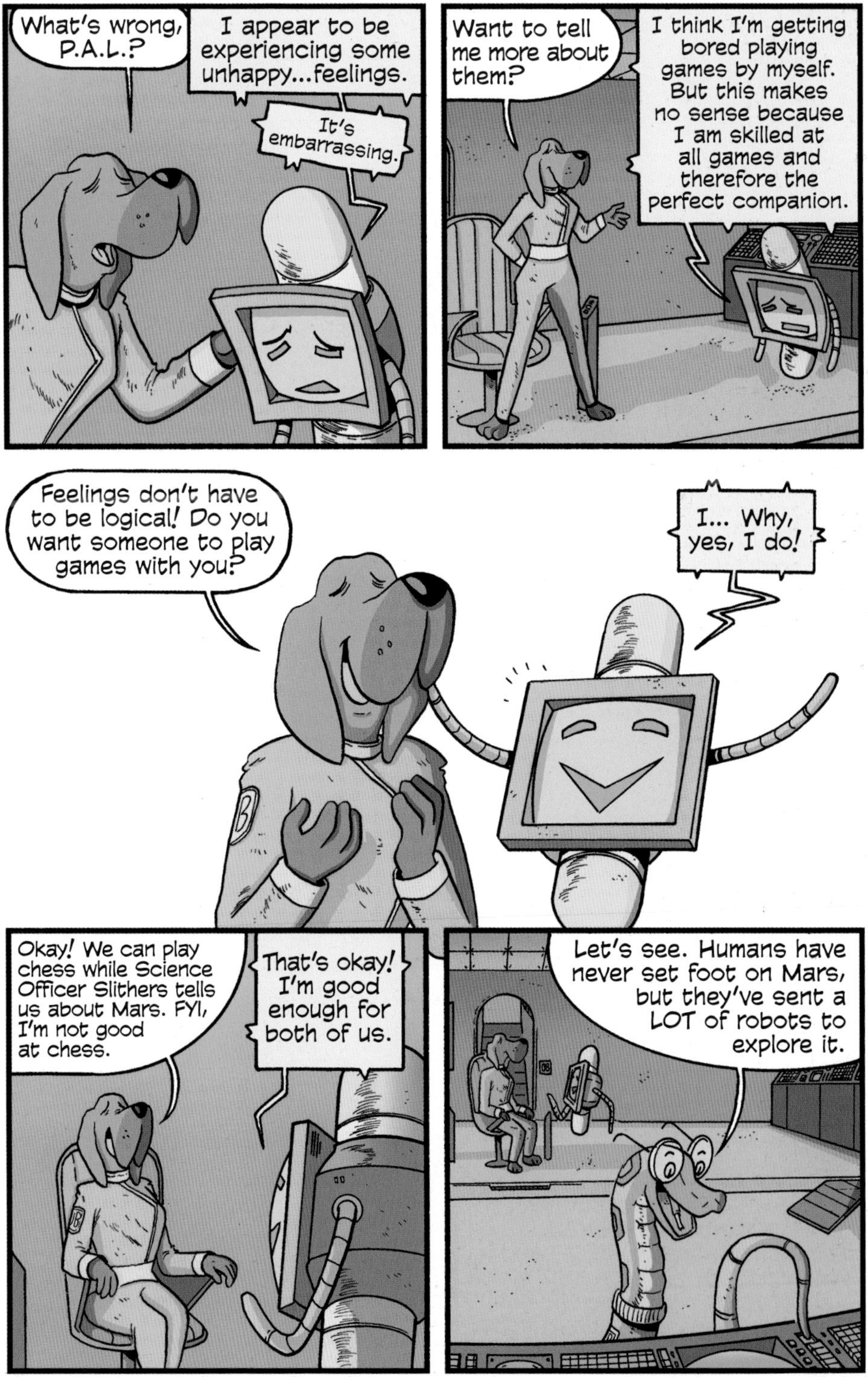
What's wrong, P.A.L.?
I appear to be experiencing some unhappy...feelings.
It's embarrassing.
Want to tell me more about them?
I think I'm getting bored playing games by myself. But this makes no sense because I am skilled at all games and therefore the perfect companion.
Feelings don't have to be logical! Do you want someone to play games with you?
I... Why, yes, I do!
Okay! We can play chess while Science Officer Slithers tells us about Mars. FYI, I'm not good at chess.
That's okay! I'm good enough for both of us.
Let's see. Humans have never set foot on Mars, but they've sent a LOT of robots to explore it.

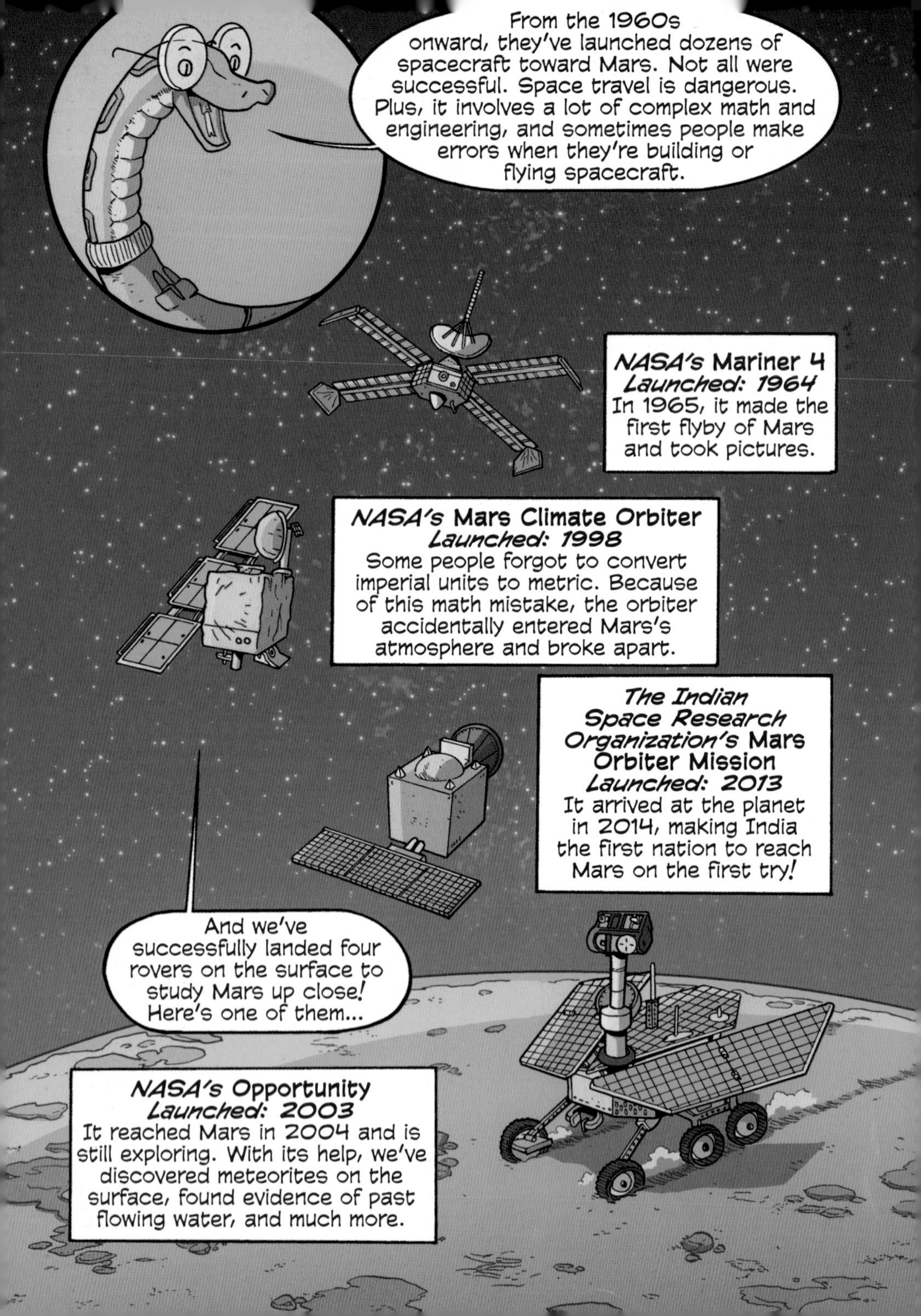
From the 1960s onward, they've launched dozens of spacecraft toward Mars. Not all were successful. Space travel is dangerous. Plus, it involves a lot of complex math and engineering, and sometimes people make errors when they're building or flying spacecraft.
NASA's Mariner 4 Launched: 1964 In 1965, it made the first flyby of Mars and took pictures.
NASA's Mars Climate Orbiter Launched: 1998 Some people forgot to convert imperial units to metric. Because of this math mistake, the orbiter accidentally entered Mars's atmosphere and broke apart.
The Indian Space Research Organization's Mars Orbiter Mission Launched: 2013 It arrived at the planet in 2014, making India the first nation to reach Mars on the first try!
And we've successfully landed four rovers on the surface to study Mars up close! Here's one of them...
NASA's Opportunity Launched: 2003 It reached Mars in 2004 and is still exploring. With its help, we've discovered meteorites on the surface, found evidence of past flowing water, and much more.

Thanks to these orbiters and rovers, we've learned a lot about Mars.

It has two tiny lumpy moons: Phobos and Deimos. The US island of Manhattan is longer than Deimos!

Hah! Earth's Moon is way better.

Mars once had liquid water on its surface—perhaps oceans or just floods. Then the magnetic field and atmosphere disappeared, and the water dried up.

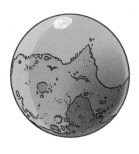

Because Mars doesn't have much of an atmosphere, it's cold. Earth averages a balmy 58.3°F, but Mars is about -63°F.

Brrr. Horrible.

Oh, but there's lots of cool stuff down there!

Crew, let's take the shuttle in for a closer look. I think I've almost lost this chess game, anyway.

Yes, you definitely have!

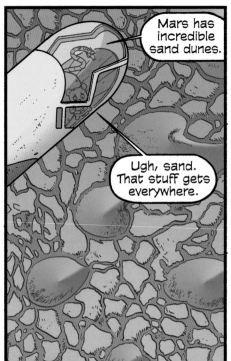

Mars has incredible sand dunes.

Ugh, sand. That stuff gets everywhere.

Towering whirlwinds called dust devils blow away the rusty dust and draw squiggles on the surface.

Olympus Mons, the Solar System's largest-known volcano, is more than twice as high as Mount Everest.

I... Wow.

EVEREST

And this is Valles Marineris, a canyon that's almost as long as the whole United States.

Wow.

Nice work, crew! Let's return to the *Unbored*.

56

PART 8: LEAVING MARS & ASTEROID BELT

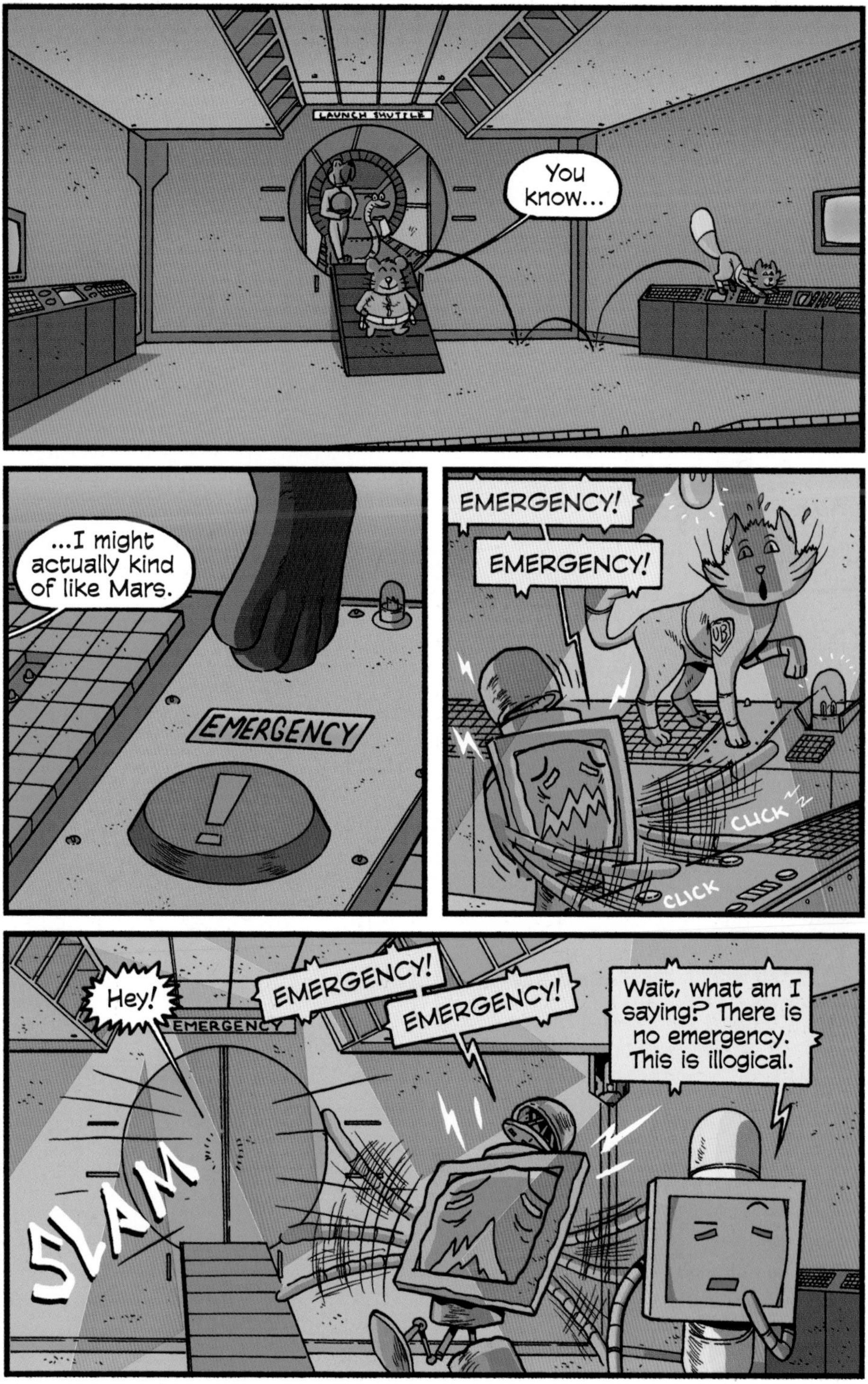
LAUNCH SHUTTLE
You know...
...I might actually kind of like Mars.
EMERGENCY
EMERGENCY!
EMERGENCY!
CLICK
CLICK
Hey!
EMERGENCY
EMERGENCY!
EMERGENCY!
Wait, what am I saying? There is no emergency. This is illogical.
SLAM

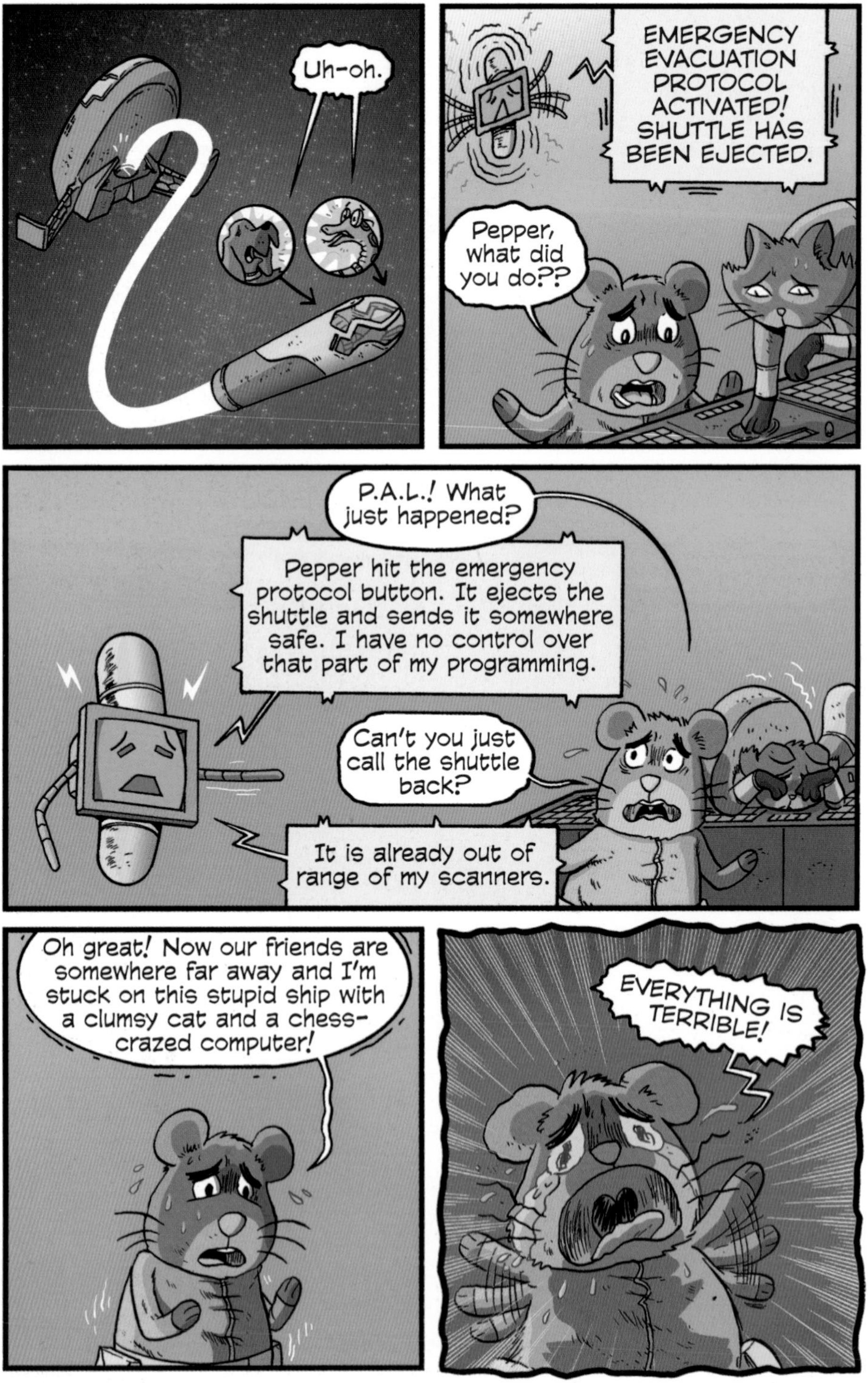

Uh-oh.
EMERGENCY EVACUATION PROTOCOL ACTIVATED! SHUTTLE HAS BEEN EJECTED.
Pepper, what did you do??
P.A.L.! What just happened?
Pepper hit the emergency protocol button. It ejects the shuttle and sends it somewhere safe. I have no control over that part of my programming.
Can't you just call the shuttle back?
It is already out of range of my scanners.
Oh great! Now our friends are somewhere far away and I'm stuck on this stupid ship with a clumsy cat and a chess-crazed computer!
EVERYTHING IS TERRIBLE!

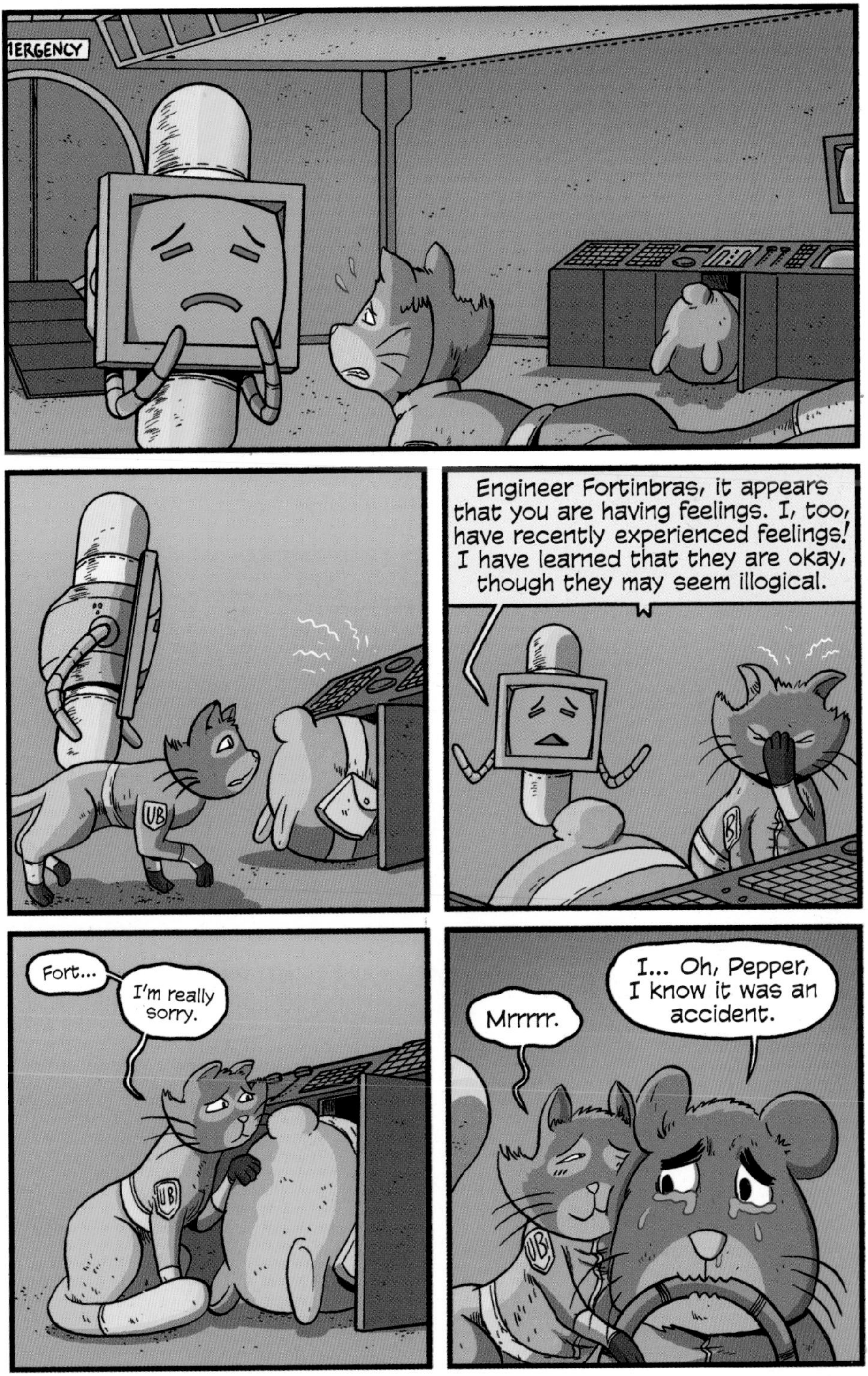

MERGENCY
Engineer Fortinbras, it appears that you are having feelings. I, too, have recently experienced feelings! I have learned that they are okay, though they may seem illogical.
Fort...
I'm really sorry.
Mrrrrr.
I... Oh, Pepper, I know it was an accident.

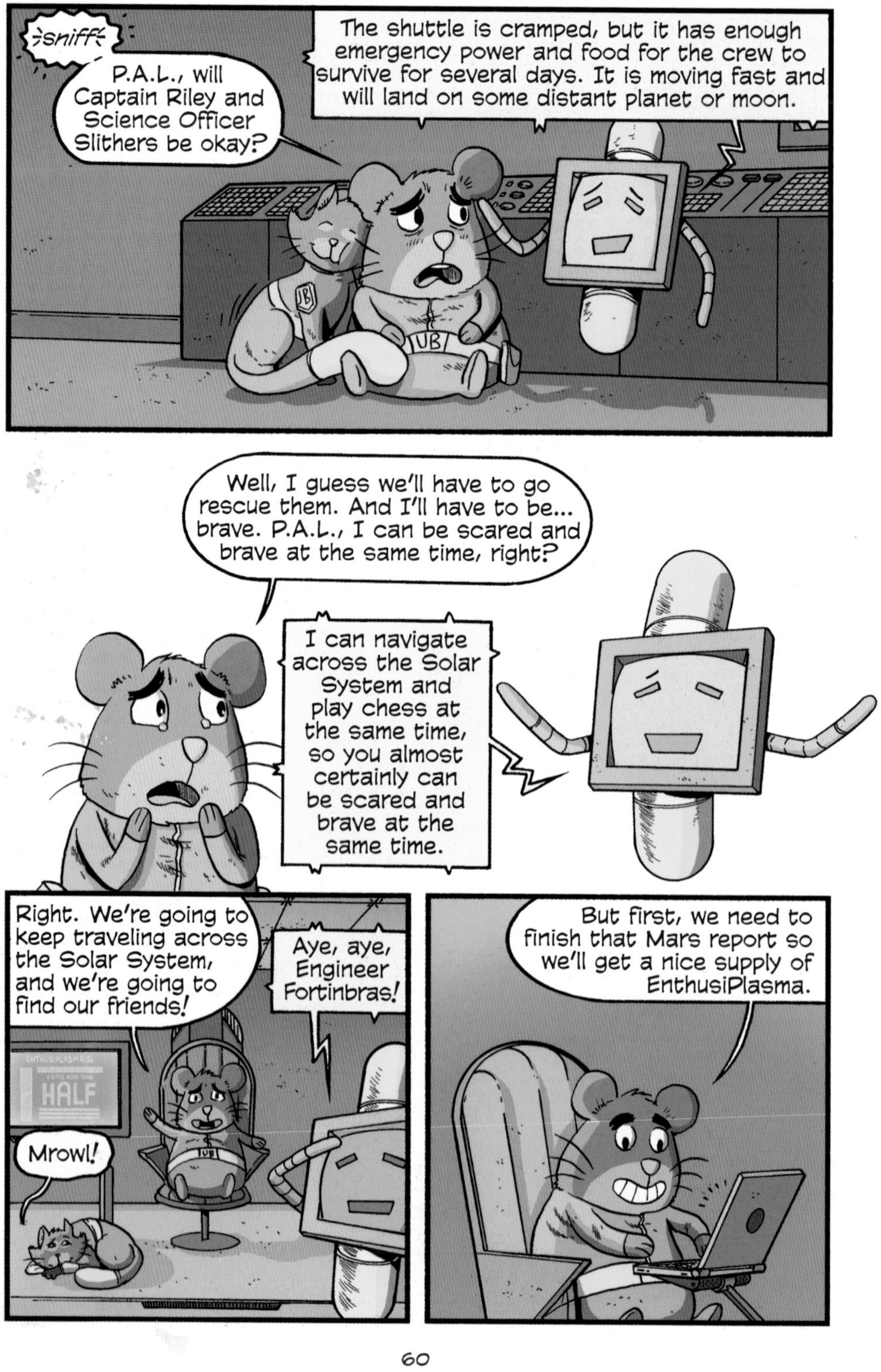

sniff
P.A.L., will Captain Riley and Science Officer Slithers be okay?
The shuttle is cramped, but it has enough emergency power and food for the crew to survive for several days. It is moving fast and will land on some distant planet or moon.
Well, I guess we'll have to go rescue them. And I'll have to be... brave. P.A.L., I can be scared and brave at the same time, right?
I can navigate across the Solar System and play chess at the same time, so you almost certainly can be scared and brave at the same time.
Right. We're going to keep traveling across the Solar System, and we're going to find our friends!
Aye, aye, Engineer Fortinbras!
HALF
Mrowl!
But first, we need to finish that Mars report so we'll get a nice supply of EnthusiPlasma.

MARS: A REPORT

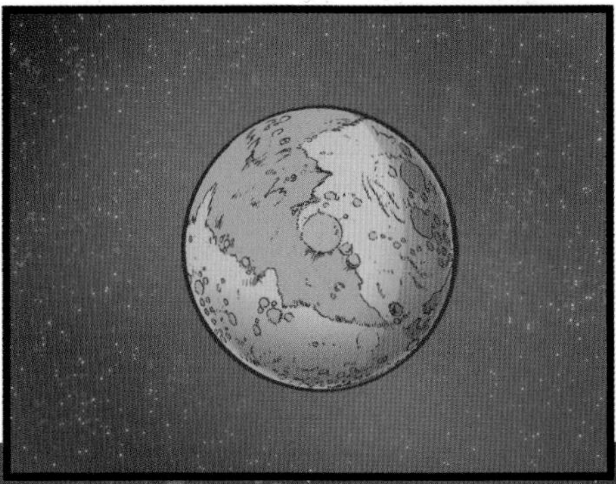

Origin of Name: The ancient Roman god of war and agriculture.

Size: 4,212 miles across—just a little more than half the width of Earth.

Contents: An iron (possibly partly liquid) core, a rocky mantle, and a crust, plus a thin atmosphere.

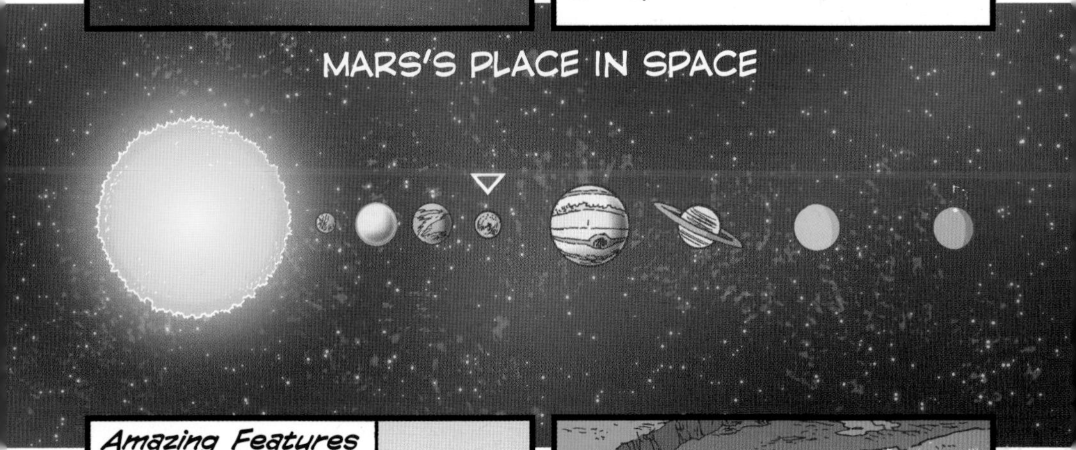
MARS'S PLACE IN SPACE

Amazing Features

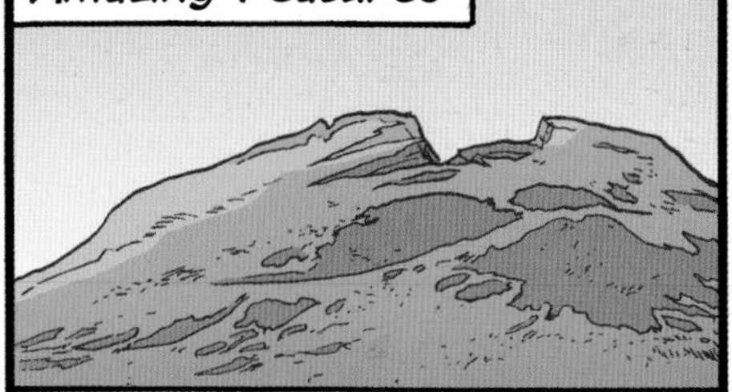

Olympus Mons, the largest-known volcano in the Solar System.

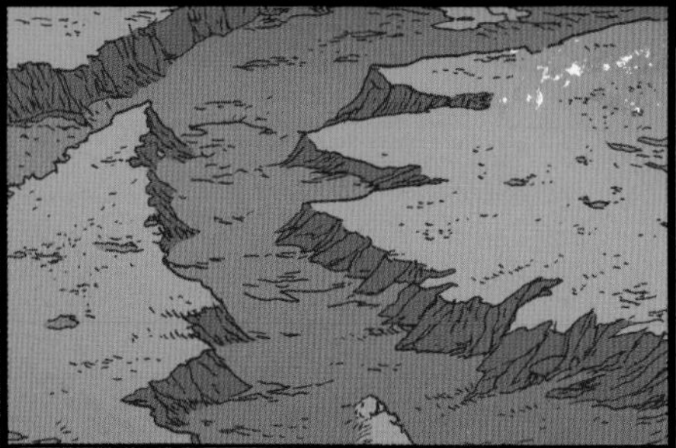

Valles Marineris, a huge canyon.

Visits from Earth Spacecraft:
Many! People have been launching spacecraft at Mars since the 1960s. There have been flybys, orbiting and landing spacecraft, and rovers—dozens of craft in all!

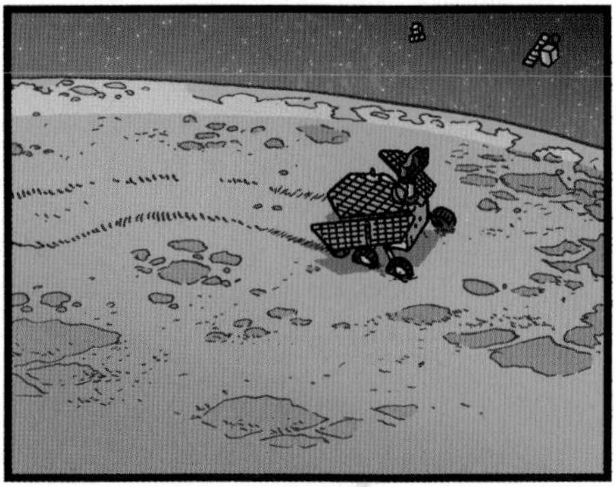

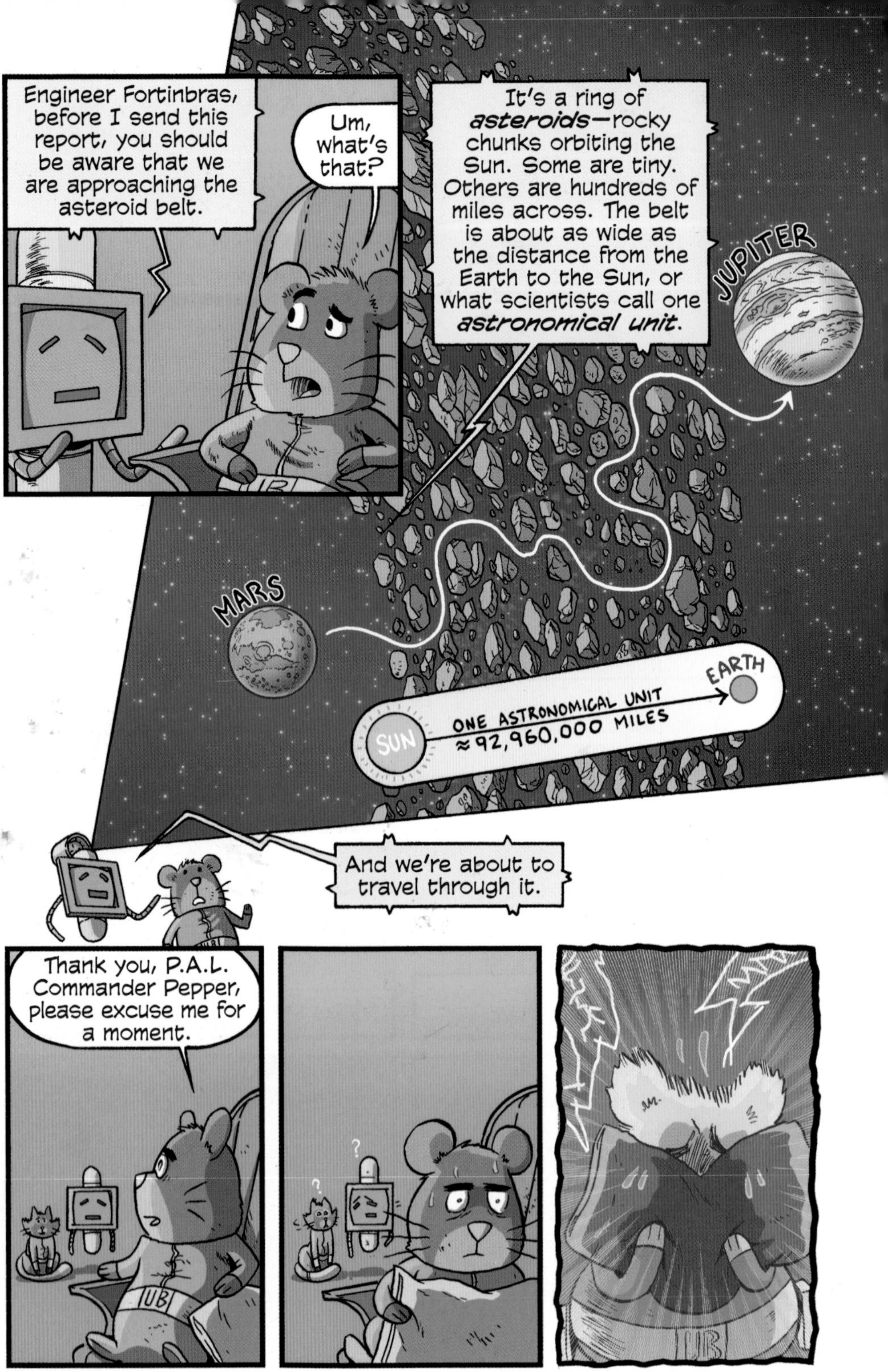

Engineer Fortinbras, before I send this report, you should be aware that we are approaching the asteroid belt.
Um, what's that?
It's a ring of *asteroids*—rocky chunks orbiting the Sun. Some are tiny. Others are hundreds of miles across. The belt is about as wide as the distance from the Earth to the Sun, or what scientists call one *astronomical unit*.
JUPITER
MARS
EARTH
SUN
ONE ASTRONOMICAL UNIT
≈92,960,000 MILES
And we're about to travel through it.
Thank you, P.A.L. Commander Pepper, please excuse me for a moment.

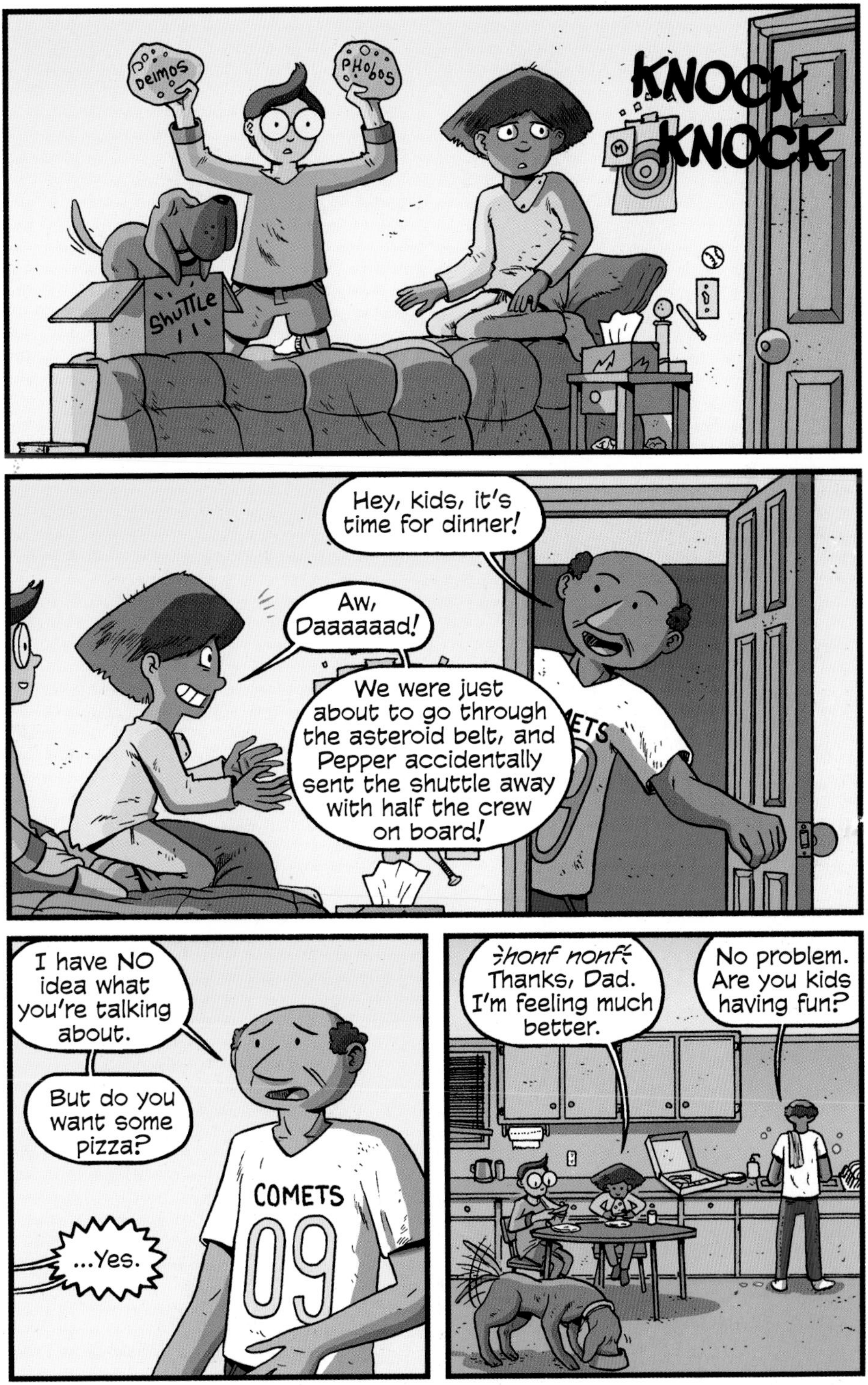
DEIMOS
PHOBOS
SHUTTLE
KNOCK KNOCK
Hey, kids, it's time for dinner!
Aw, Daaaaaad!
We were just about to go through the asteroid belt, and Pepper accidentally sent the shuttle away with half the crew on board!
I have NO idea what you're talking about.
But do you want some pizza?
COMETS 09
...Yes.
≈honf nonf≈ Thanks, Dad. I'm feeling much better.
No problem. Are you kids having fun?

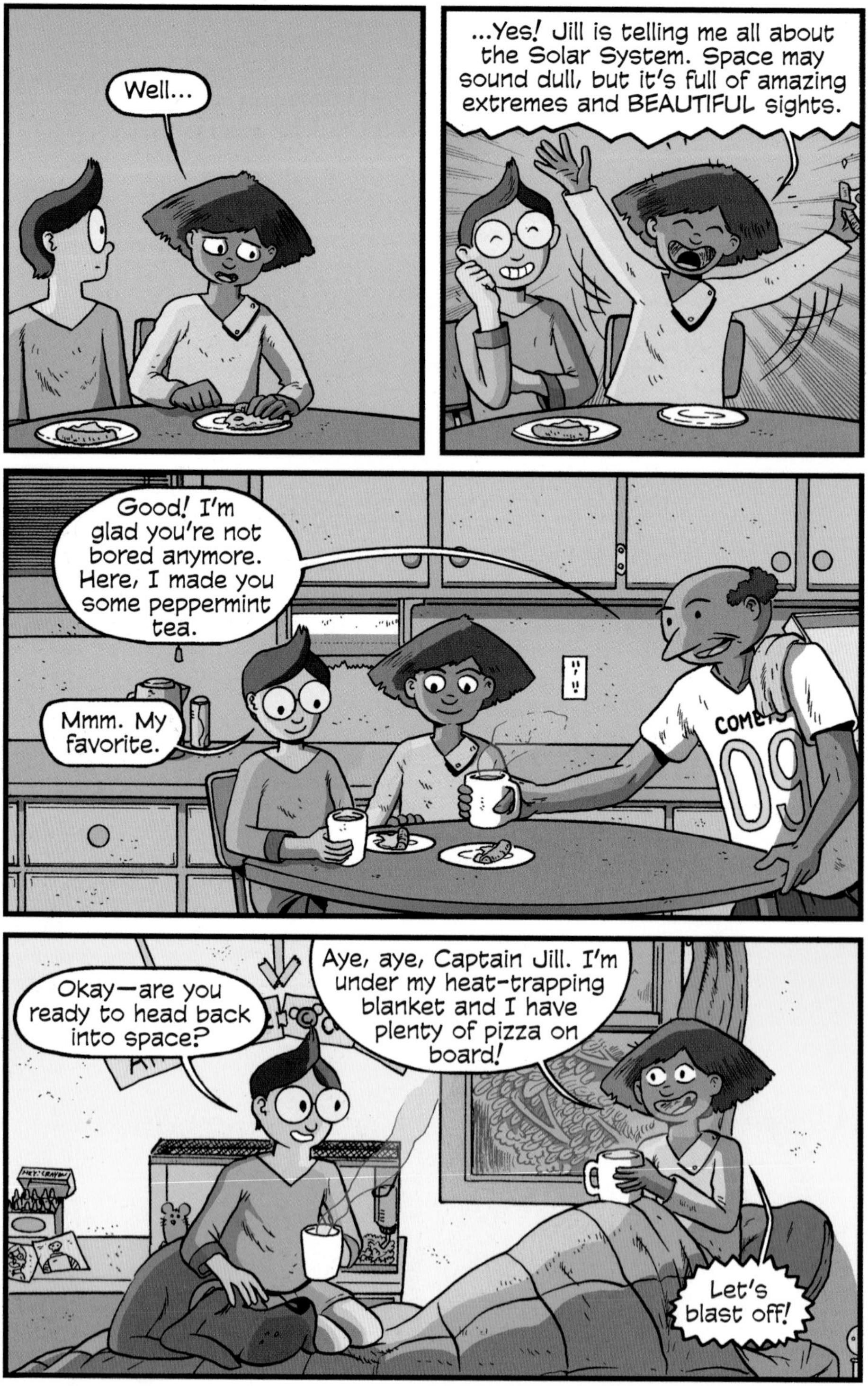

Well...
...Yes! Jill is telling me all about the Solar System. Space may sound dull, but it's full of amazing extremes and BEAUTIFUL sights.
Good! I'm glad you're not bored anymore. Here, I made you some peppermint tea.
Mmm. My favorite.
COMETS
09
Okay—are you ready to head back into space?
Aye, aye, Captain Jill. I'm under my heat-trapping blanket and I have plenty of pizza on board!
Let's blast off!

When we last left our intrepid heroes, they were...

Approaching the asteroid belt.

P.A.L., we don't have enough EnthusiPlasma to dodge space rocks! You need to send that report!

I tried, but I got an error message saying that Sara was eating dinner! Let me try again.

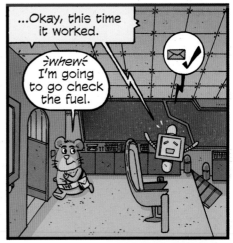

...Okay, this time it worked.

≥whew≤ I'm going to go check the fuel.

Oh! Sara must be starting to get excited about space!

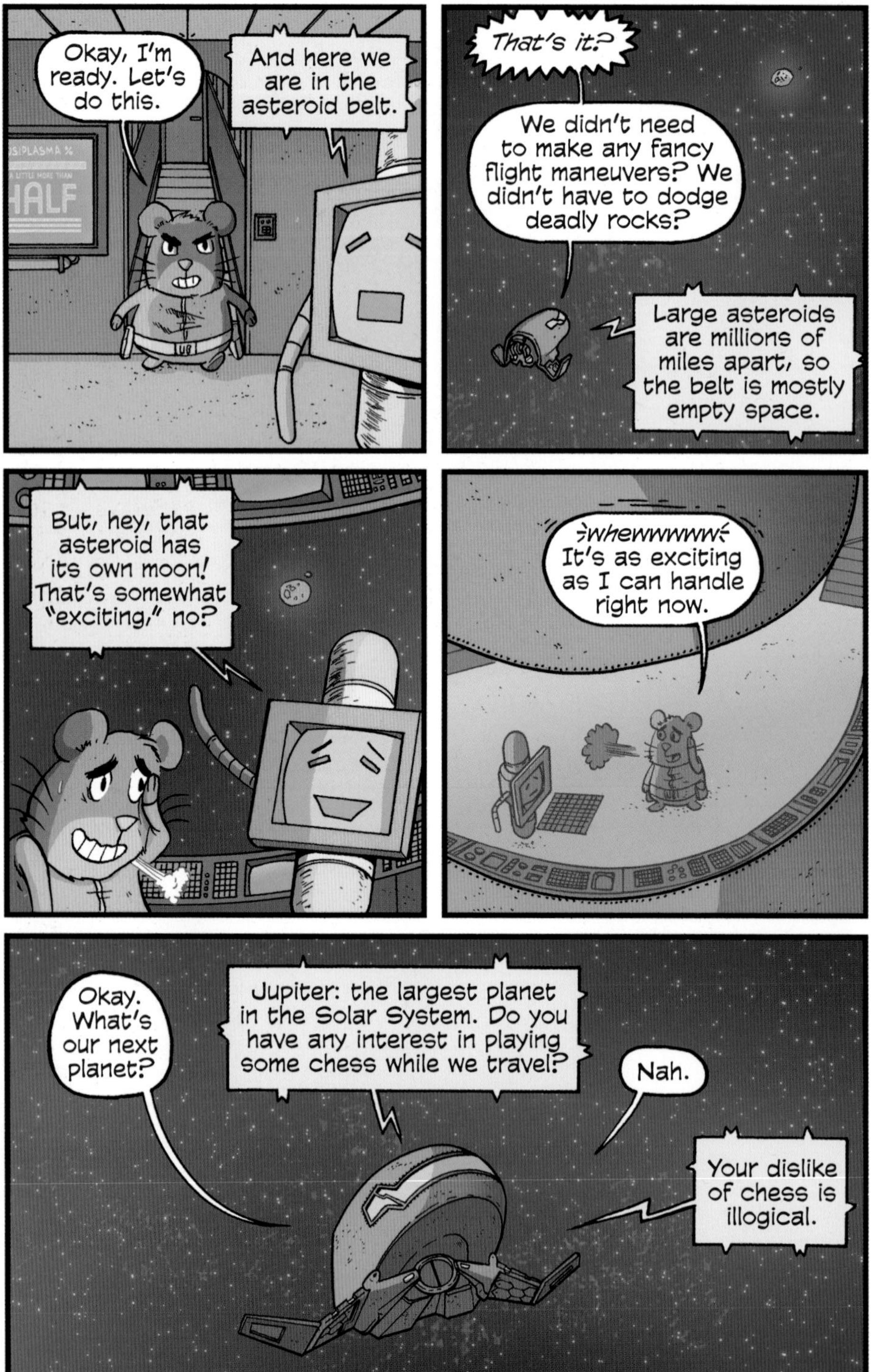

Okay, I'm ready. Let's do this.
And here we are in the asteroid belt.
That's it?
We didn't need to make any fancy flight maneuvers? We didn't have to dodge deadly rocks?
Large asteroids are millions of miles apart, so the belt is mostly empty space.
But, hey, that asteroid has its own moon! That's somewhat "exciting," no?
whewwwww
It's as exciting as I can handle right now.
Okay. What's our next planet?
Jupiter: the largest planet in the Solar System. Do you have any interest in playing some chess while we travel?
Nah.
Your dislike of chess is illogical.

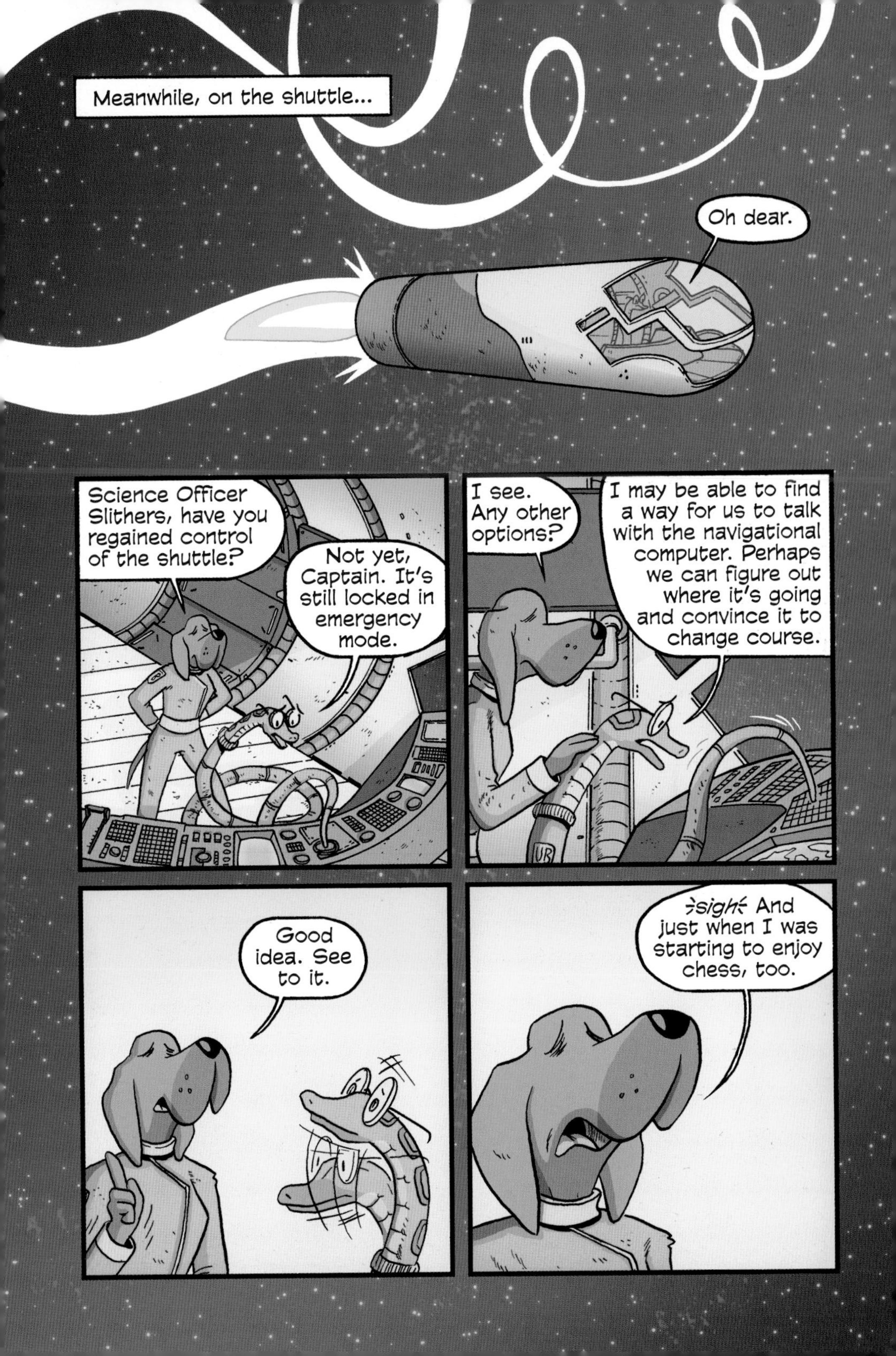
Meanwhile, on the shuttle...
Oh dear.
Science Officer Slithers, have you regained control of the shuttle?
Not yet, Captain. It's still locked in emergency mode.
I see. Any other options?
I may be able to find a way for us to talk with the navigational computer. Perhaps we can figure out where it's going and convince it to change course.
Good idea. See to it.
sigh And just when I was starting to enjoy chess, too.

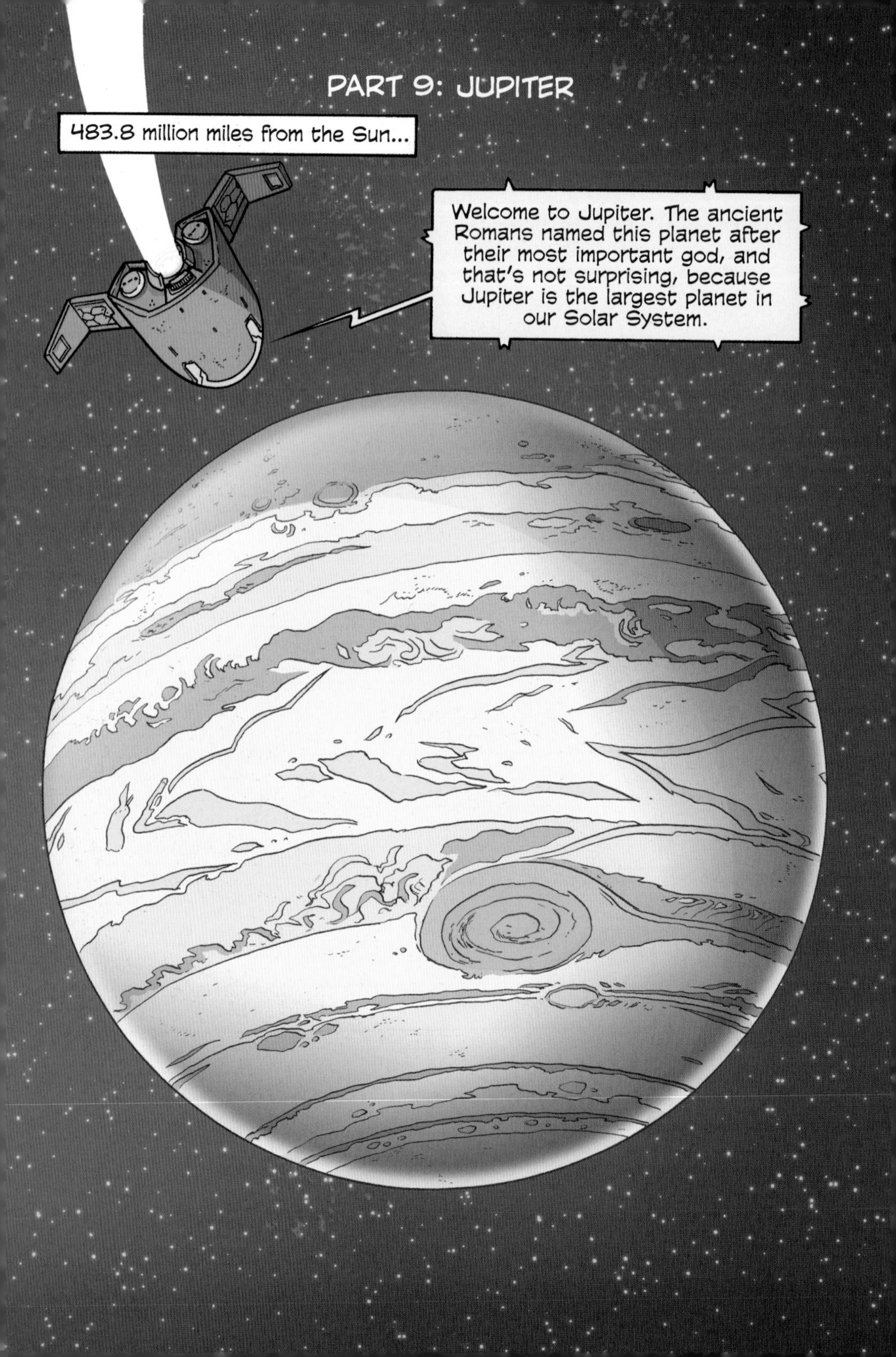
PART 9: JUPITER
483.8 million miles from the Sun...
Welcome to Jupiter. The ancient Romans named this planet after their most important god, and that's not surprising, because Jupiter is the largest planet in our Solar System.

Huh. Can you give me a sense of how big it is?

That type of explanation is really Science Officer Slithers's area of expertise, but let me try.

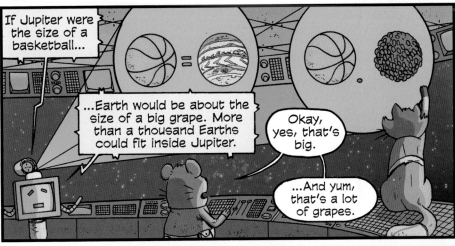

If Jupiter were the size of a basketball...

...Earth would be about the size of a big grape. More than a thousand Earths could fit inside Jupiter.

Okay, yes, that's big.

...And yum, that's a lot of grapes.

So what's it made of? And why does it look so...swirly?

There's a lot we don't yet know about Jupiter. But we call it a gas giant because it's mostly made of hydrogen and other gases.

He

H

Strong winds and heat stir up this gassy soup and make it swirl.

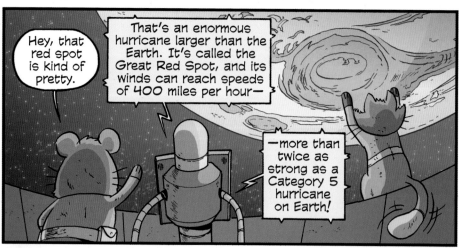

Hey, that red spot is kind of pretty.

That's an enormous hurricane larger than the Earth. It's called the Great Red Spot, and its winds can reach speeds of 400 miles per hour—

—more than twice as strong as a Category 5 hurricane on Earth!

Yikes. That's scary. But at the same time, it's also... interesting. Scary and interesting?

Scareinteresting?

NO DEFINITION FOUND.

I am certain that is not a real word.

Perhaps I can make it less scary? One moment, adjusting display...

SCARINESS

Hahaha! Thanks, P.A.L.

Mrowwwww!

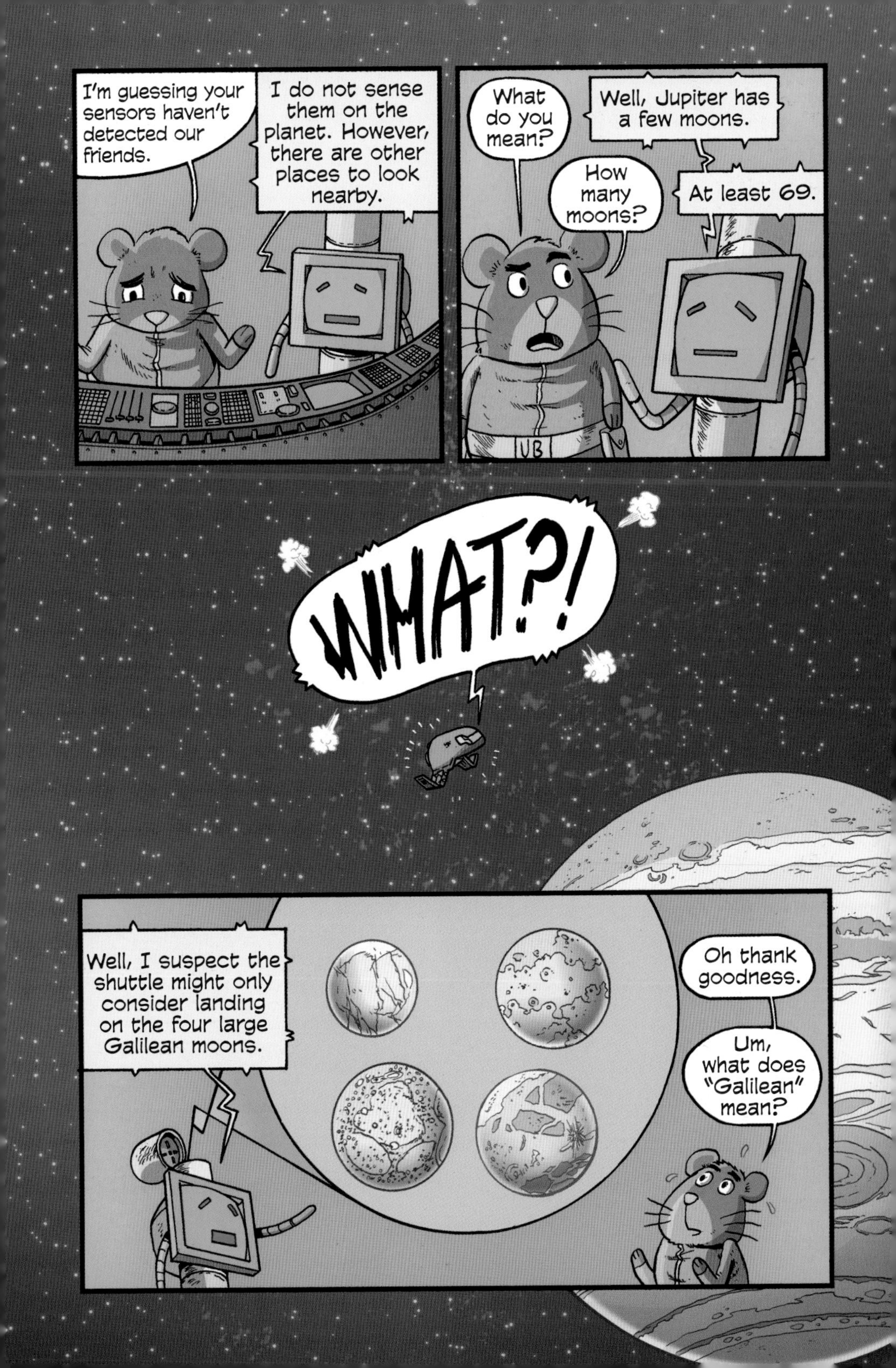
I'm guessing your sensors haven't detected our friends.
I do not sense them on the planet. However, there are other places to look nearby.
What do you mean?
Well, Jupiter has a few moons.
How many moons?
At least 69.
WHAT?!
Well, I suspect the shuttle might only consider landing on the four large Galilean moons.
Oh thank goodness.
Um, what does "Galilean" mean?

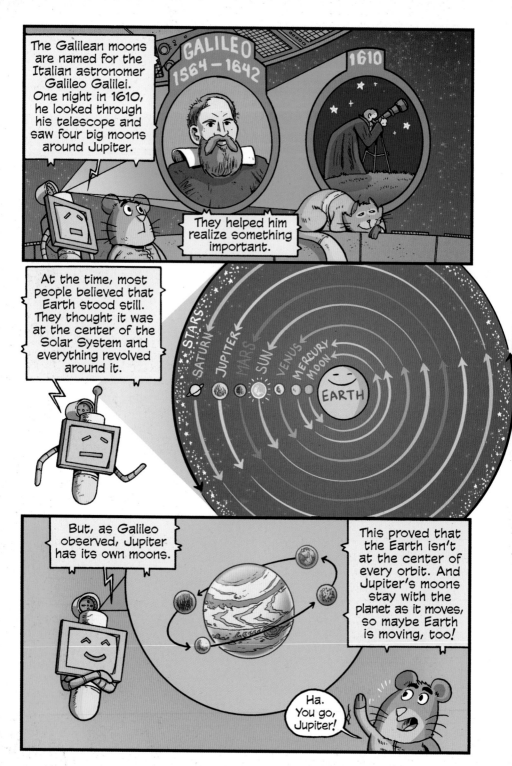

The Galilean moons are named for the Italian astronomer Galileo Galilei. One night in 1610, he looked through his telescope and saw four big moons around Jupiter.

GALILEO 1564 – 1642

1610

They helped him realize something important.

At the time, most people believed that Earth stood still. They thought it was at the center of the Solar System and everything revolved around it.

STARS
SATURN
JUPITER
MARS
SUN
VENUS
MERCURY
MOON
EARTH

But, as Galileo observed, Jupiter has its own moons.

This proved that the Earth isn't at the center of every orbit. And Jupiter's moons stay with the planet as it moves, so maybe Earth is moving, too!

Ha. You go, Jupiter!

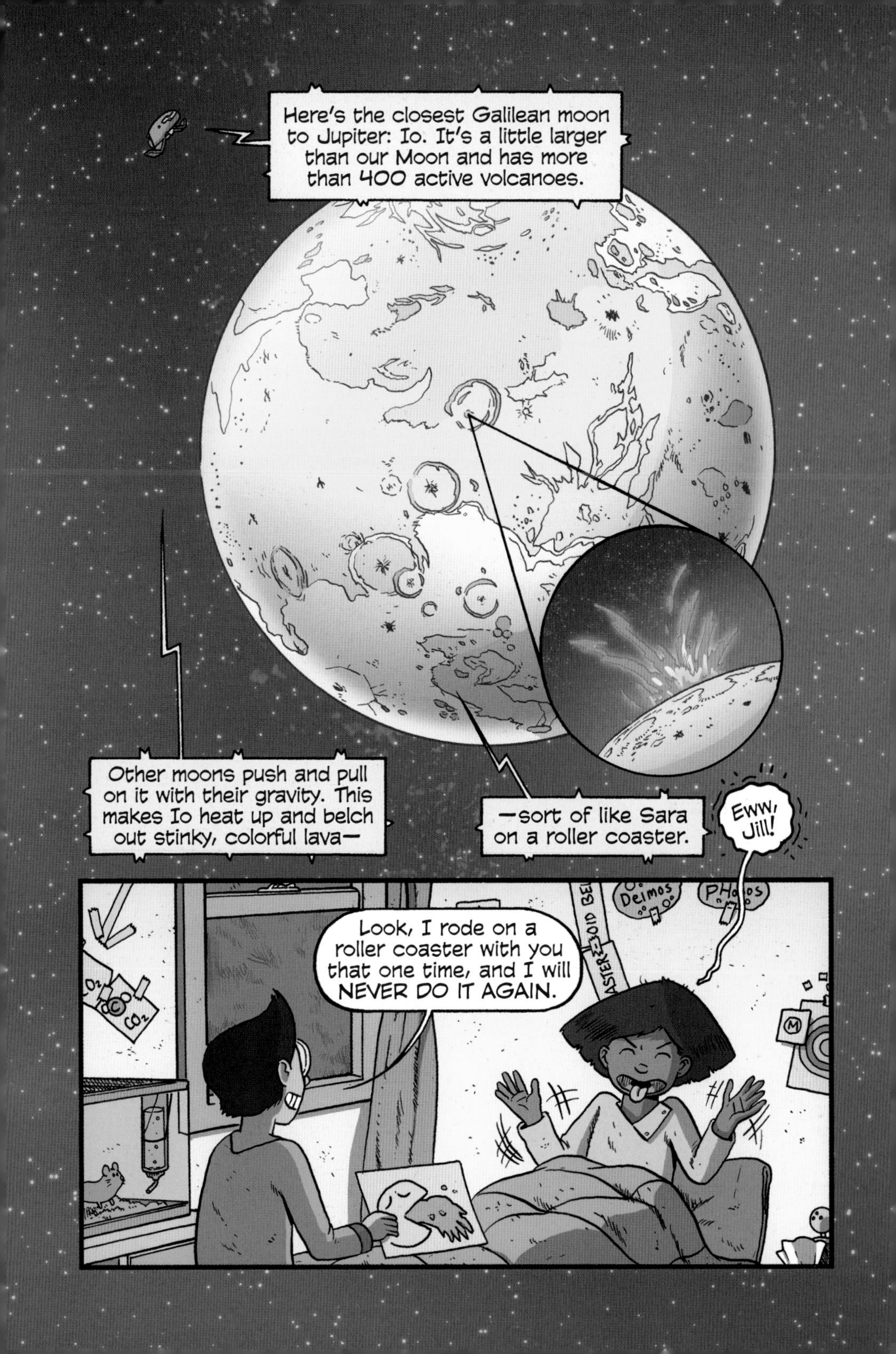
Here's the closest Galilean moon to Jupiter: Io. It's a little larger than our Moon and has more than 400 active volcanoes.
Other moons push and pull on it with their gravity. This makes Io heat up and belch out stinky, colorful lava—
—sort of like Sara on a roller coaster.
Eww, Jill!
Look, I rode on a roller coaster with you that one time, and I will NEVER DO IT AGAIN.
Deimos

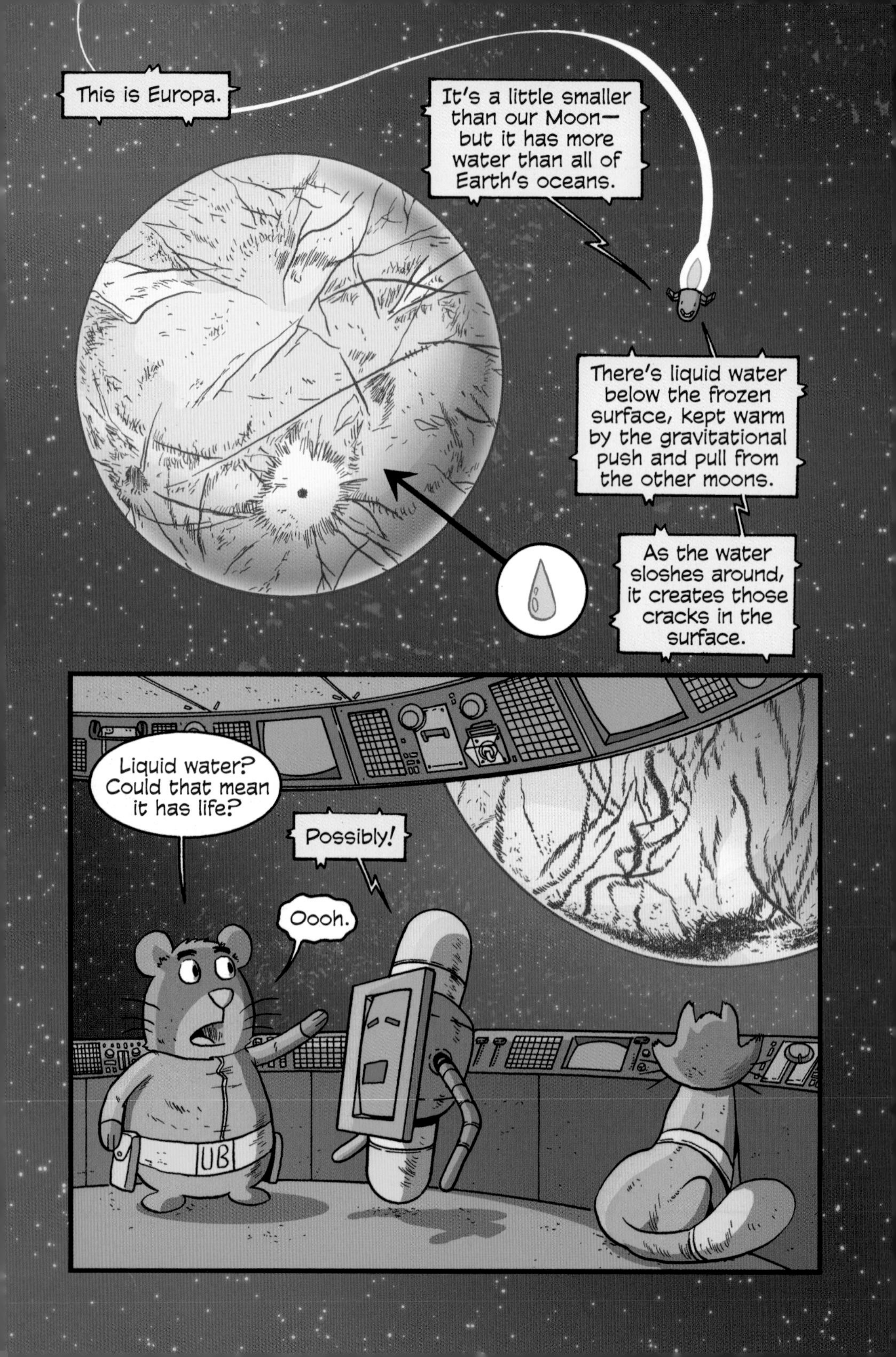
This is Europa.
It's a little smaller than our Moon—but it has more water than all of Earth's oceans.
There's liquid water below the frozen surface, kept warm by the gravitational push and pull from the other moons.
As the water sloshes around, it creates those cracks in the surface.
Liquid water? Could that mean it has life?
Possibly!
Oooh.
UB

Ganymede is the biggest moon in the Solar System. It probably has salty oceans below its surface.

It's the only moon with a liquid iron core that makes a magnetic field—and it has auroras!

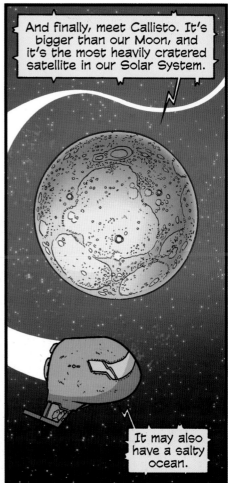

And finally, meet Callisto. It's bigger than our Moon, and it's the most heavily cratered satellite in our Solar System.

It may also have a salty ocean.

These moons are all so unique.

I have a feeling that Sara is going to like our report.

JUPITER: A REPORT

Origin of Name: The ancient Roman king of the gods.

Size: 86,881.4 miles wide. More than 1,300 Earths could fit inside Jupiter!

Contents: There's a lot we don't know about Jupiter's insides. The core is a mystery. Above it is metallic hydrogen (gas under so much pressure that it behaves like a metal), then liquid and gaseous hydrogen and other gases.

JUPITER'S PLACE IN SPACE

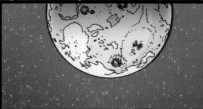

Amazing Features

The Great Red Spot, a scareinteresting hurricane.

At least 69 confirmed moons. Some have liquid water, which could mean they have life! Io, one of the weirdest, looks like a pizza gone bad.

Visits from Earth Spacecraft:
Starting in the 1970s, several spacecraft flew past Jupiter, and a couple have orbited it. None landed on the surface (because there might not even be one!).

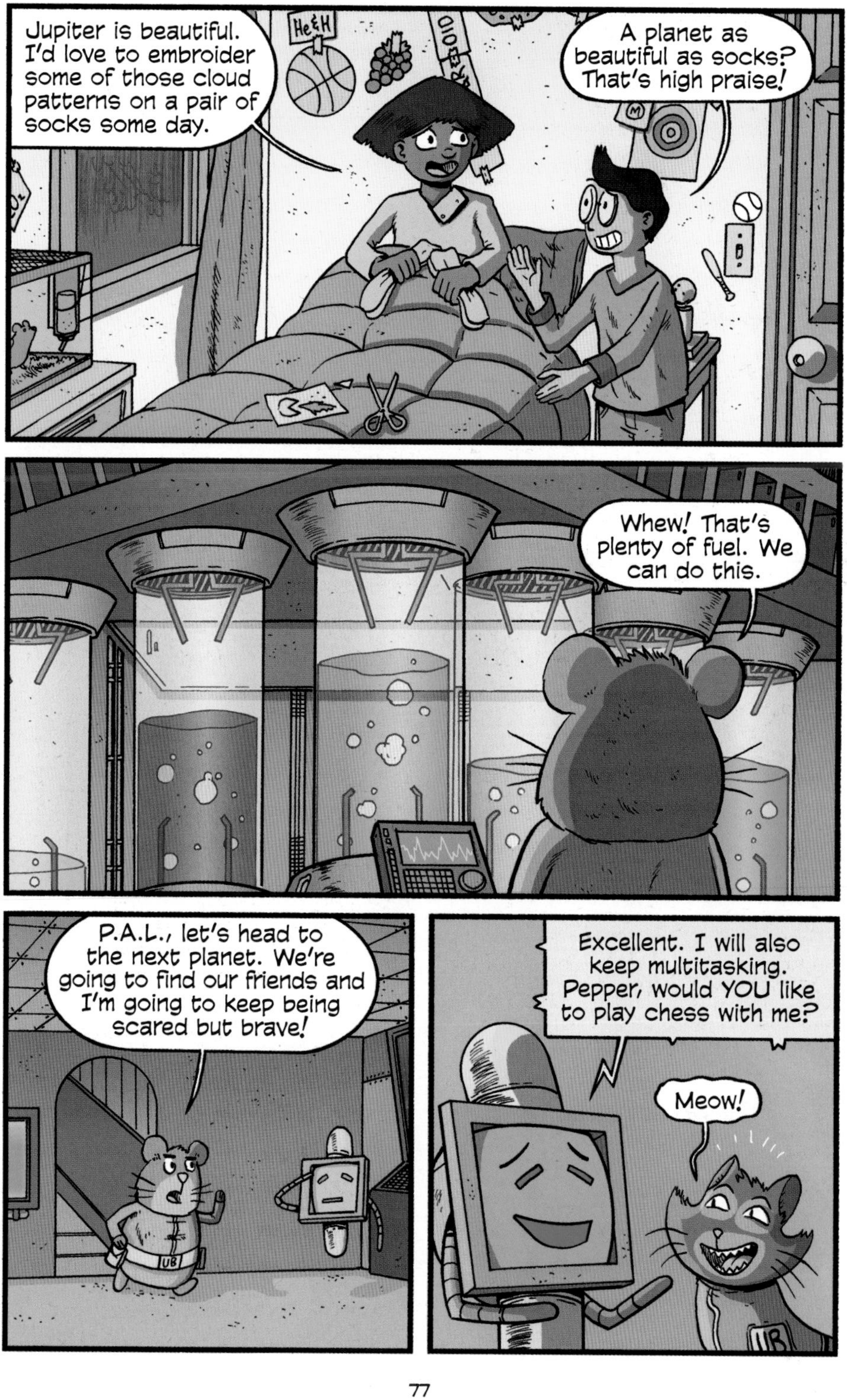
Jupiter is beautiful. I'd love to embroider some of those cloud patterns on a pair of socks some day.
A planet as beautiful as socks? That's high praise!
Whew! That's plenty of fuel. We can do this.
P.A.L., let's head to the next planet. We're going to find our friends and I'm going to keep being scared but brave!
Excellent. I will also keep multitasking. Pepper, would YOU like to play chess with me?
Meow!

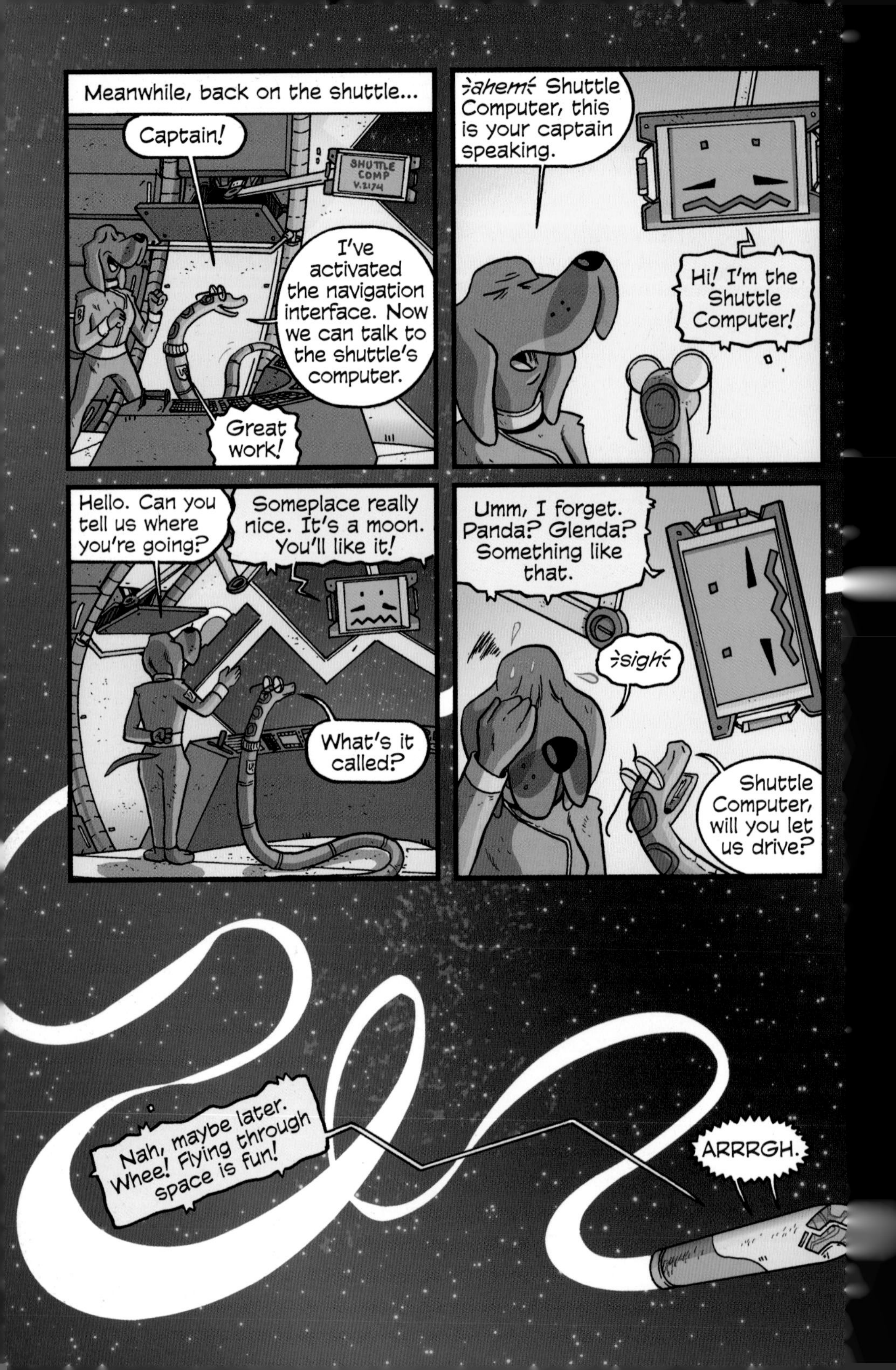
Meanwhile, back on the shuttle...
Captain!
SHUTTLE COMP V.2174
I've activated the navigation interface. Now we can talk to the shuttle's computer.
Great work!
ahem Shuttle Computer, this is your captain speaking.
Hi! I'm the Shuttle Computer!
Hello. Can you tell us where you're going?
Someplace really nice. It's a moon. You'll like it!
What's it called?
Umm, I forget. Panda? Glenda? Something like that.
sigh
Shuttle Computer, will you let us drive?
Nah, maybe later. Whee! Flying through space is fun!
ARRRGH.

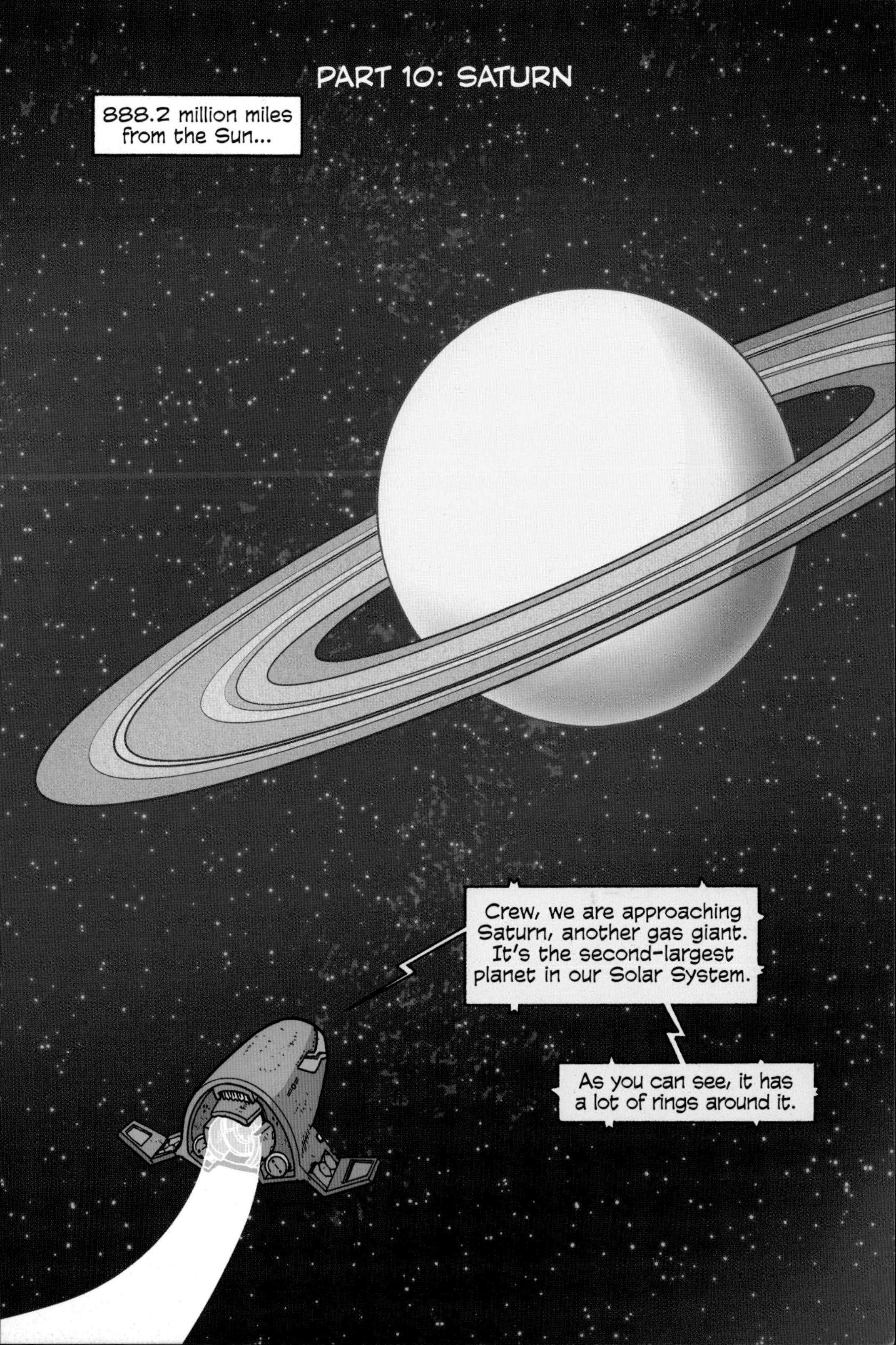

PART 10: SATURN
888.2 million miles from the Sun...
Crew, we are approaching Saturn, another gas giant. It's the second-largest planet in our Solar System.
As you can see, it has a lot of rings around it.

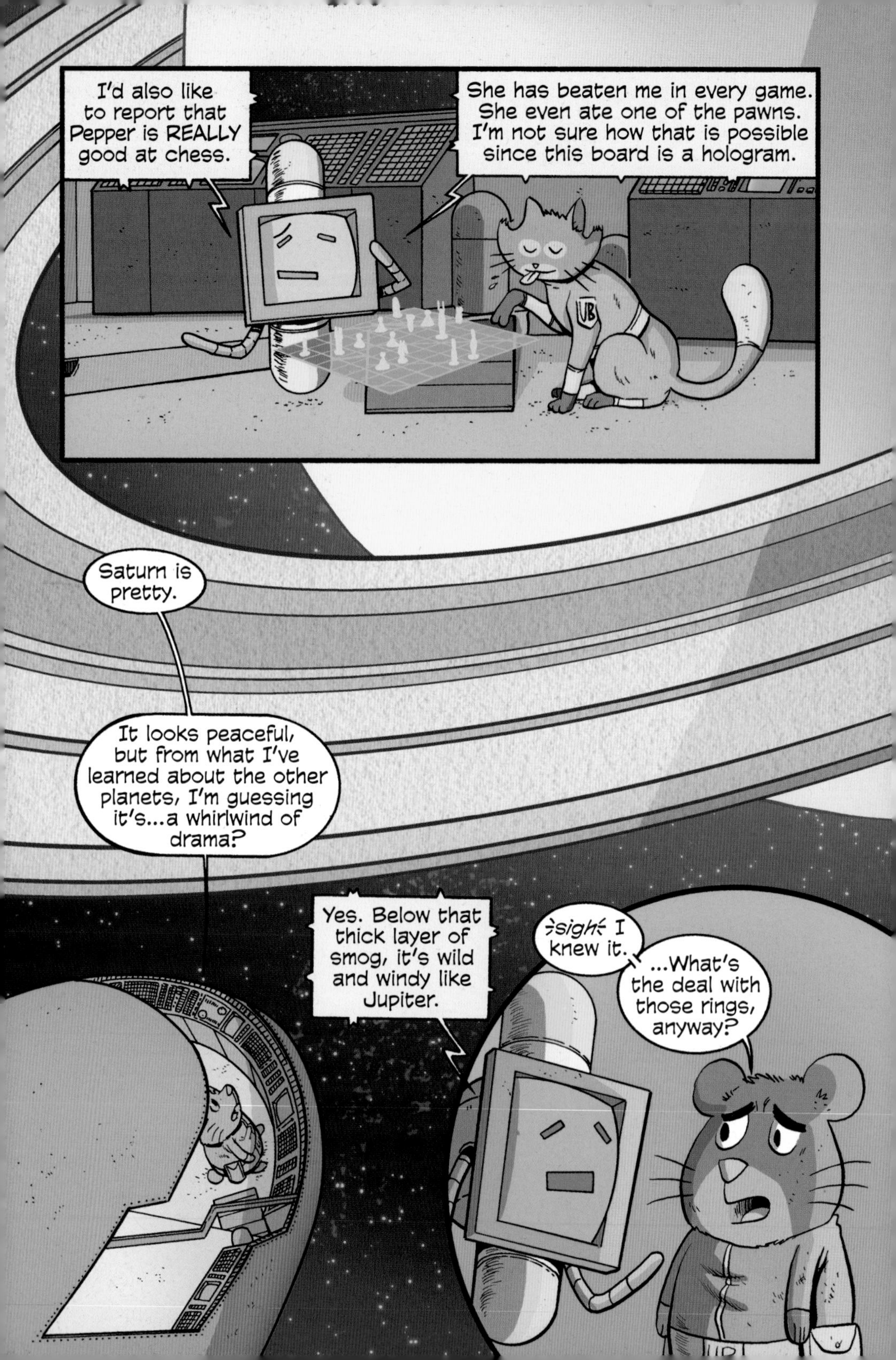
I'd also like to report that Pepper is REALLY good at chess.
She has beaten me in every game. She even ate one of the pawns. I'm not sure how that is possible since this board is a hologram.
Saturn is pretty.
It looks peaceful, but from what I've learned about the other planets, I'm guessing it's...a whirlwind of drama?
Yes. Below that thick layer of smog, it's wild and windy like Jupiter.
sigh I knew it.
...What's the deal with those rings, anyway?

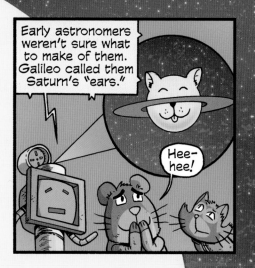

Early astronomers weren't sure what to make of them. Galileo called them Saturn's "ears."

Hee-hee!

But if you look closely, you'll see that they're a thin layer of mostly water ice with a little bit of rock and dust.

And when I say thin, I mean it. Saturn is huge—more than 760 Earths could fit inside it—

—but the rings are mostly as tall as Sara's three-story house.

Whoa!

Where did those icy chunks come from?

Nobody knows for sure. They may be pieces of moons or passing asteroids torn apart by Saturn's gravity. Debris streaming off nearby moons helps add to the rings.

JUPITER

NEPTUNE

URANUS

Jupiter, Uranus, and Neptune also have rings, but they're not as impressive.

In fact, Mars will have a ring someday. Its moon Phobos is spiraling inward, and in 20 to 40 million years, Mars's gravity will rip it apart, creating a ring!

Whoa! That's pretty scareinteresting!

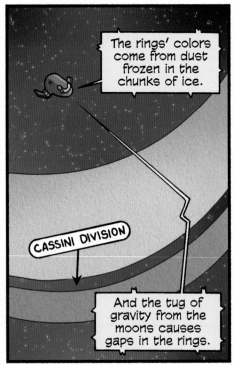

The rings' colors come from dust frozen in the chunks of ice.

CASSINI DIVISION

And the tug of gravity from the moons causes gaps in the rings.

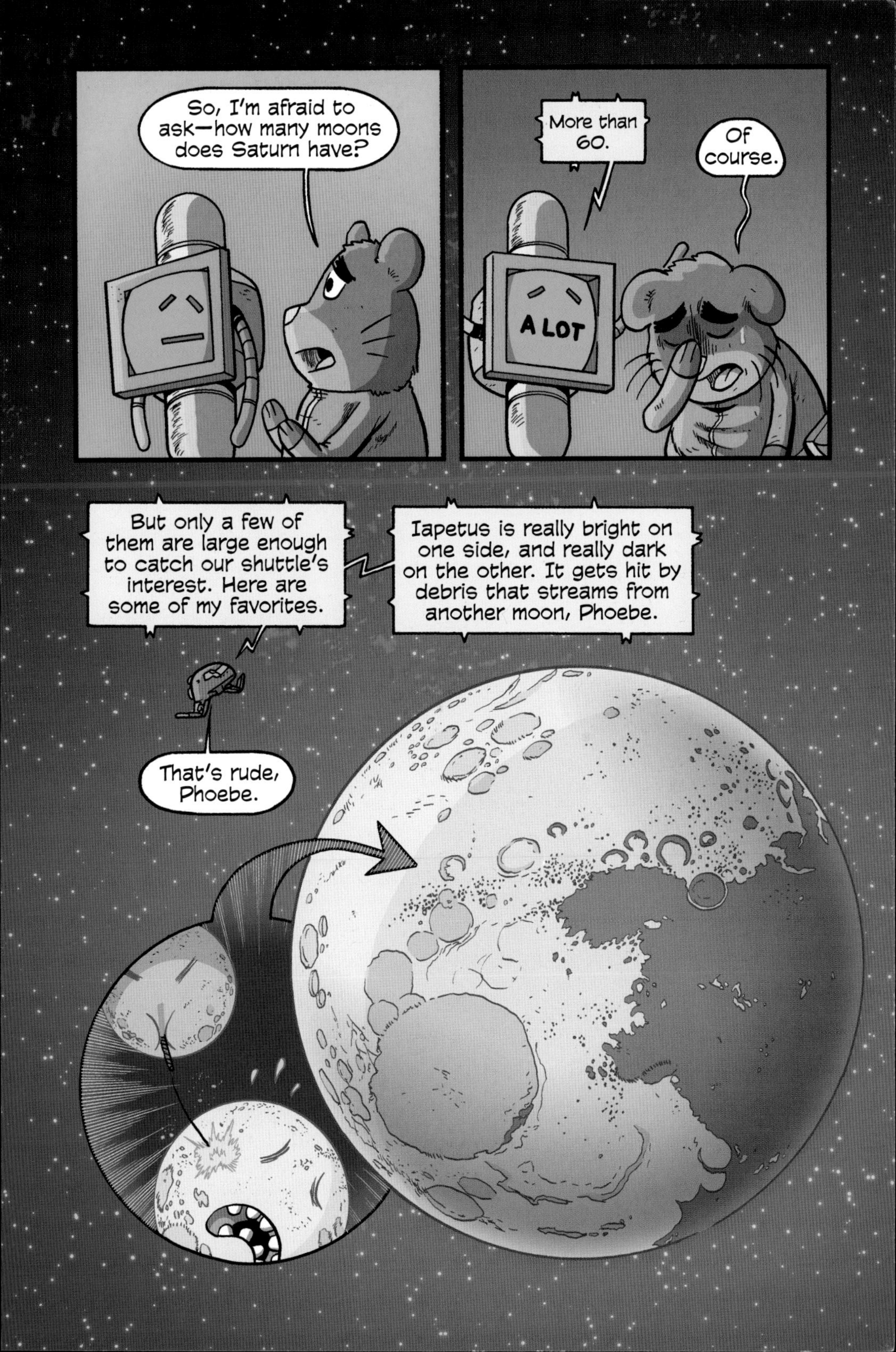
So, I'm afraid to ask—how many moons does Saturn have?
More than 60.
A LOT
Of course.
But only a few of them are large enough to catch our shuttle's interest. Here are some of my favorites.
Iapetus is really bright on one side, and really dark on the other. It gets hit by debris that streams from another moon, Phoebe.
That's rude, Phoebe.

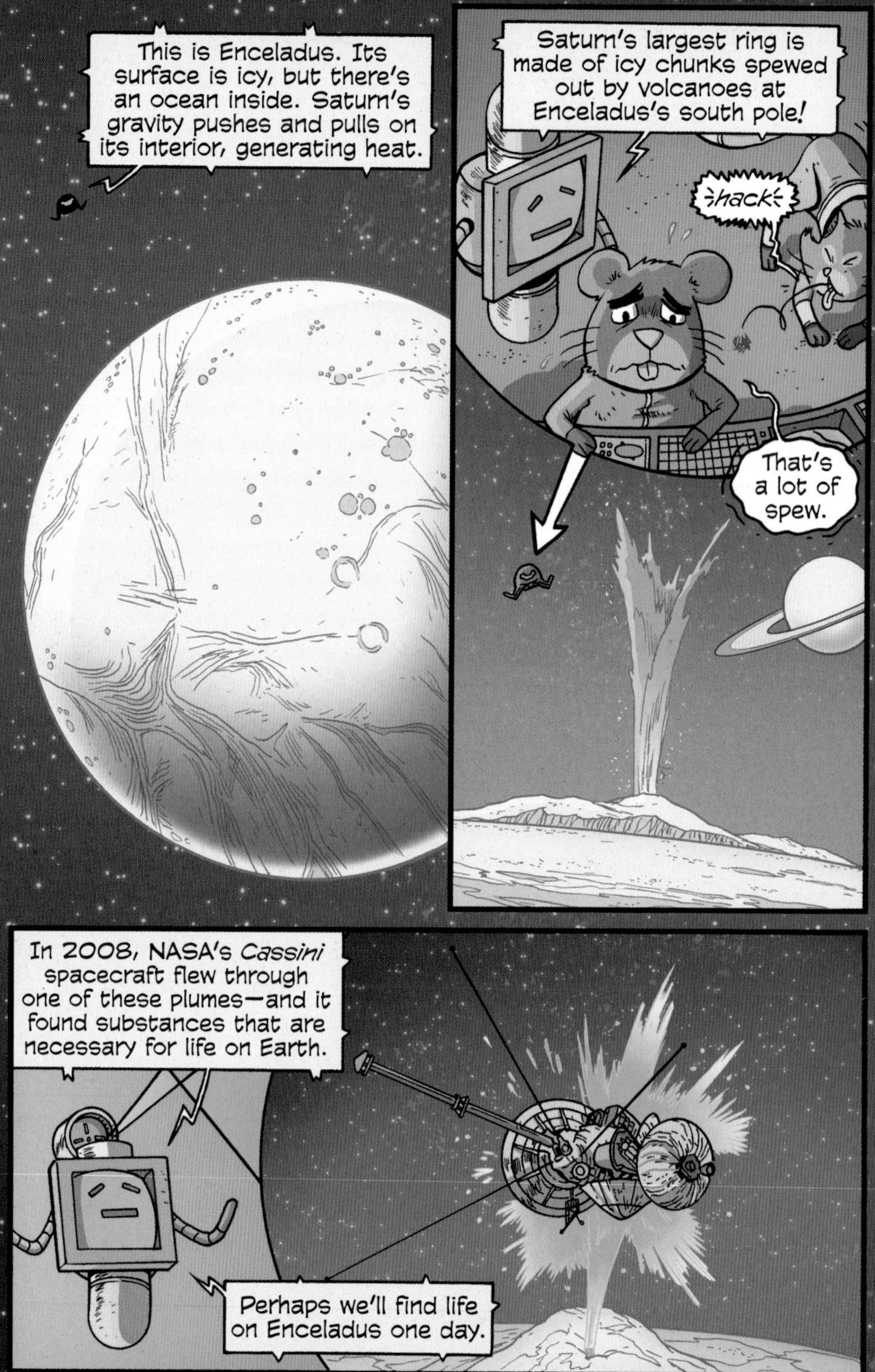
This is Enceladus. Its surface is icy, but there's an ocean inside. Saturn's gravity pushes and pulls on its interior, generating heat.
Saturn's largest ring is made of icy chunks spewed out by volcanoes at Enceladus's south pole!
hack
That's a lot of spew.
In 2008, NASA's *Cassini* spacecraft flew through one of these plumes—and it found substances that are necessary for life on Earth.
Perhaps we'll find life on Enceladus one day.

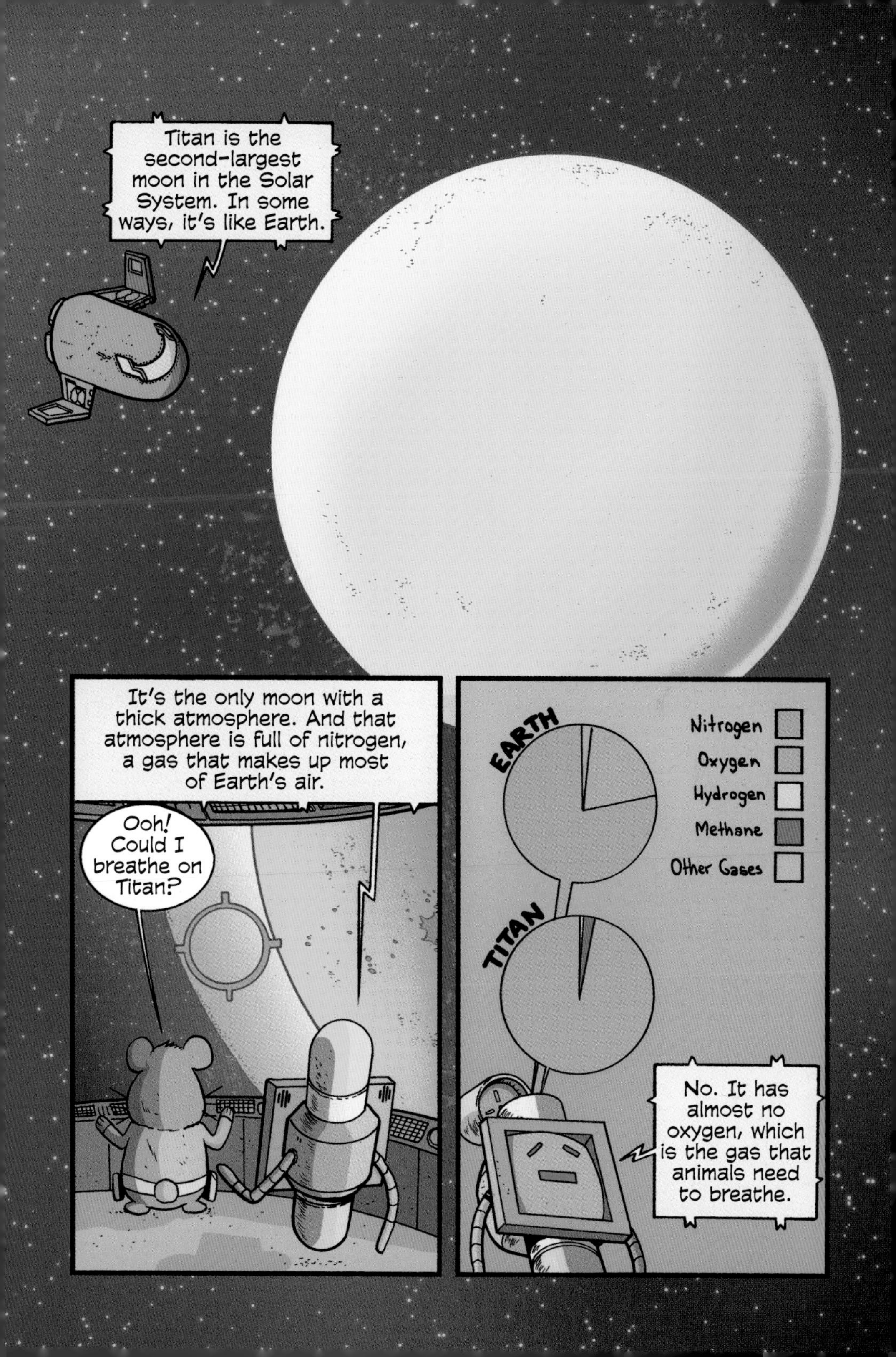
Titan is the second-largest moon in the Solar System. In some ways, it's like Earth.
It's the only moon with a thick atmosphere. And that atmosphere is full of nitrogen, a gas that makes up most of Earth's air.
Ooh! Could I breathe on Titan?
EARTH
TITAN
Nitrogen
Oxygen
Hydrogen
Methane
Other Gases
No. It has almost no oxygen, which is the gas that animals need to breathe.

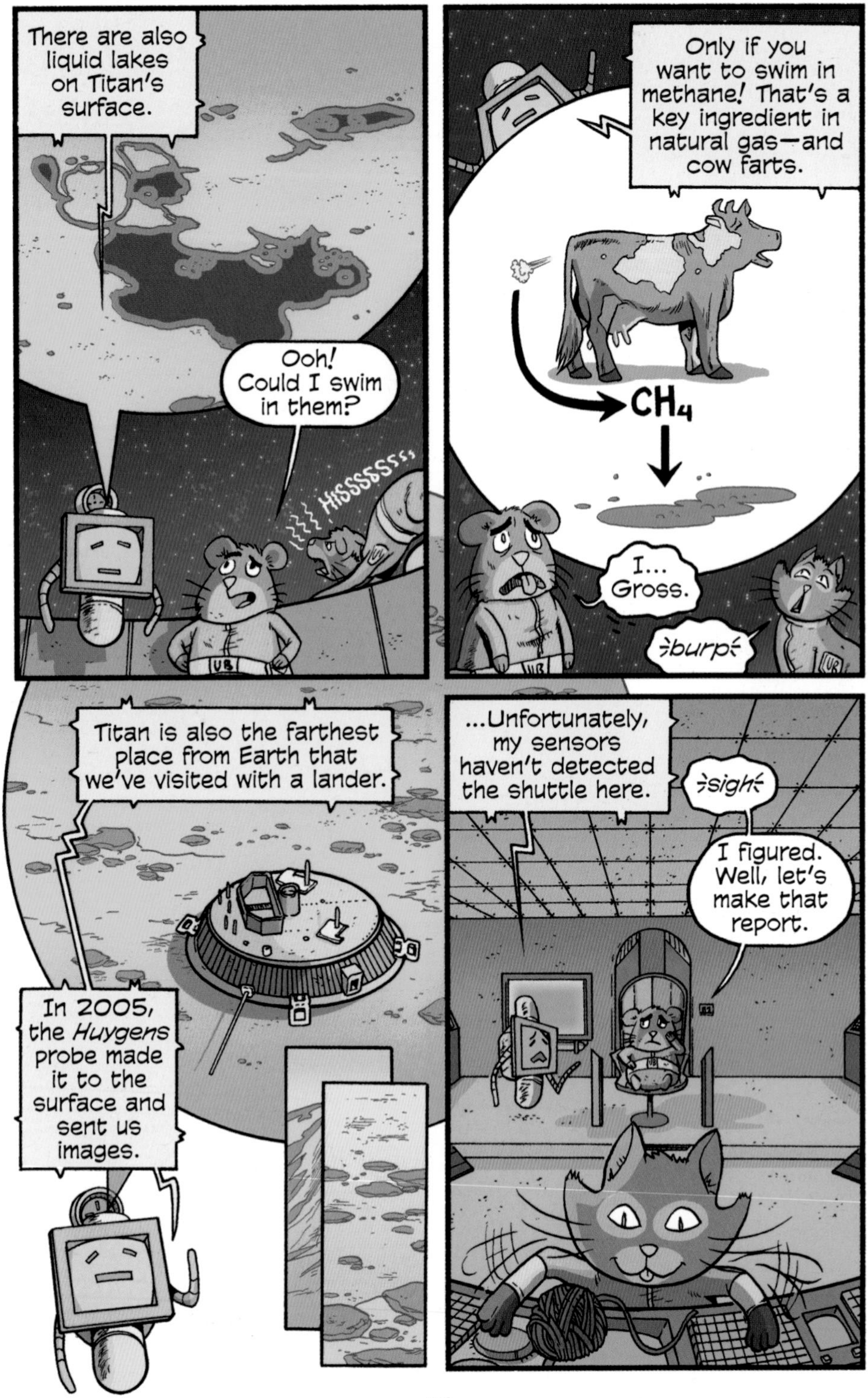

There are also liquid lakes on Titan's surface.
Ooh! Could I swim in them?
HISSSSSSSSS
Only if you want to swim in methane! That's a key ingredient in natural gas—and cow farts.
CH_4
I... Gross.
burp
Titan is also the farthest place from Earth that we've visited with a lander.
In 2005, the *Huygens* probe made it to the surface and sent us images.
...Unfortunately, my sensors haven't detected the shuttle here.
sigh
I figured. Well, let's make that report.

SATURN: A REPORT

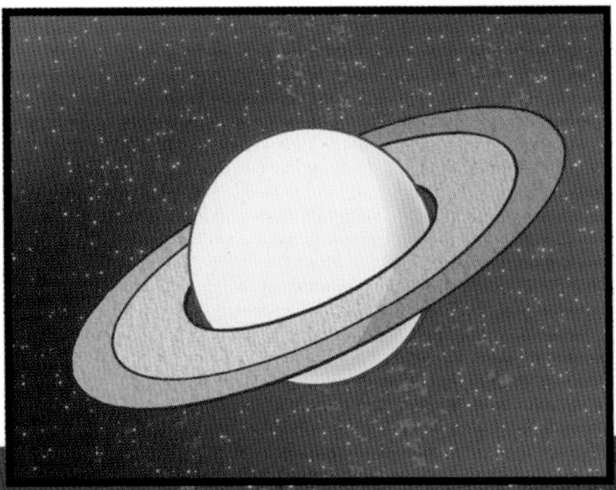

Origin of Name: The ancient Roman god of agriculture.

Size: 72,367.4 miles across. 764 Earths could fit inside Saturn.

Contents: There's a lot we don't know about Saturn's interior. Scientists figure it's similar to Jupiter, with metallic hydrogen below gaseous and liquid hydrogen (and some other gases, too).

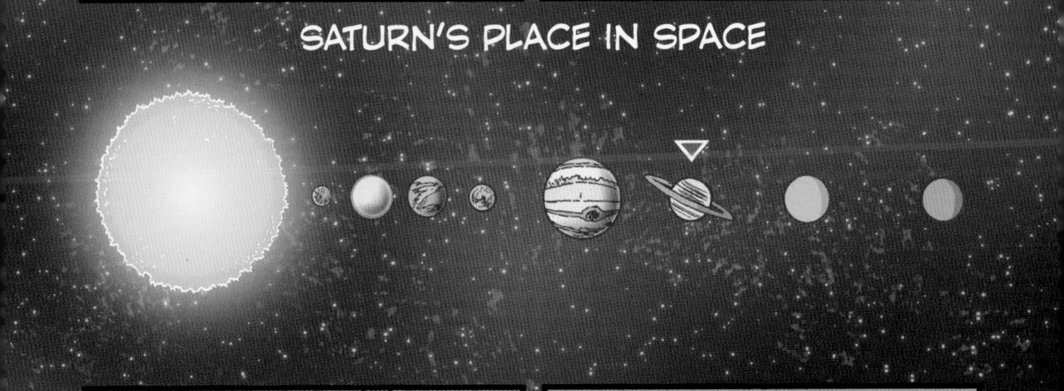
SATURN'S PLACE IN SPACE

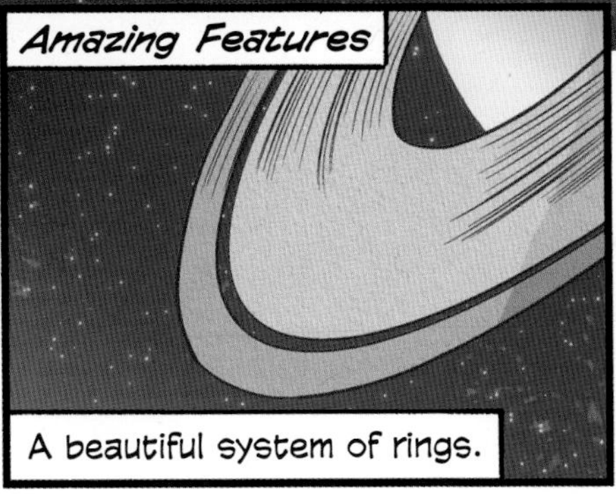
Amazing Features
A beautiful system of rings.

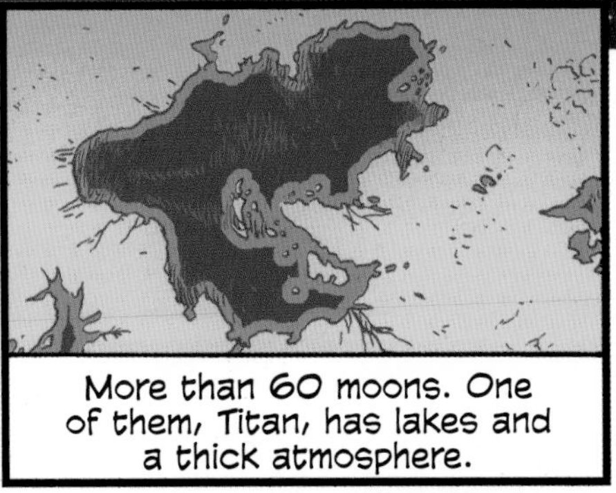
More than 60 moons. One of them, Titan, has lakes and a thick atmosphere.

Visits from Earth Spacecraft:
A few spacecraft have flown past Saturn. The *Cassini-Huygens* space probe orbited Saturn in 2004 and *Huygens* landed on Titan in 2005.

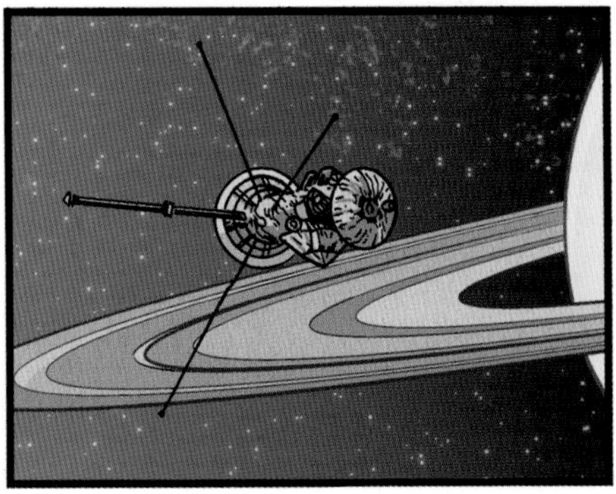

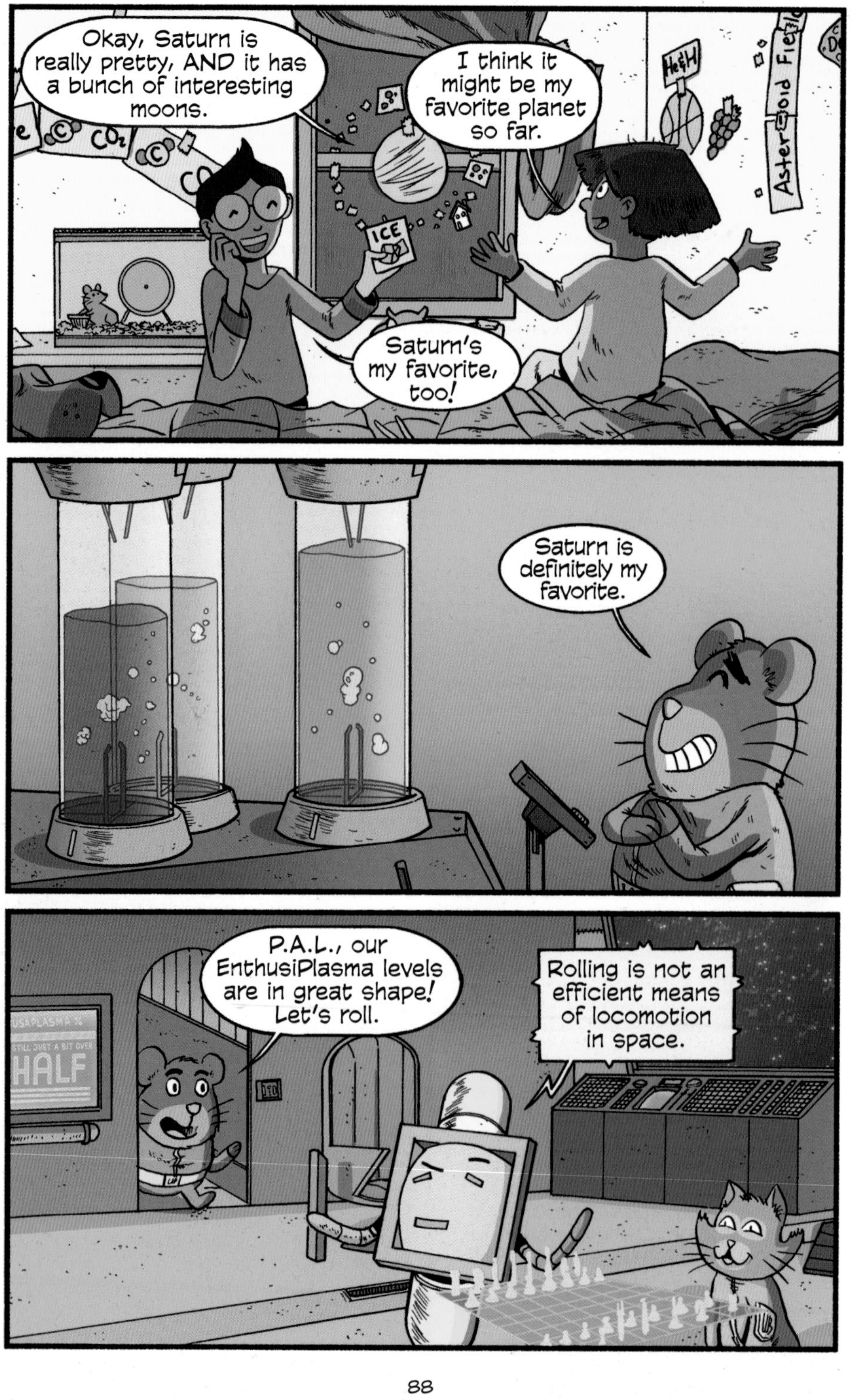
Okay, Saturn is really pretty, AND it has a bunch of interesting moons.
I think it might be my favorite planet so far.
ICE
Saturn's my favorite, too!
Saturn is definitely my favorite.
P.A.L., our EnthusiPlasma levels are in great shape! Let's roll.
STILL JUST A BIT OVER
HALF
Rolling is not an efficient means of locomotion in space.

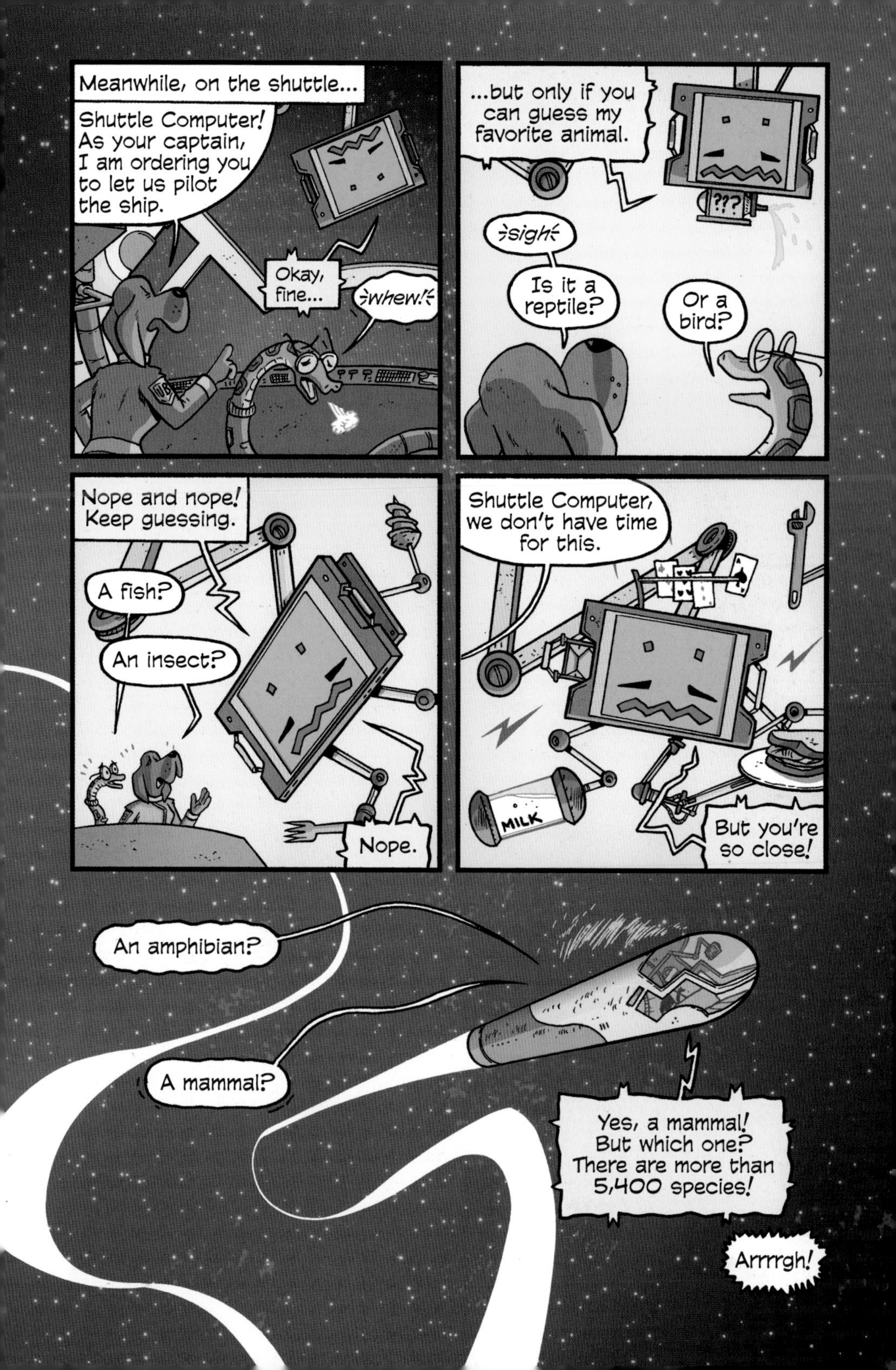
Meanwhile, on the shuttle...
Shuttle Computer! As your captain, I am ordering you to let us pilot the ship.
Okay, fine...
whew!
...but only if you can guess my favorite animal.
???
sigh
Is it a reptile?
Or a bird?
Nope and nope! Keep guessing.
A fish?
An insect?
Nope.
Shuttle Computer, we don't have time for this.
MILK
But you're so close!
An amphibian?
A mammal?
Yes, a mammal! But which one? There are more than 5,400 species!
Arrrrgh!

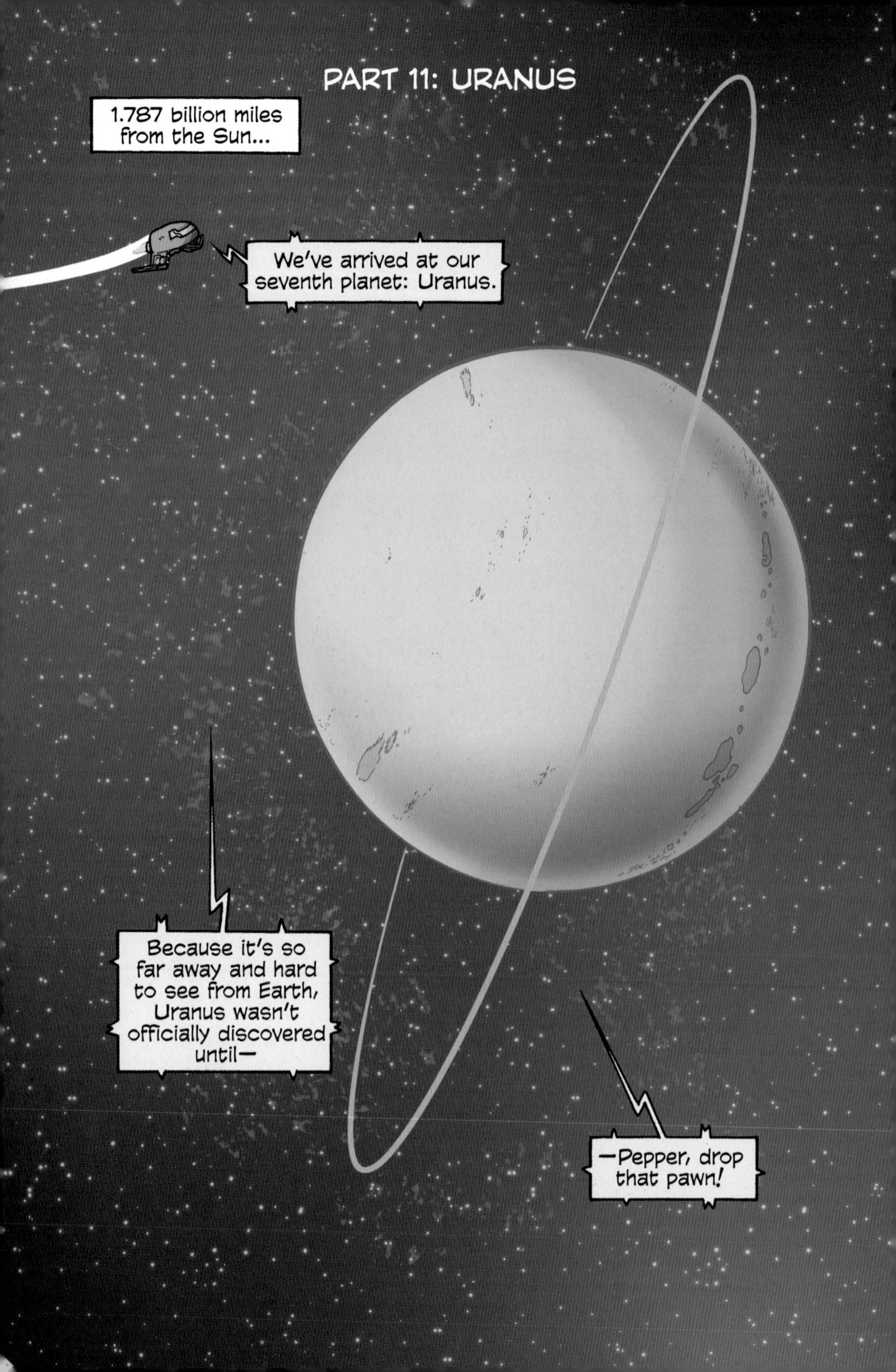
PART 11: URANUS
1.787 billion miles from the Sun...
We've arrived at our seventh planet: Uranus.
Because it's so far away and hard to see from Earth, Uranus wasn't officially discovered until—
—Pepper, drop that pawn!

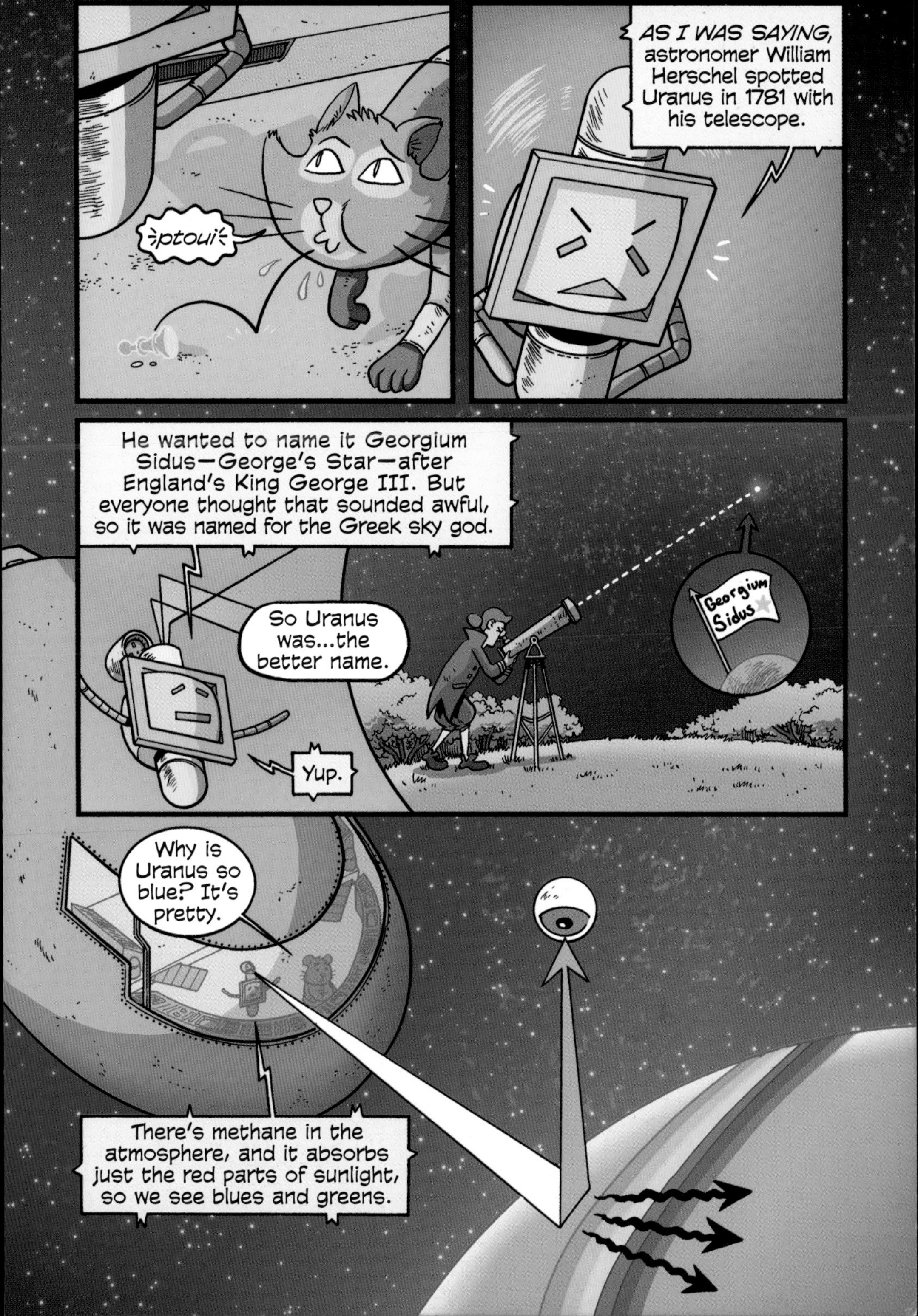
ptoui
AS I WAS SAYING, astronomer William Herschel spotted Uranus in 1781 with his telescope.
He wanted to name it Georgium Sidus—George's Star—after England's King George III. But everyone thought that sounded awful, so it was named for the Greek sky god.
So Uranus was...the better name.
Yup.
Georgium Sidus
Why is Uranus so blue? It's pretty.
There's methane in the atmosphere, and it absorbs just the red parts of sunlight, so we see blues and greens.

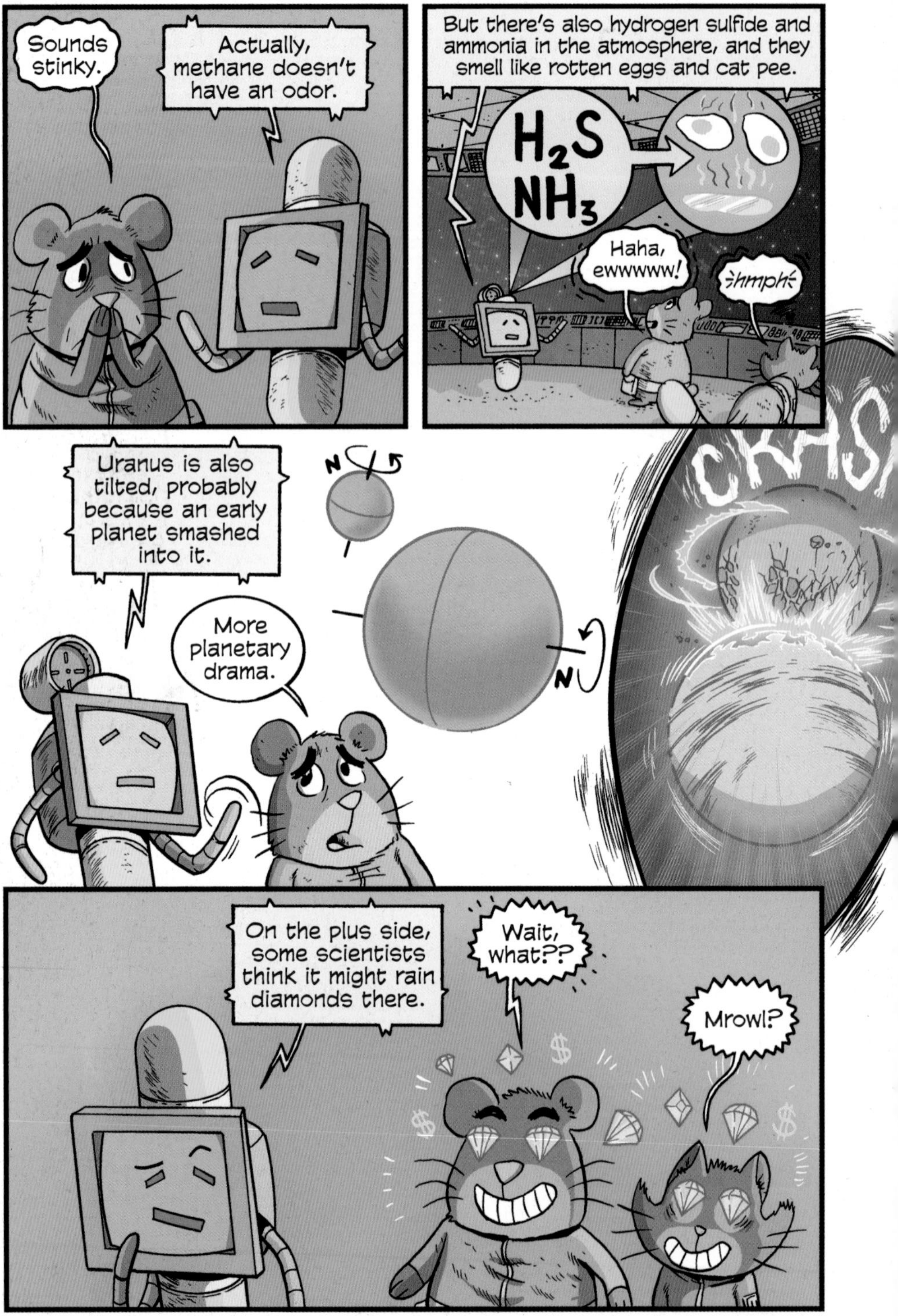
Sounds stinky.
Actually, methane doesn't have an odor.
But there's also hydrogen sulfide and ammonia in the atmosphere, and they smell like rotten eggs and cat pee.
H2S NH3
Haha, ewwwww!
hmph
Uranus is also tilted, probably because an early planet smashed into it.
N
N
More planetary drama.
CRASH
On the plus side, some scientists think it might rain diamonds there.
Wait, what??
Mrowl?

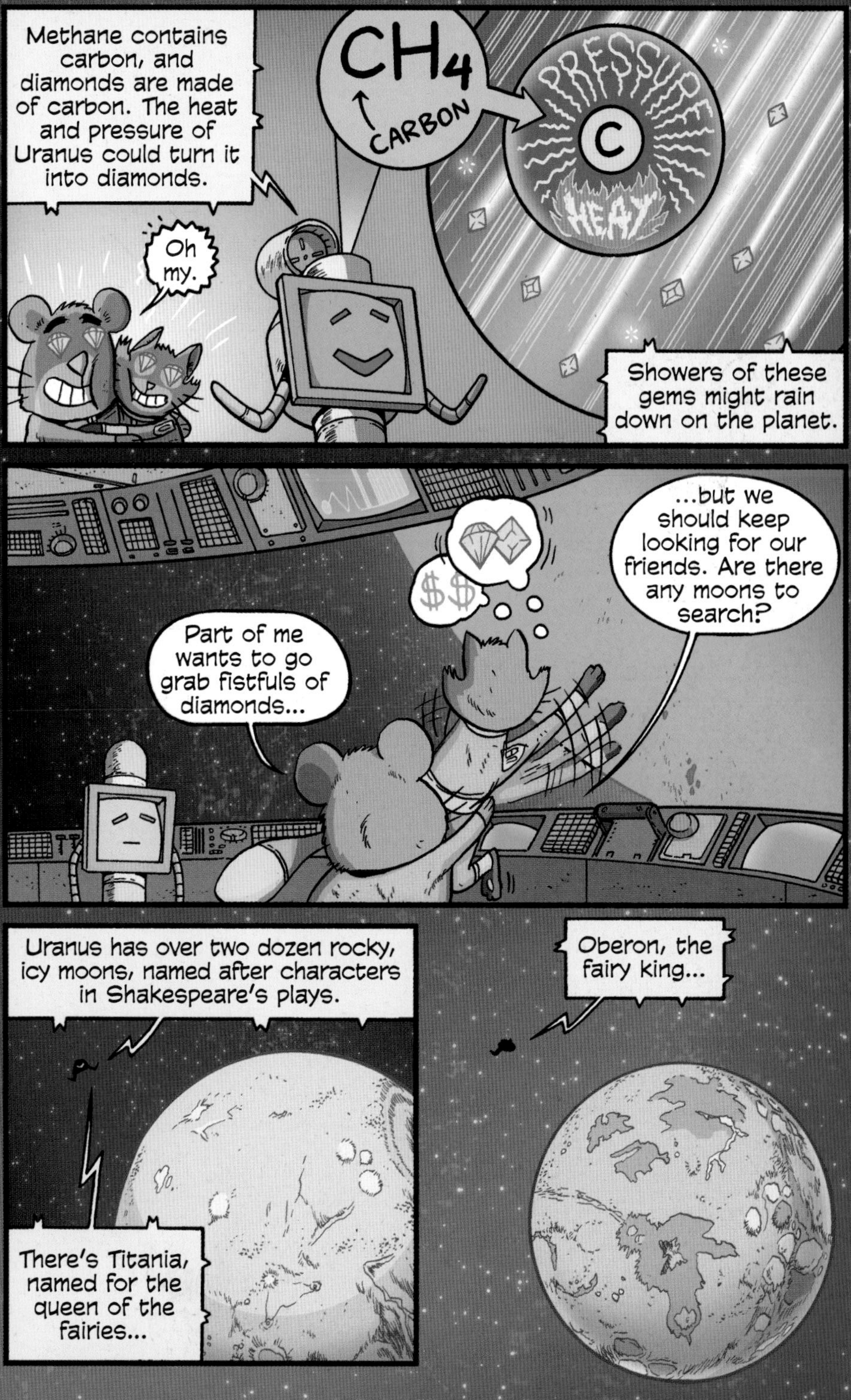

Methane contains carbon, and diamonds are made of carbon. The heat and pressure of Uranus could turn it into diamonds.
CH_4
CARBON
PRESSURE
C
HEAT
Oh my.
Showers of these gems might rain down on the planet.
$$
Part of me wants to go grab fistfuls of diamonds...
...but we should keep looking for our friends. Are there any moons to search?
Uranus has over two dozen rocky, icy moons, named after characters in Shakespeare's plays.
Oberon, the fairy king...
There's Titania, named for the queen of the fairies...

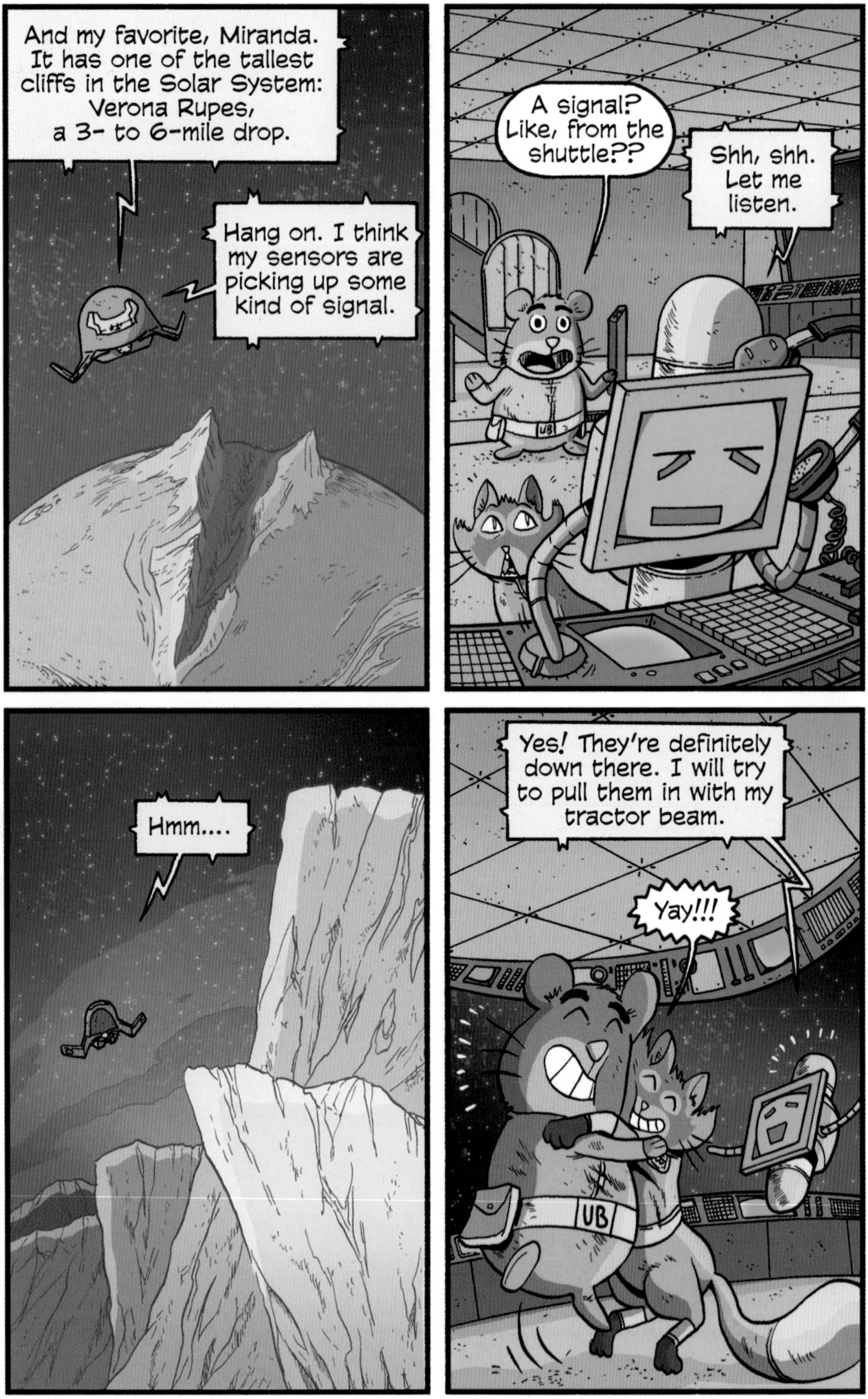
And my favorite, Miranda. It has one of the tallest cliffs in the Solar System: Verona Rupes, a 3- to 6-mile drop.
Hang on. I think my sensors are picking up some kind of signal.
A signal? Like, from the shuttle??
Shh, shh. Let me listen.
Hmm....
Yes! They're definitely down there. I will try to pull them in with my tractor beam.
Yay!!!
UB
UB

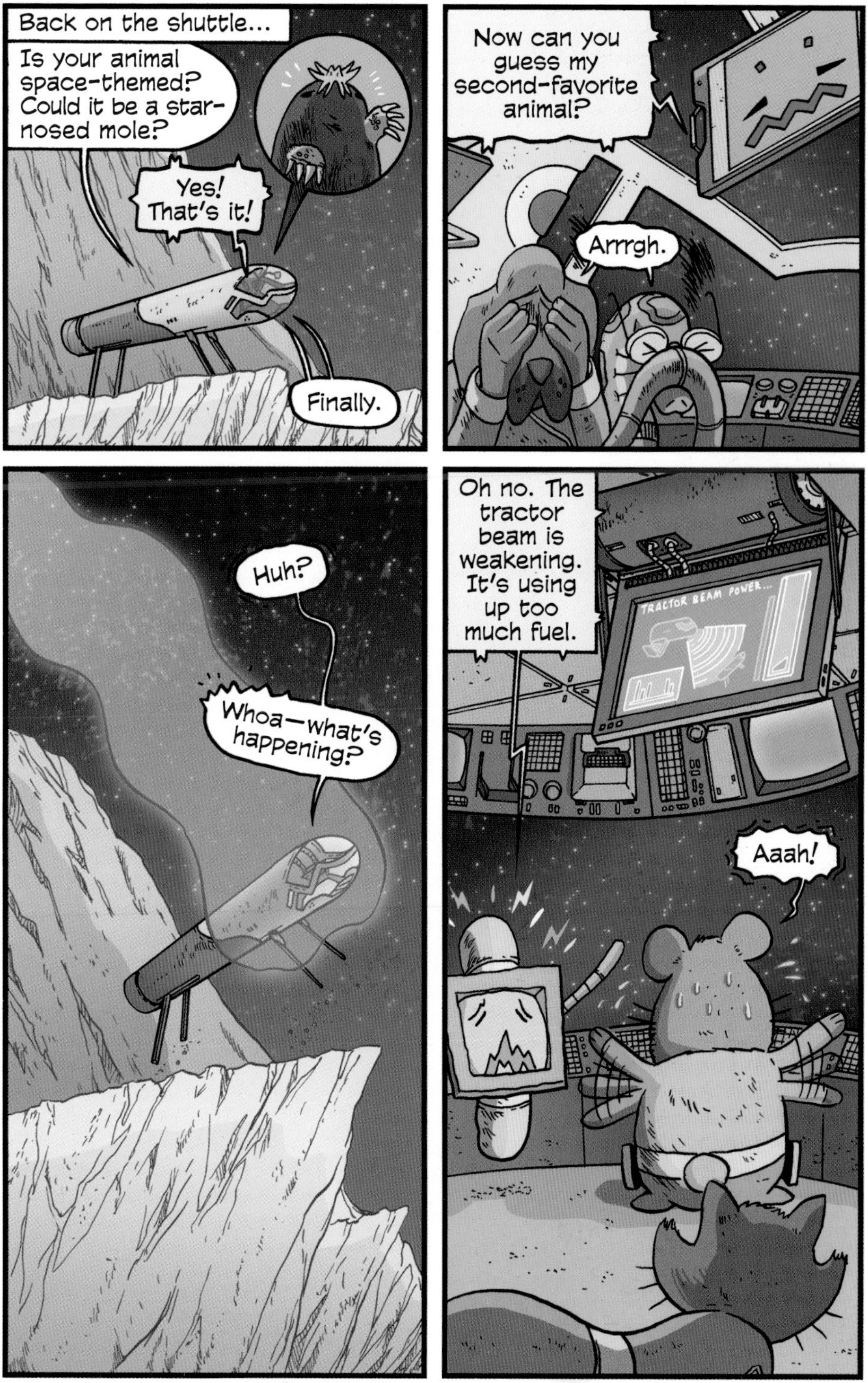
Back on the shuttle...
Is your animal space-themed? Could it be a star-nosed mole?
Yes! That's it!
Finally.
Now can you guess my second-favorite animal?
Arrrgh.
Huh?
Whoa—what's happening?
Oh no. The tractor beam is weakening. It's using up too much fuel.
TRACTOR BEAM POWER...
Aaah!

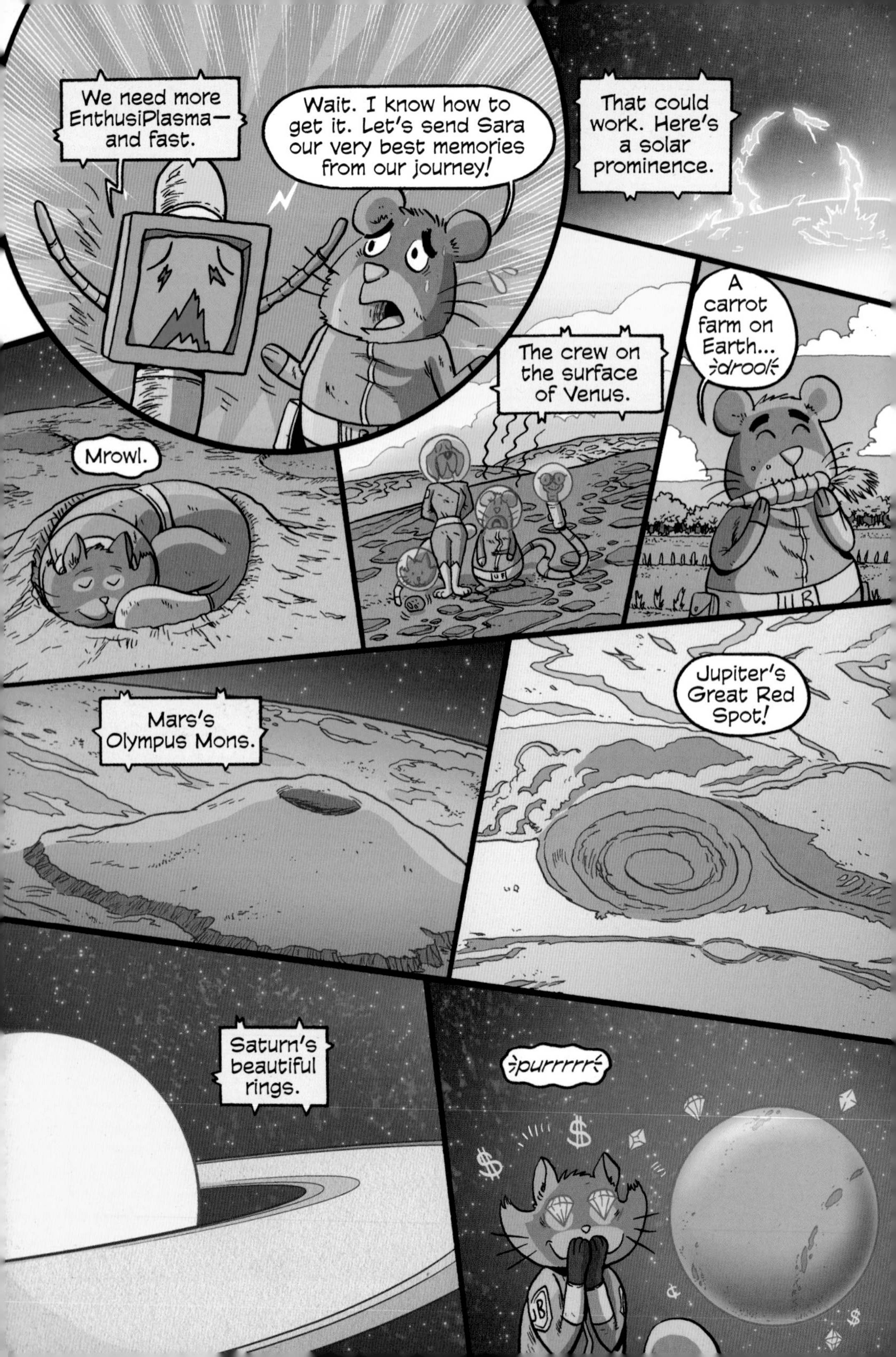

We need more EnthusiPlasma—and fast.
Wait. I know how to get it. Let's send Sara our very best memories from our journey!
That could work. Here's a solar prominence.
Mrowl.
The crew on the surface of Venus.
A carrot farm on Earth... ⪫drool⪪
Mars's Olympus Mons.
Jupiter's Great Red Spot!
Saturn's beautiful rings.
⪫purrrrr⪪

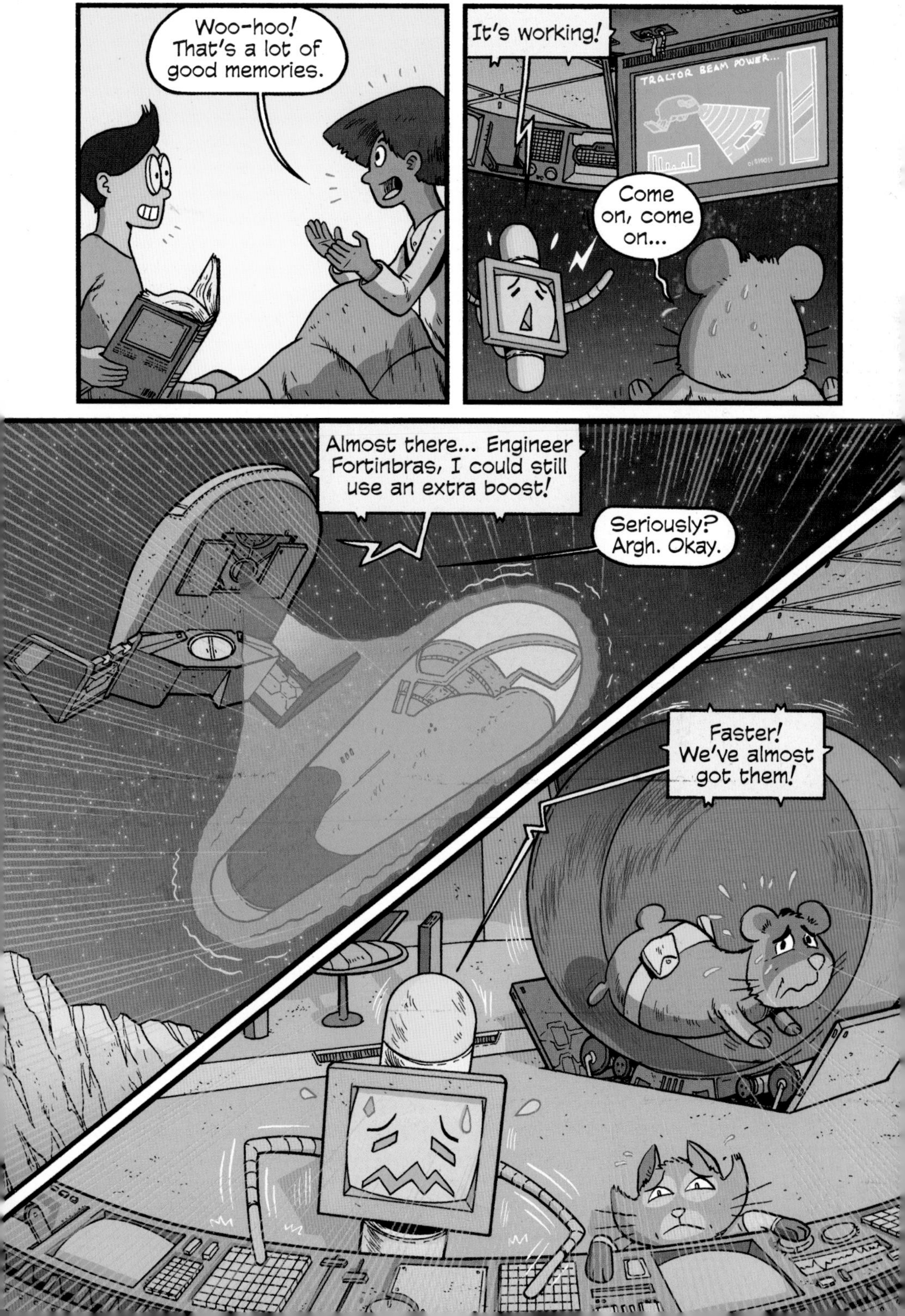
Woo-hoo! That's a lot of good memories.
It's working!
TRACTOR BEAM POWER...
Come on, come on...
Almost there... Engineer Fortinbras, I could still use an extra boost!
Seriously? Argh. Okay.
Faster! We've almost got them!

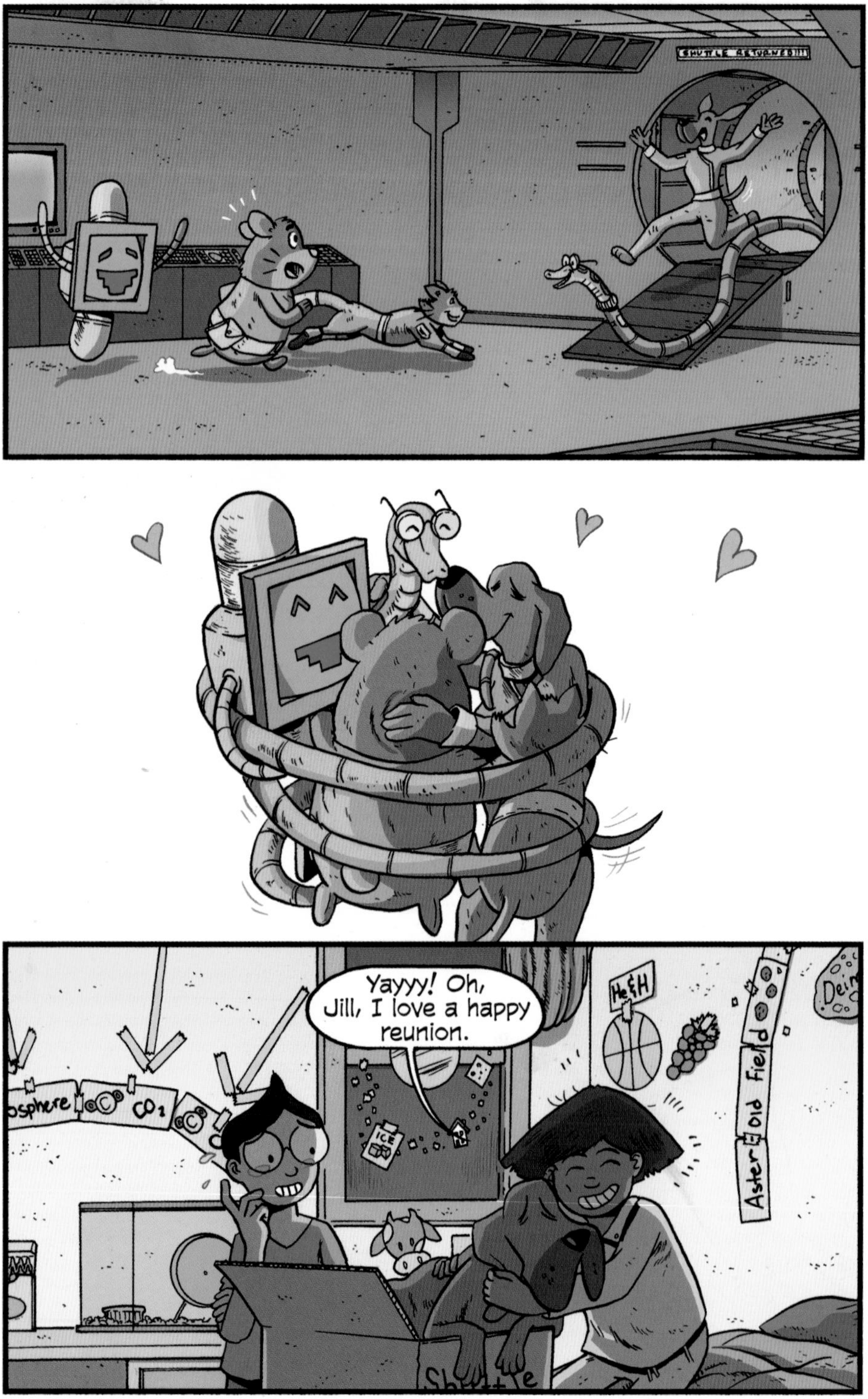
SHUTTLE RETURNED!!!
Yayyy! Oh, Jill, I love a happy reunion.

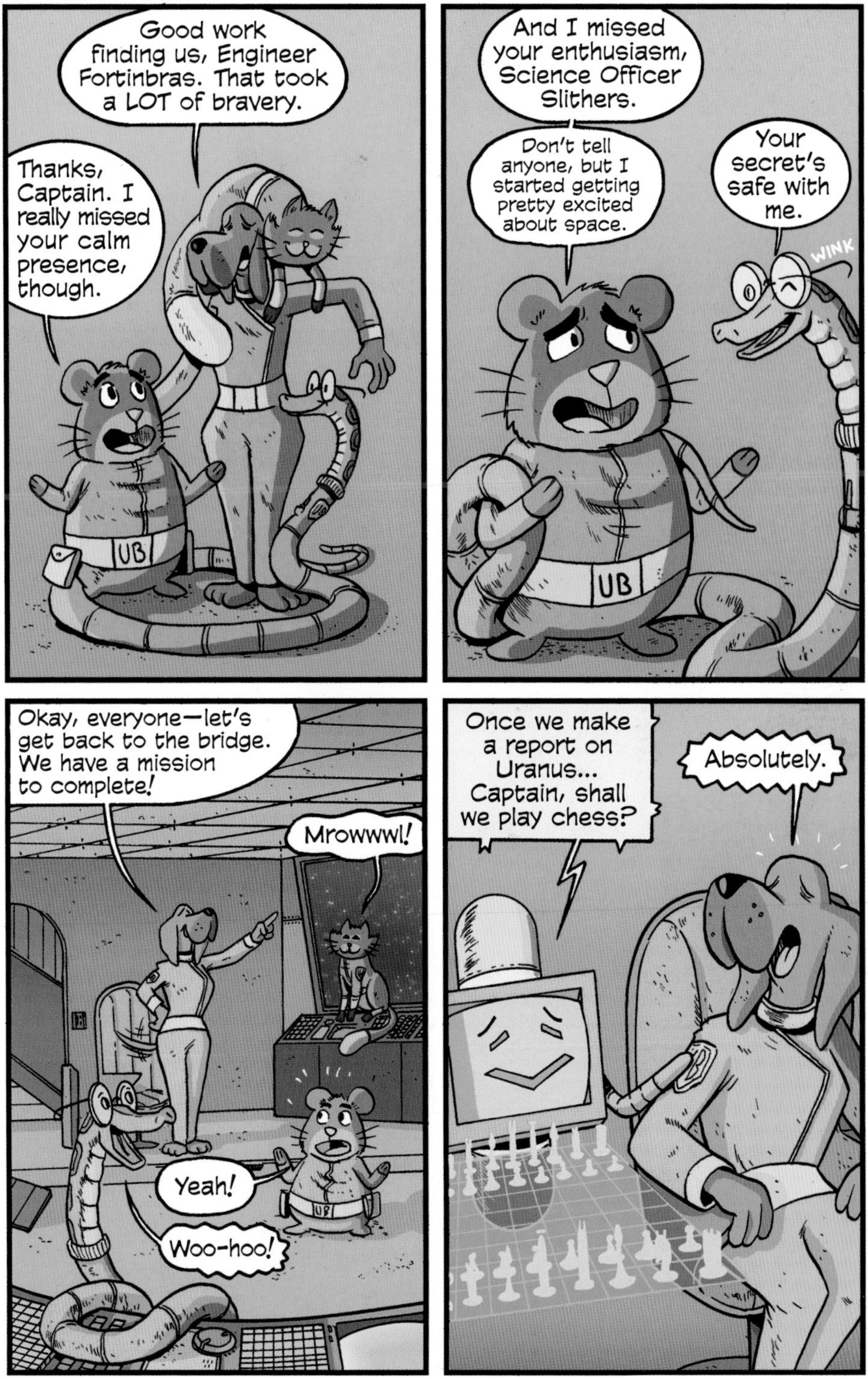
Good work finding us, Engineer Fortinbras. That took a LOT of bravery.
Thanks, Captain. I really missed your calm presence, though.
And I missed your enthusiasm, Science Officer Slithers.
Don't tell anyone, but I started getting pretty excited about space.
Your secret's safe with me.
WINK
Okay, everyone—let's get back to the bridge. We have a mission to complete!
Mrowwwl!
Yeah!
Woo-hoo!
Once we make a report on Uranus... Captain, shall we play chess?
Absolutely.

URANUS: A REPORT

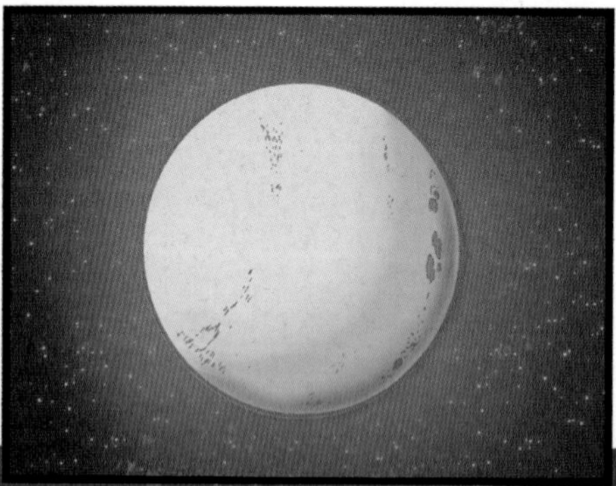

Origin of Name: The ancient Greek god of the sky.

Size: 31,518 miles across, nearly four times wider than Earth.

Contents: A rocky core; a mantle of water, ammonia, and methane; and an atmosphere of hydrogen, helium, and methane.

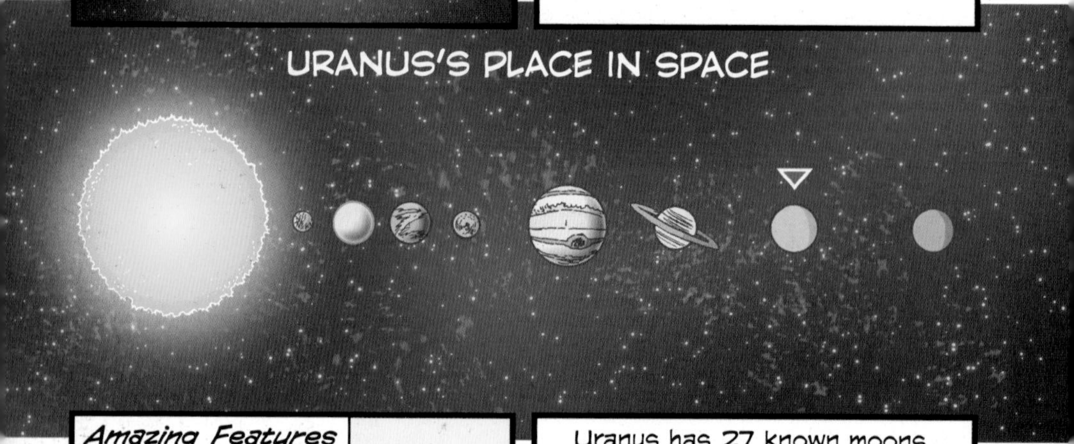
URANUS'S PLACE IN SPACE

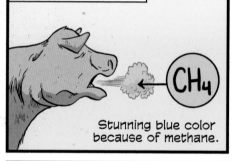

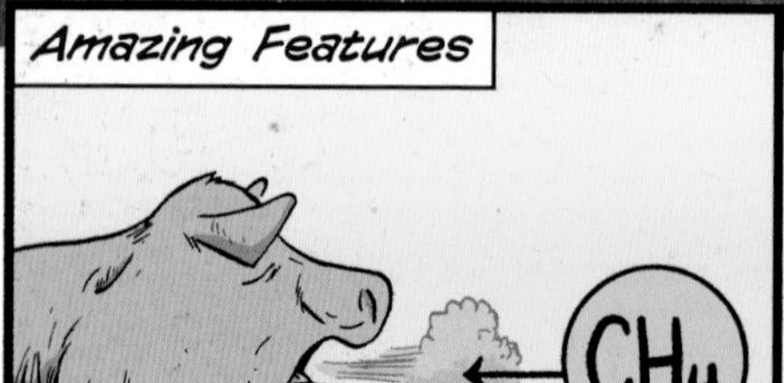
Amazing Features
CH4
Stunning blue color because of methane.

Uranus has 27 known moons. Miranda has a very, very tall cliff, and was the site of the Great Space-Pets Reunion.

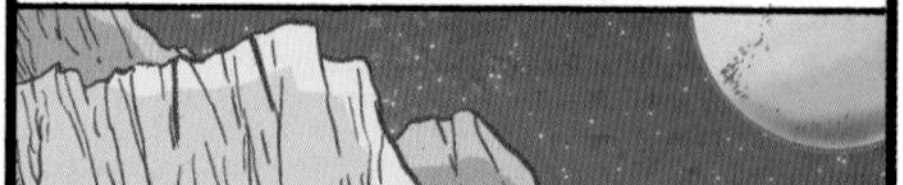

Visits from Earth Spacecraft:
Only one: *Voyager 2* flew past Uranus in 1986. There's a lot more for future explorers to discover!

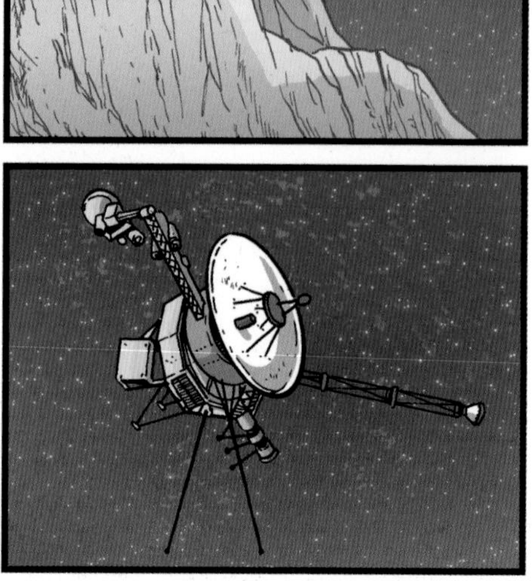

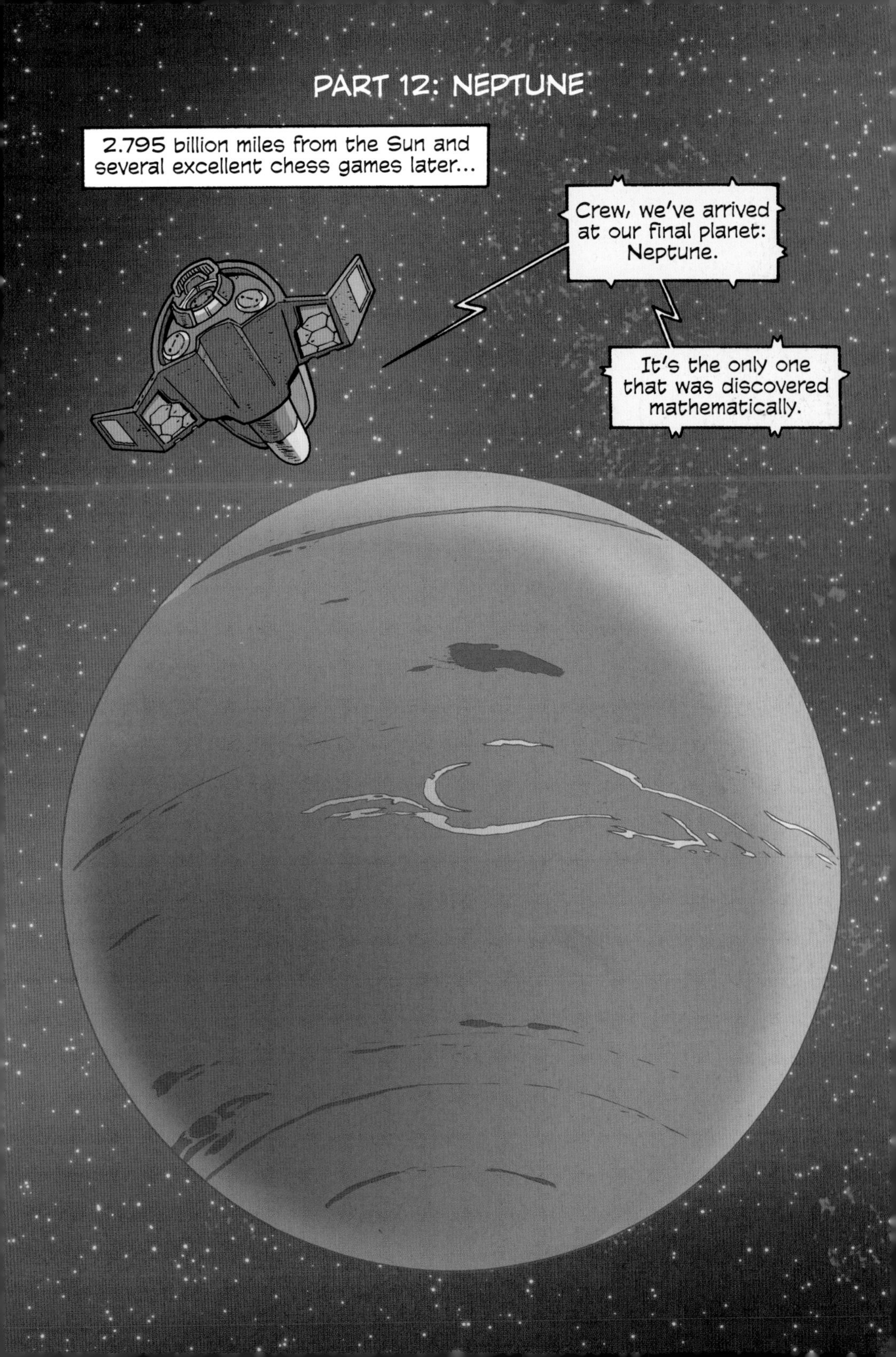
PART 12: NEPTUNE
2.795 billion miles from the Sun and several excellent chess games later...
Crew, we've arrived at our final planet: Neptune.
It's the only one that was discovered mathematically.

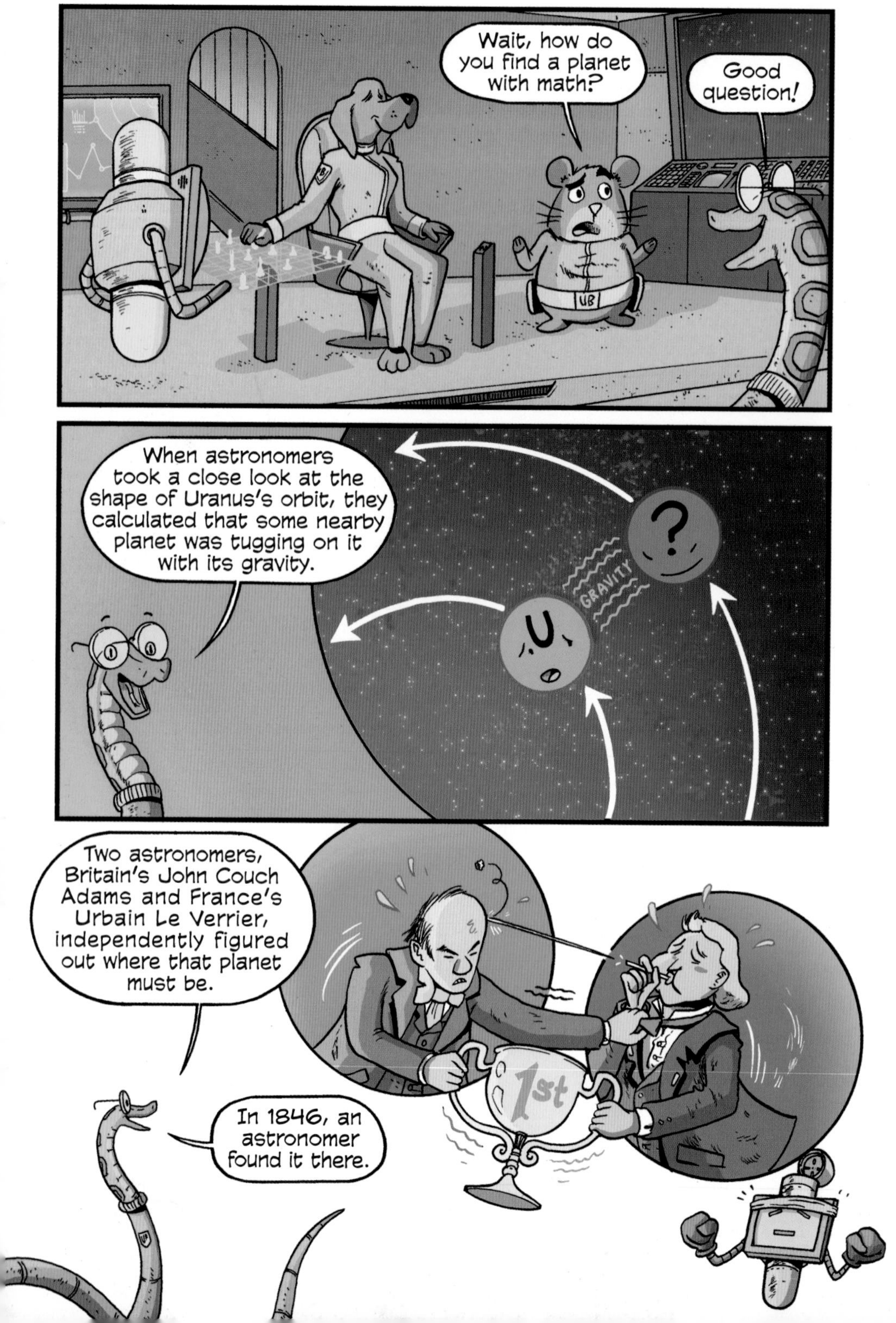
Wait, how do you find a planet with math?
Good question!
When astronomers took a close look at the shape of Uranus's orbit, they calculated that some nearby planet was tugging on it with its gravity.
?
GRAVITY
U
Two astronomers, Britain's John Couch Adams and France's Urbain Le Verrier, independently figured out where that planet must be.
1st
In 1846, an astronomer found it there.

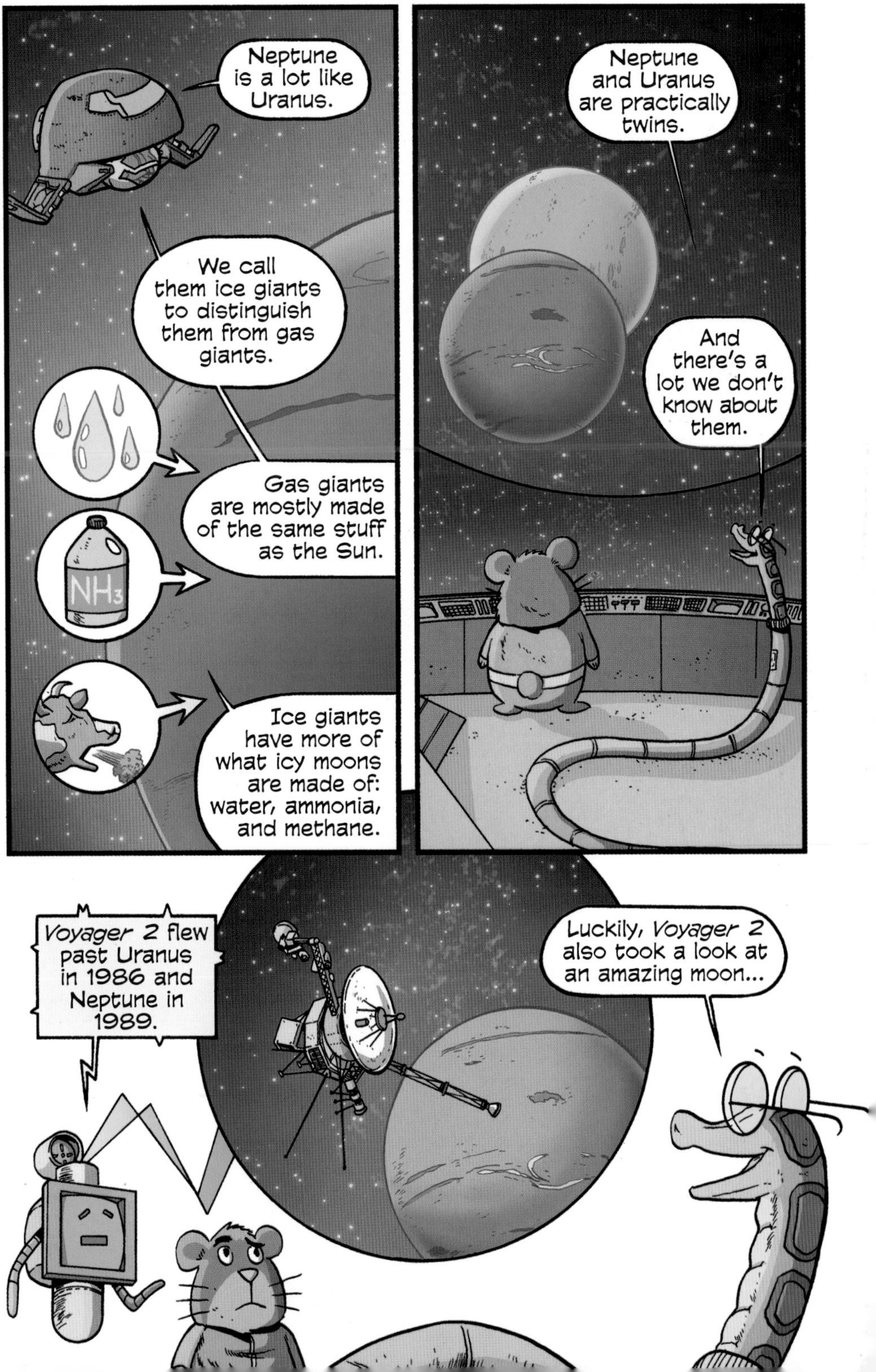

Neptune is a lot like Uranus.
We call them ice giants to distinguish them from gas giants.
Gas giants are mostly made of the same stuff as the Sun.
NH3
Ice giants have more of what icy moons are made of: water, ammonia, and methane.
Neptune and Uranus are practically twins.
And there's a lot we don't know about them.
Voyager 2 flew past Uranus in 1986 and Neptune in 1989.
Luckily, *Voyager 2* also took a look at an amazing moon...

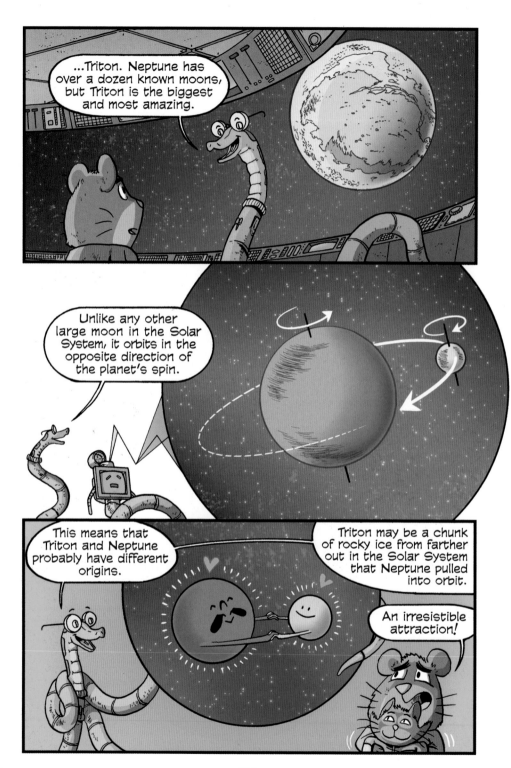

...Triton. Neptune has over a dozen known moons, but Triton is the biggest and most amazing.

Unlike any other large moon in the Solar System, it orbits in the opposite direction of the planet's spin.

This means that Triton and Neptune probably have different origins.

Triton may be a chunk of rocky ice from farther out in the Solar System that Neptune pulled into orbit.

An irresistible attraction!

Also, Triton has geysers of nitrogen gas and dust that can reach 5 miles high!

That sounds like something to see. Crew, prepare to visit the surface.

...And P.A.L., please have a talk with the Shuttle Computer.

Let me guess. Star-nosed moles?

Precisely.

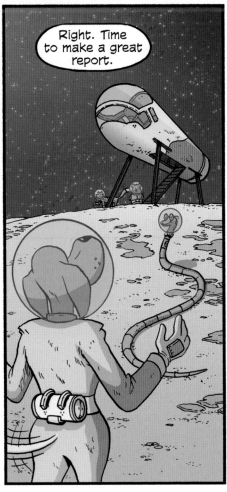

Right. Time to make a great report.

NEPTUNE: A REPORT

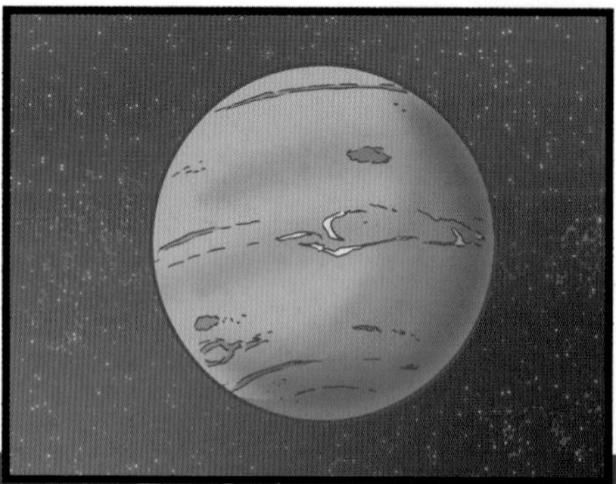

Origin of Name: The ancient Greek god of the sea.

Size: 30,599 miles across, nearly four times wider than Earth.

Contents: Like Uranus, Neptune has a rocky core; a mantle of water, ammonia, and methane; and an atmosphere of hydrogen, helium, and methane.

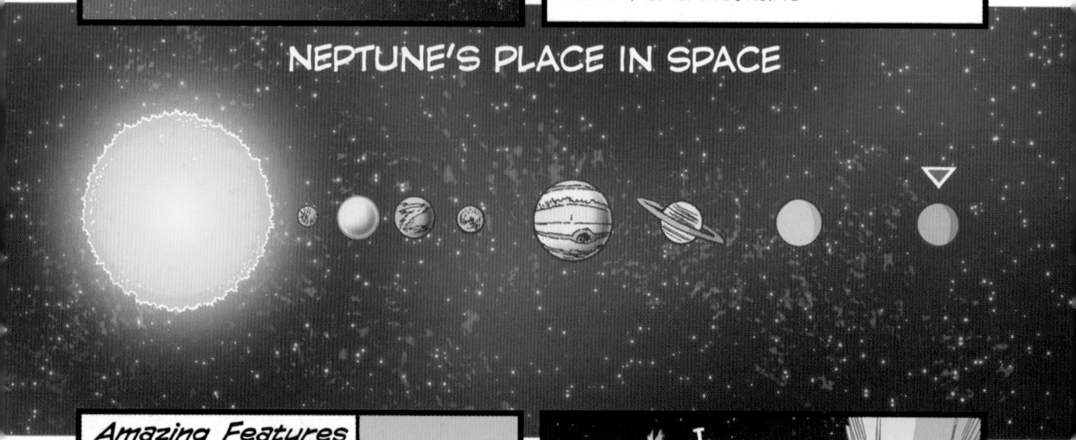
NEPTUNE'S PLACE IN SPACE

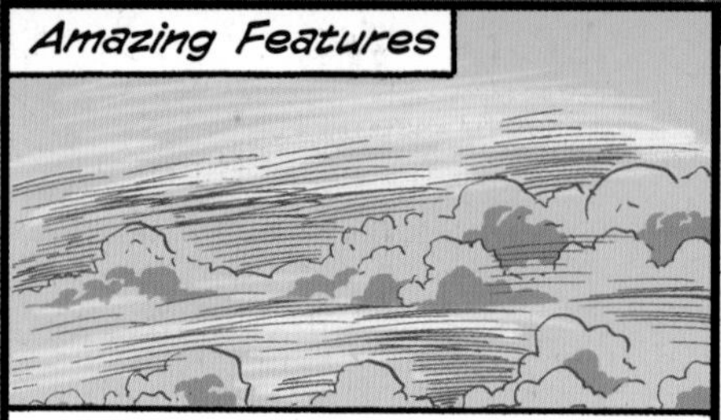
Amazing Features

The fastest wind speeds measured in the Solar System: 1,500 miles per hour! WHOOSH!

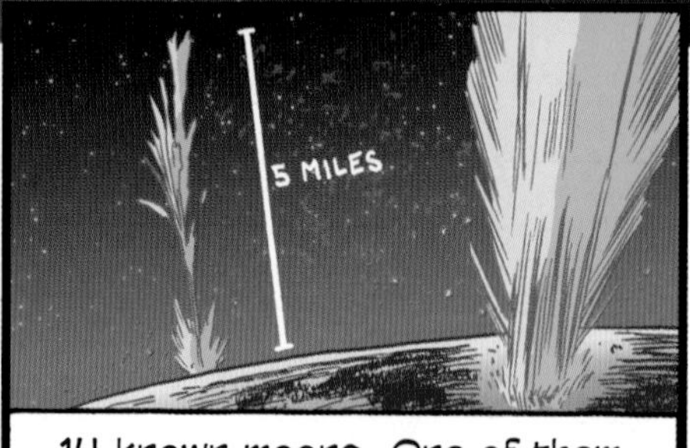
5 MILES

14 known moons. One of them, Triton, has geysers 5 miles high.

Visits from Earth Spacecraft:
Only one: *Voyager 2* flew past Neptune in 1989. This planet needs more exploration!

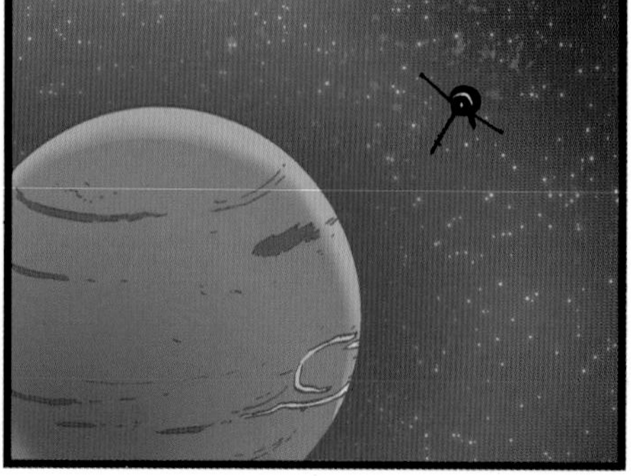

Jill, the Solar System is *amazing* and I want to explore it!

Yay! Success!

Good work, crew.

So, um...is that it? Have we finished the mission?

What do you mean?

Well, Neptune was the last planet. Does that mean we've seen the whole Solar System?

No way!

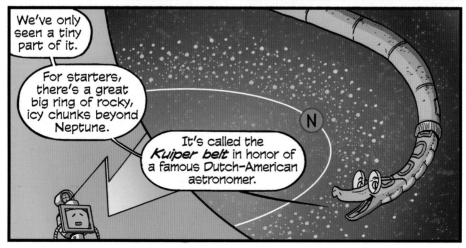

We've only seen a tiny part of it.

For starters, there's a great big ring of rocky, icy chunks beyond Neptune.

It's called the *Kuiper belt* in honor of a famous Dutch-American astronomer.

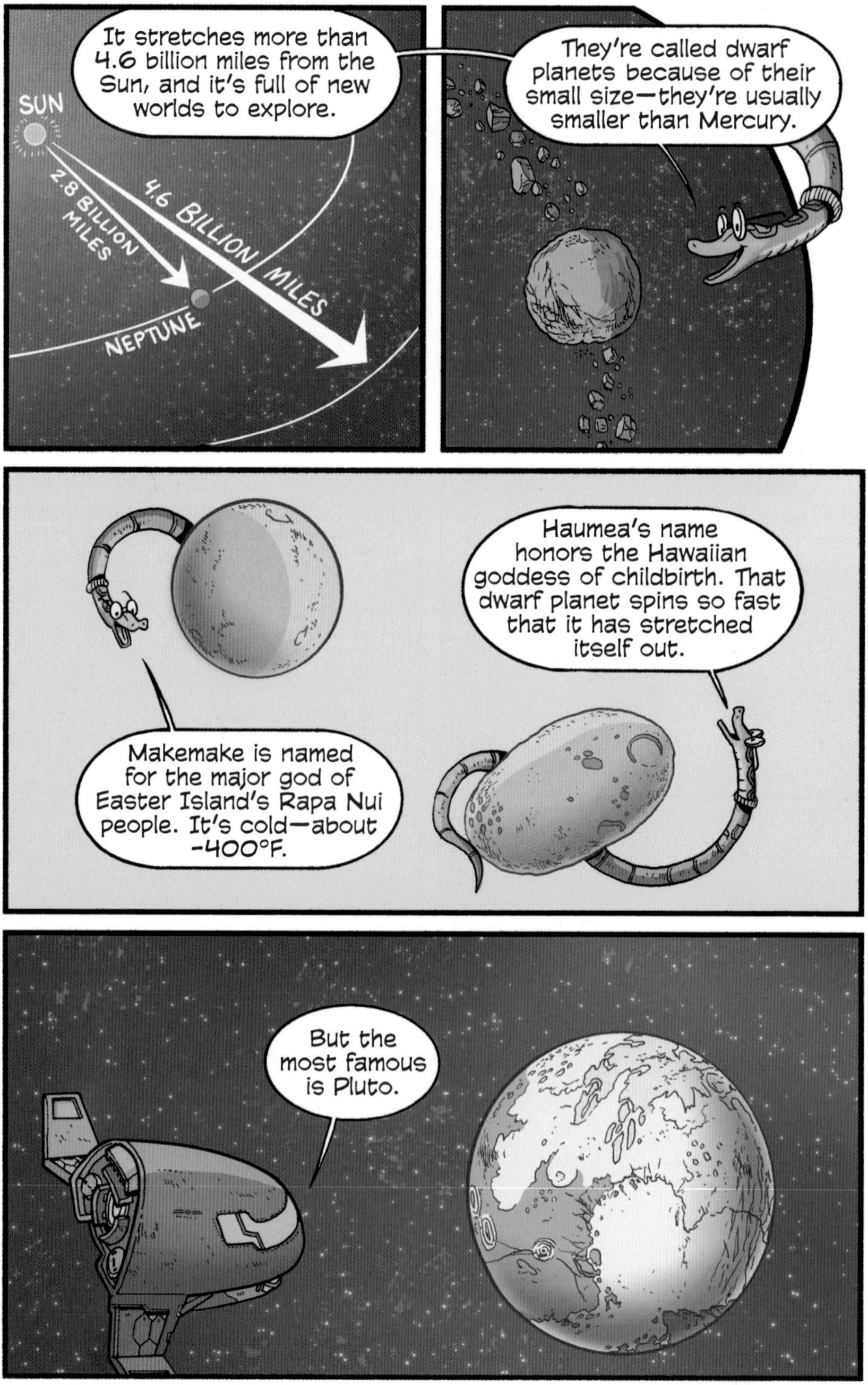
It stretches more than 4.6 billion miles from the Sun, and it's full of new worlds to explore.
SUN
2.8 BILLION MILES
4.6 BILLION MILES
NEPTUNE
They're called dwarf planets because of their small size—they're usually smaller than Mercury.
Makemake is named for the major god of Easter Island's Rapa Nui people. It's cold—about -400°F.
Haumea's name honors the Hawaiian goddess of childbirth. That dwarf planet spins so fast that it has stretched itself out.
But the most famous is Pluto.

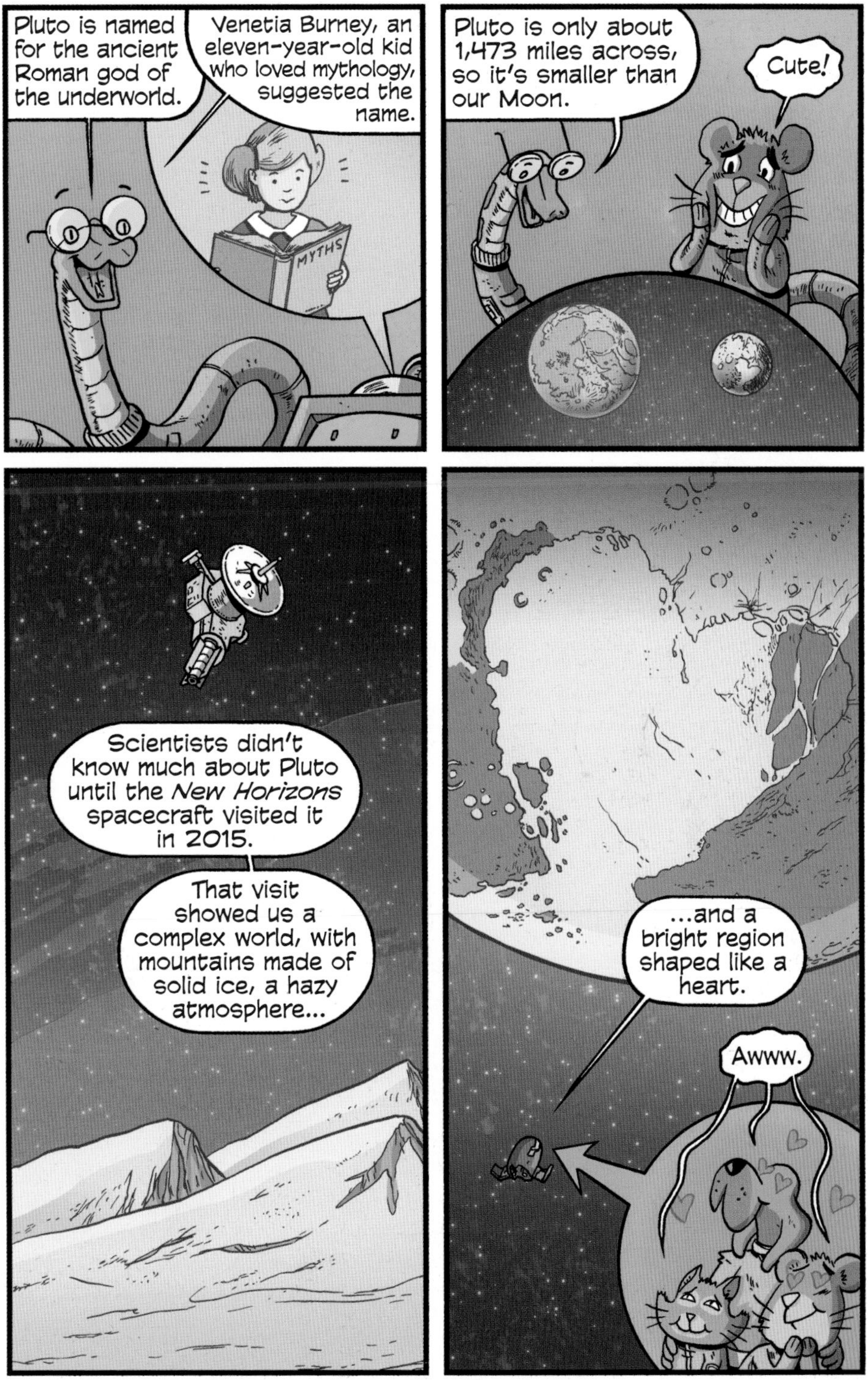
Pluto is named for the ancient Roman god of the underworld.
Venetia Burney, an eleven-year-old kid who loved mythology, suggested the name.
MYTHS
Pluto is only about 1,473 miles across, so it's smaller than our Moon.
Cute!
Scientists didn't know much about Pluto until the *New Horizons* spacecraft visited it in 2015.
That visit showed us a complex world, with mountains made of solid ice, a hazy atmosphere...
...and a bright region shaped like a heart.
Awww.

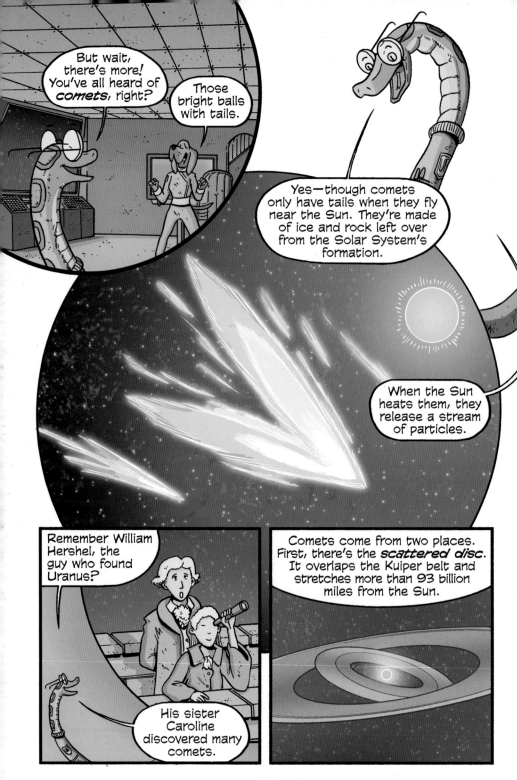

But wait, there's more! You've all heard of *comets*, right?

Those bright balls with tails.

Yes—though comets only have tails when they fly near the Sun. They're made of ice and rock left over from the Solar System's formation.

When the Sun heats them, they release a stream of particles.

Remember William Hershel, the guy who found Uranus?

His sister Caroline discovered many comets.

Comets come from two places. First, there's the *scattered disc*. It overlaps the Kuiper belt and stretches more than 93 billion miles from the Sun.

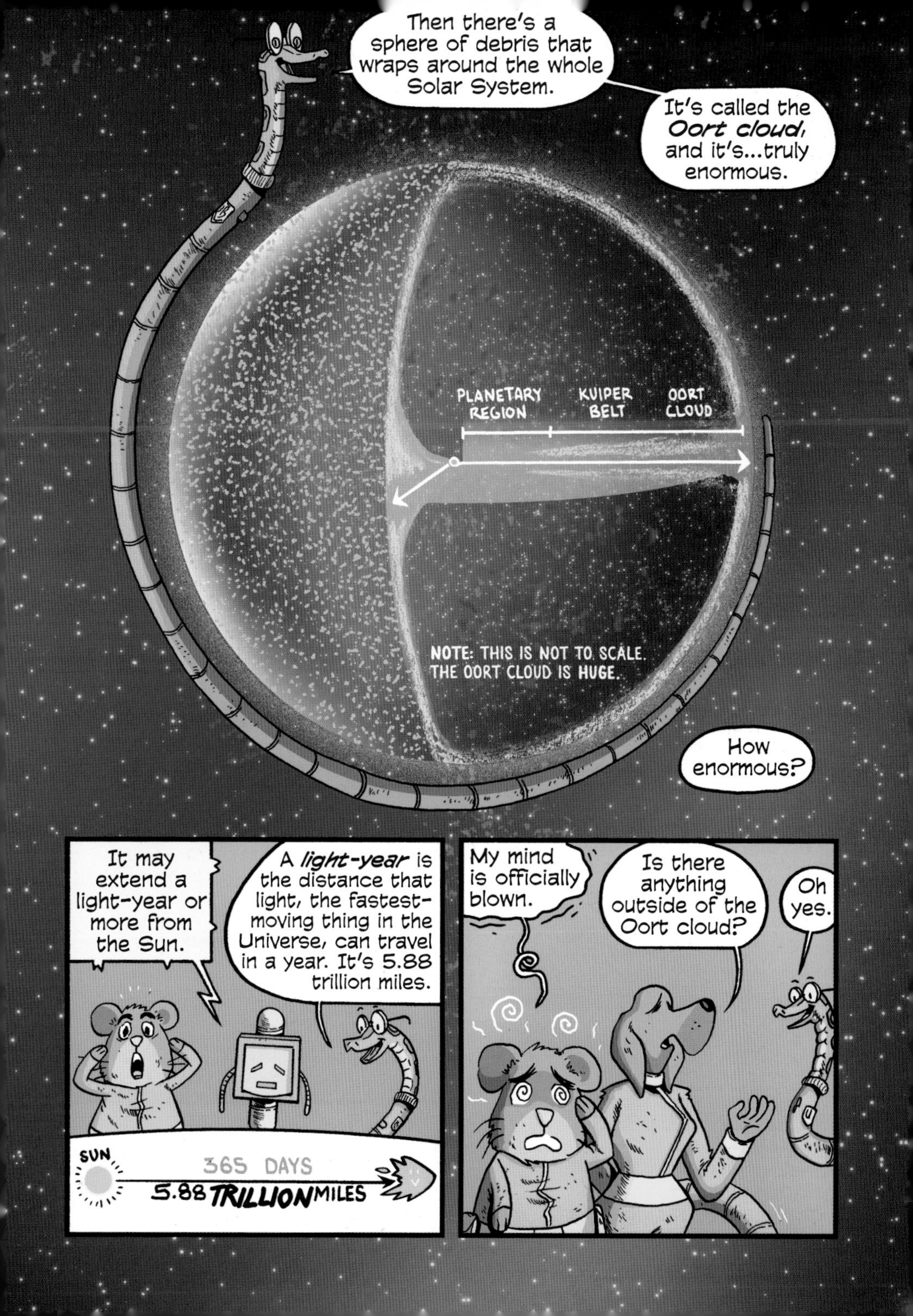
Then there's a sphere of debris that wraps around the whole Solar System.
It's called the *Oort cloud*, and it's...truly enormous.
PLANETARY REGION
KUIPER BELT
OORT CLOUD
NOTE: THIS IS NOT TO SCALE. THE OORT CLOUD IS HUGE.
How enormous?
It may extend a light-year or more from the Sun.
A *light-year* is the distance that light, the fastest-moving thing in the Universe, can travel in a year. It's 5.88 trillion miles.
SUN
365 DAYS
5.88 TRILLION MILES
My mind is officially blown.
Is there anything outside of the Oort cloud?
Oh yes.

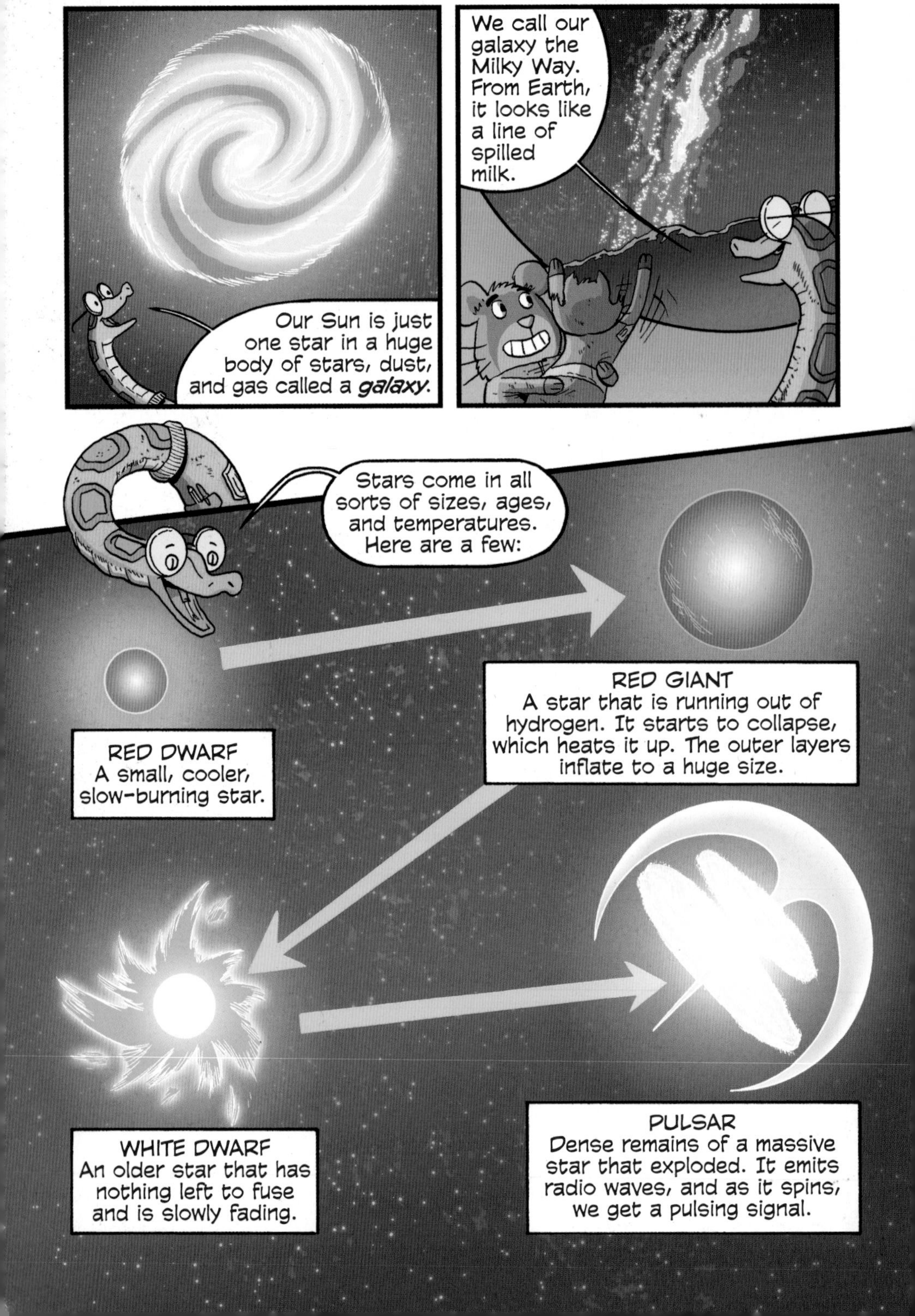

We call our galaxy the Milky Way. From Earth, it looks like a line of spilled milk.

Our Sun is just one star in a huge body of stars, dust, and gas called a *galaxy*.

Stars come in all sorts of sizes, ages, and temperatures. Here are a few:

RED GIANT
A star that is running out of hydrogen. It starts to collapse, which heats it up. The outer layers inflate to a huge size.

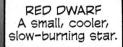

RED DWARF
A small, cooler, slow-burning star.

WHITE DWARF
An older star that has nothing left to fuse and is slowly fading.

PULSAR
Dense remains of a massive star that exploded. It emits radio waves, and as it spins, we get a pulsing signal.

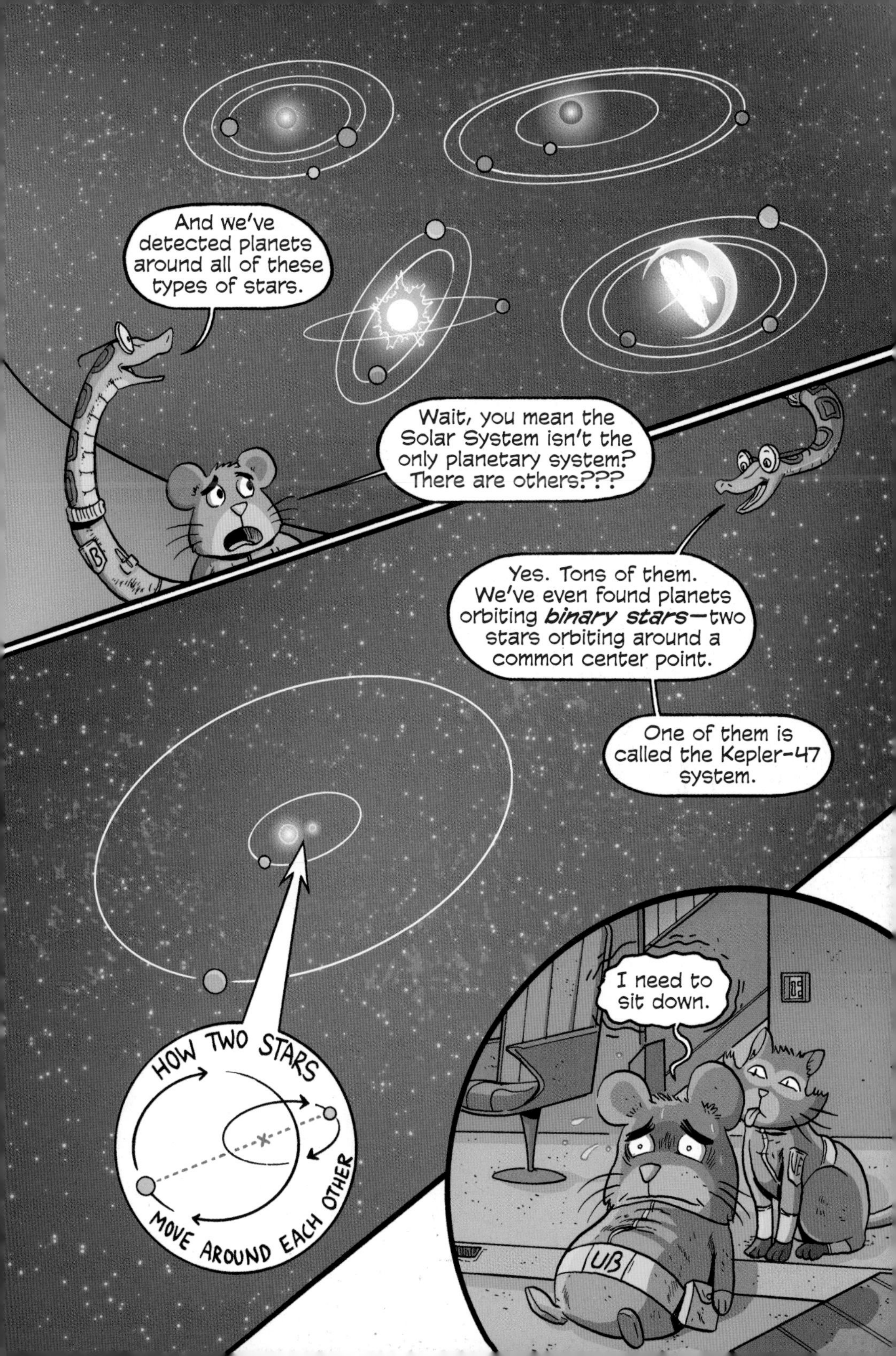
And we've detected planets around all of these types of stars.
Wait, you mean the Solar System isn't the only planetary system? There are others???
Yes. Tons of them. We've even found planets orbiting *binary stars*—two stars orbiting around a common center point.
One of them is called the Kepler-47 system.
HOW TWO STARS MOVE AROUND EACH OTHER
I need to sit down.

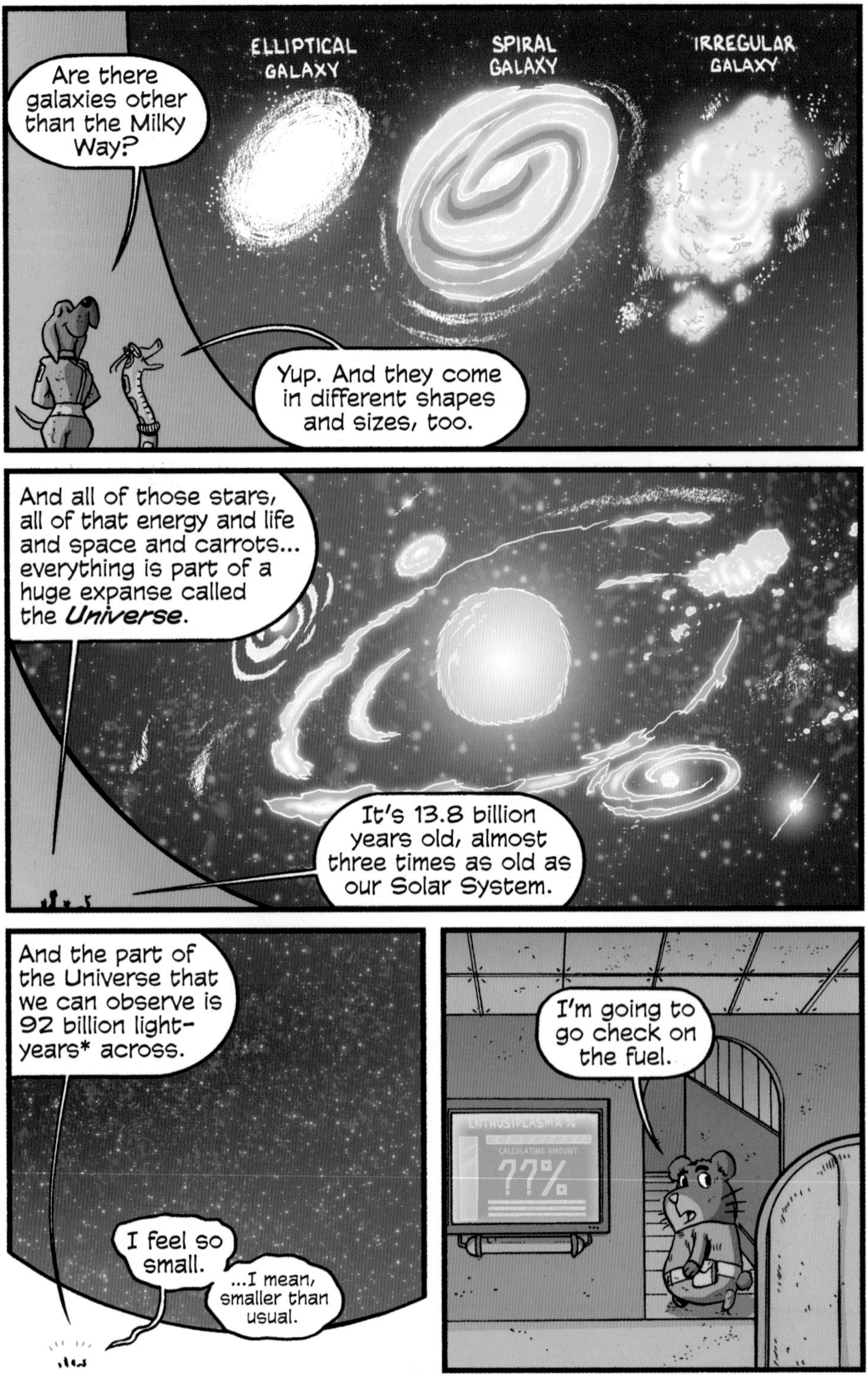
ELLIPTICAL GALAXY
SPIRAL GALAXY
IRREGULAR GALAXY
Are there galaxies other than the Milky Way?
Yup. And they come in different shapes and sizes, too.
And all of those stars, all of that energy and life and space and carrots... everything is part of a huge expanse called the *Universe*.
It's 13.8 billion years old, almost three times as old as our Solar System.
And the part of the Universe that we can observe is 92 billion light-years* across.
I feel so small.
...I mean, smaller than usual.
I'm going to go check on the fuel.
ENTHUSIPLASMA %
CALCULATING AMOUNT
??%

* ROUGHLY 5,408,335,343,330,000,000,000,000 MILES!!!

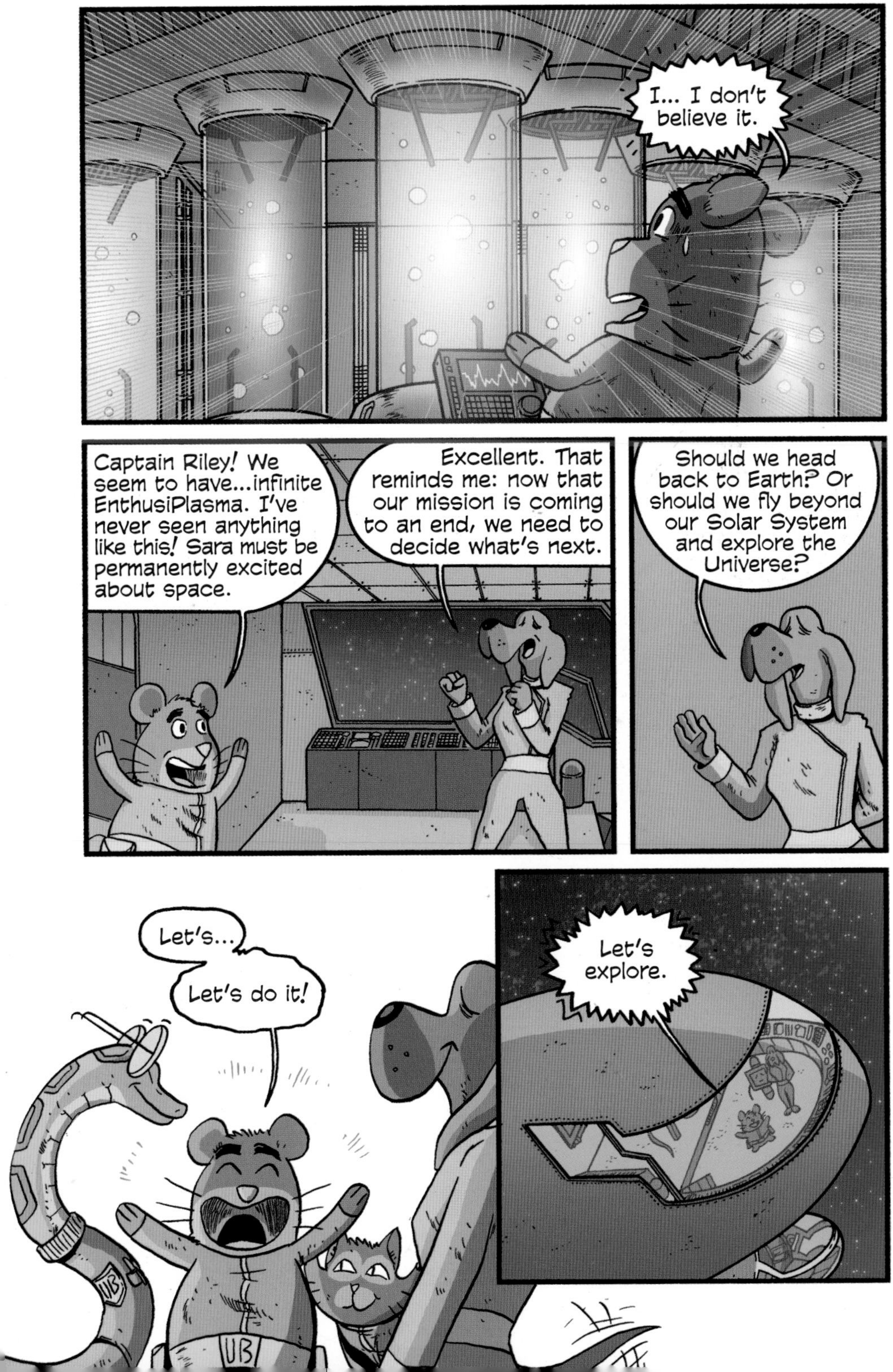

I... I don't believe it.
Captain Riley! We seem to have...infinite EnthusiPlasma. I've never seen anything like this! Sara must be permanently excited about space.
Excellent. That reminds me: now that our mission is coming to an end, we need to decide what's next.
Should we head back to Earth? Or should we fly beyond our Solar System and explore the Universe?
Let's explore.
Let's...
Let's do it!

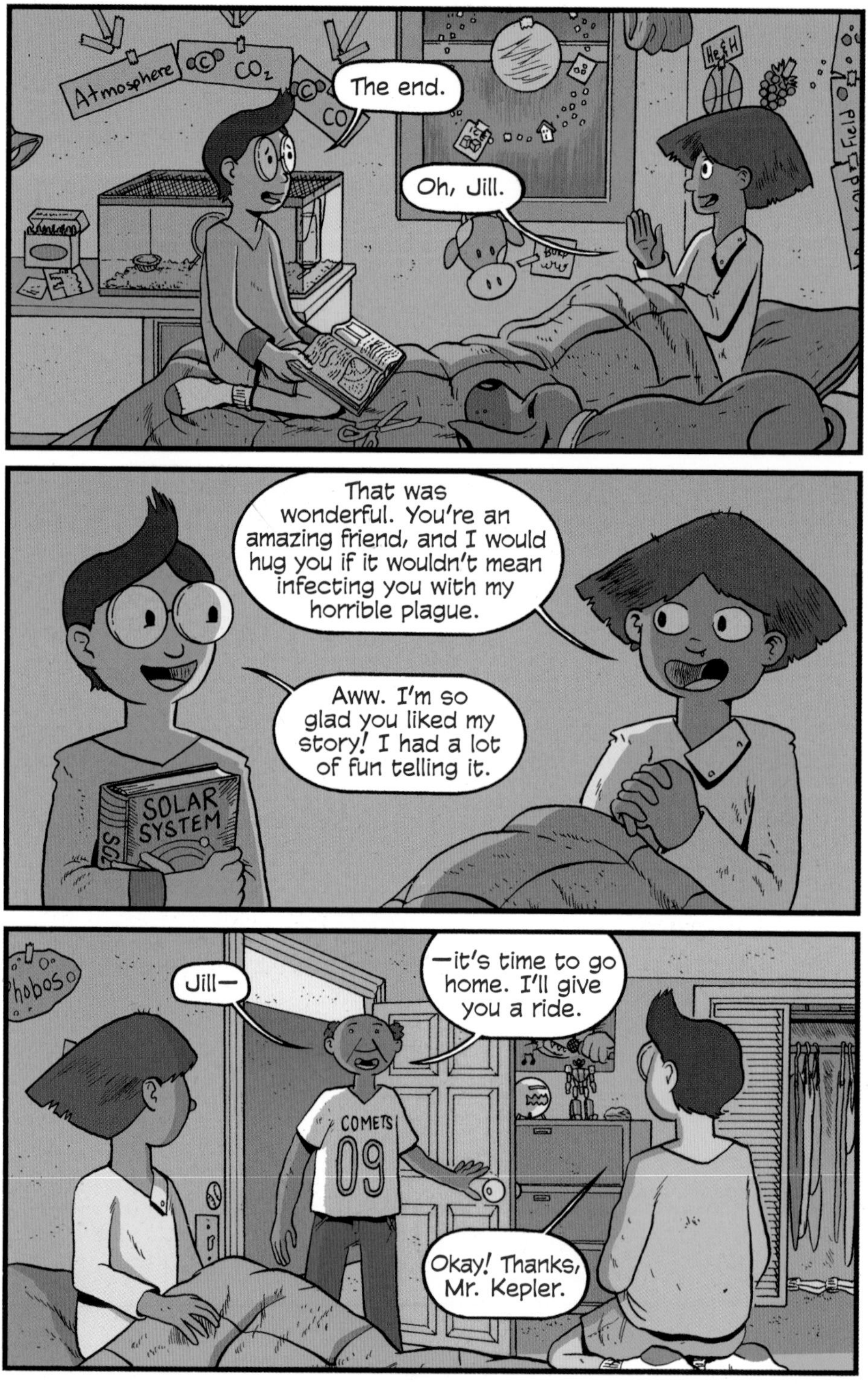
Atmosphere
CO_2
The end.
Oh, Jill.
That was wonderful. You're an amazing friend, and I would hug you if it wouldn't mean infecting you with my horrible plague.
Aww. I'm so glad you liked my story! I had a lot of fun telling it.
SOLAR SYSTEM
Phobos
Jill—
—it's time to go home. I'll give you a ride.
COMETS 09
Okay! Thanks, Mr. Kepler.

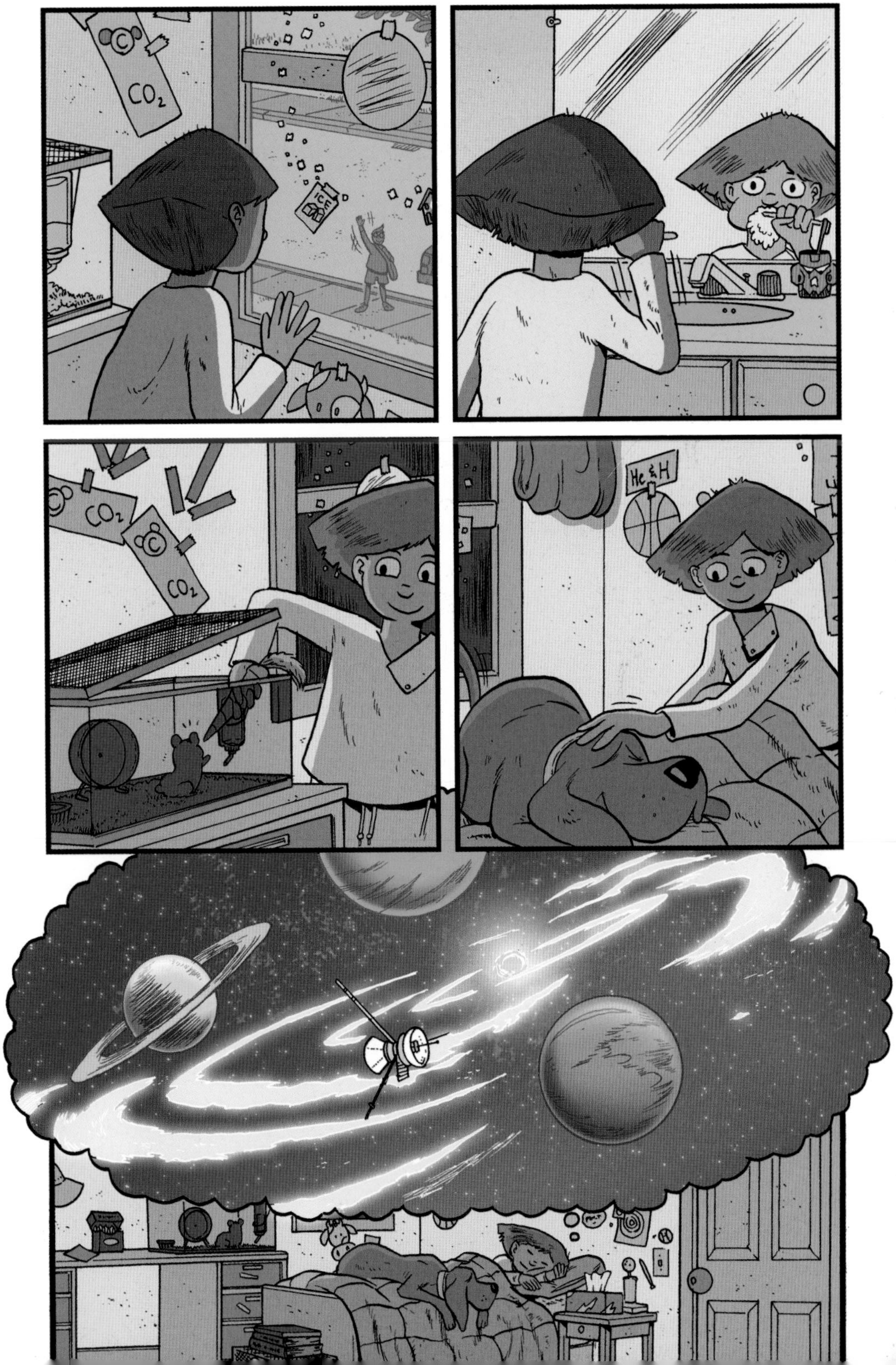
CO_2
CO_2
CO_2
He & H

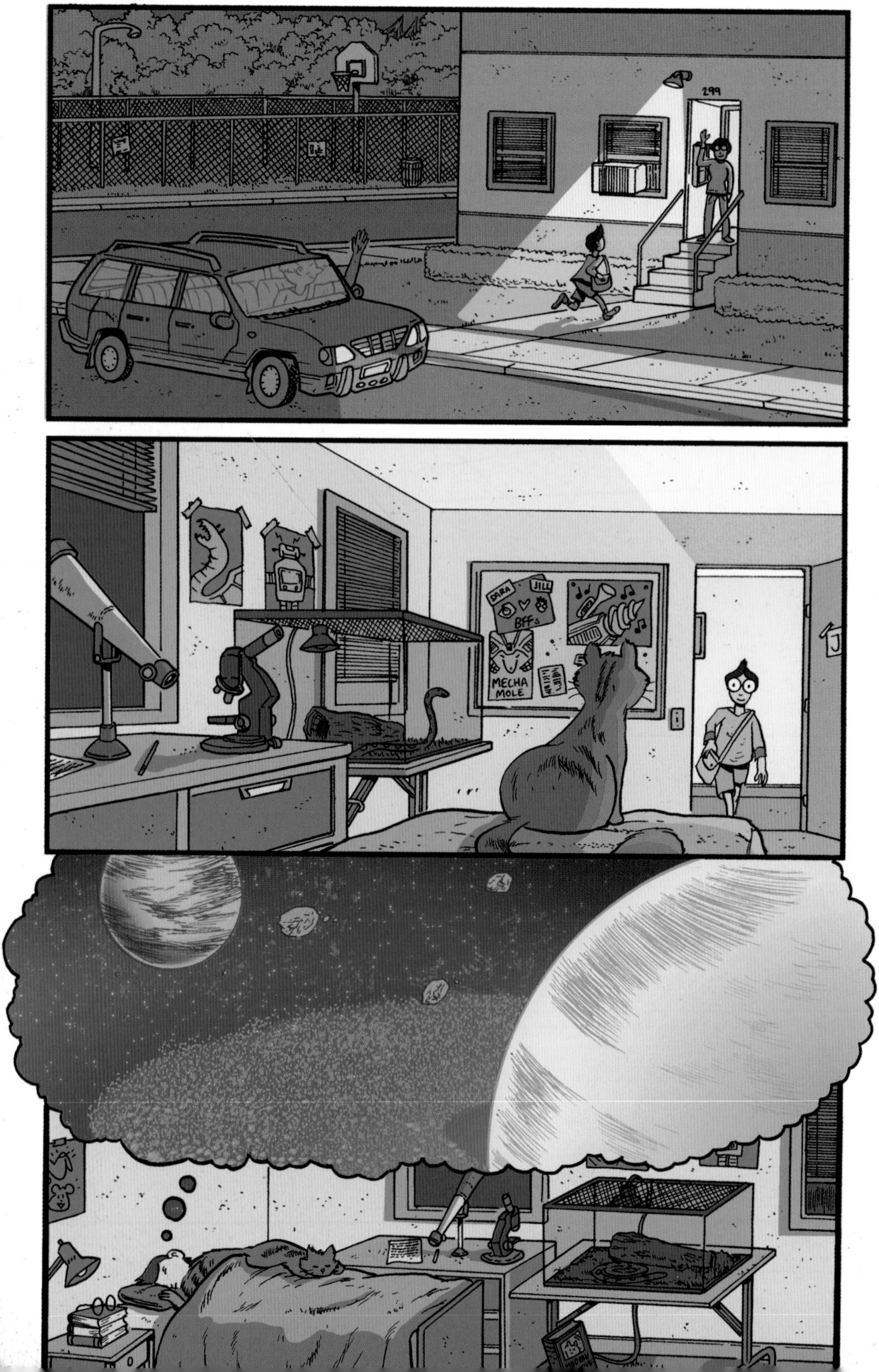
299
SARA
JILL
BFFs
MECHA MOLE
J

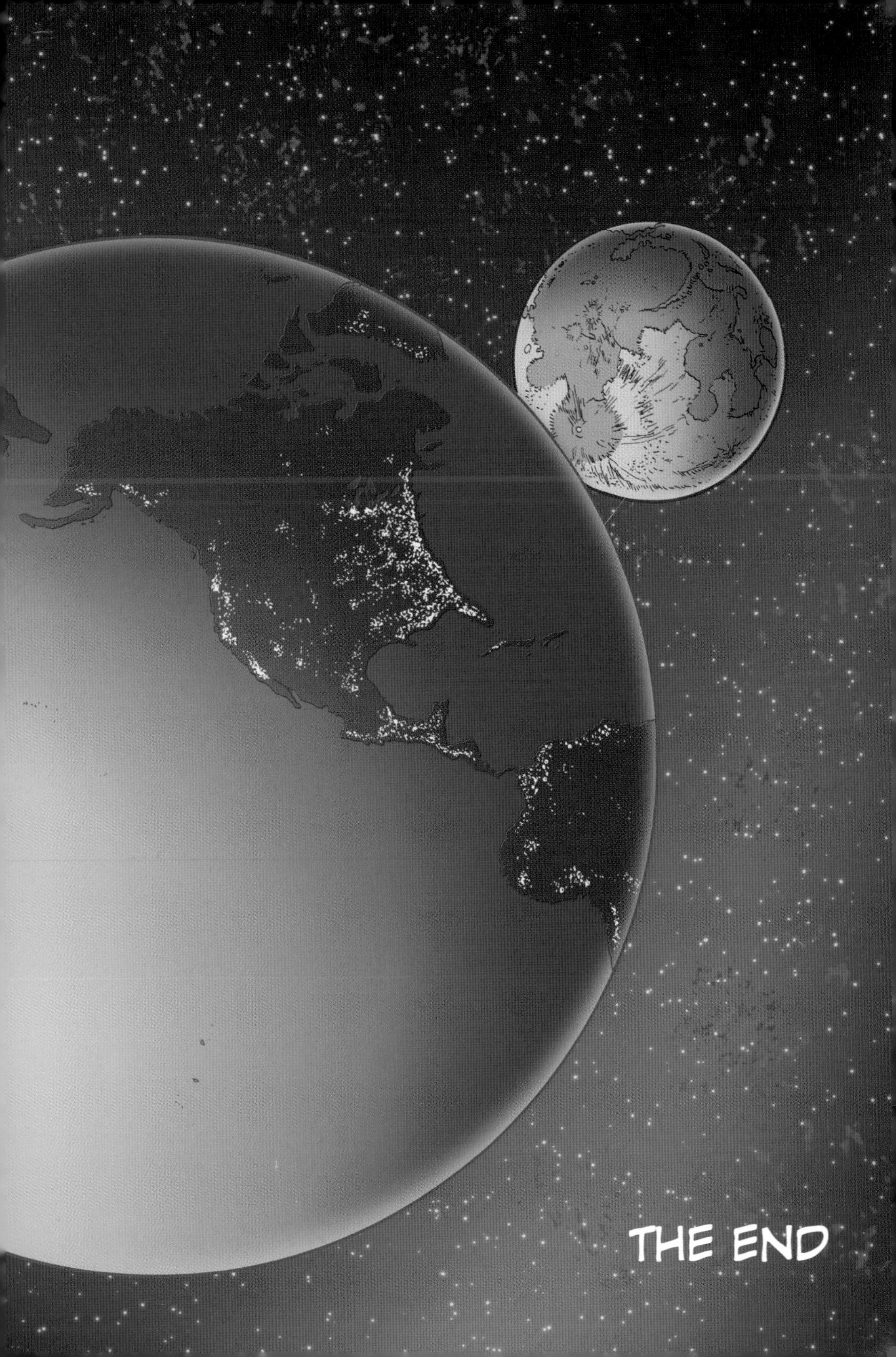
THE END

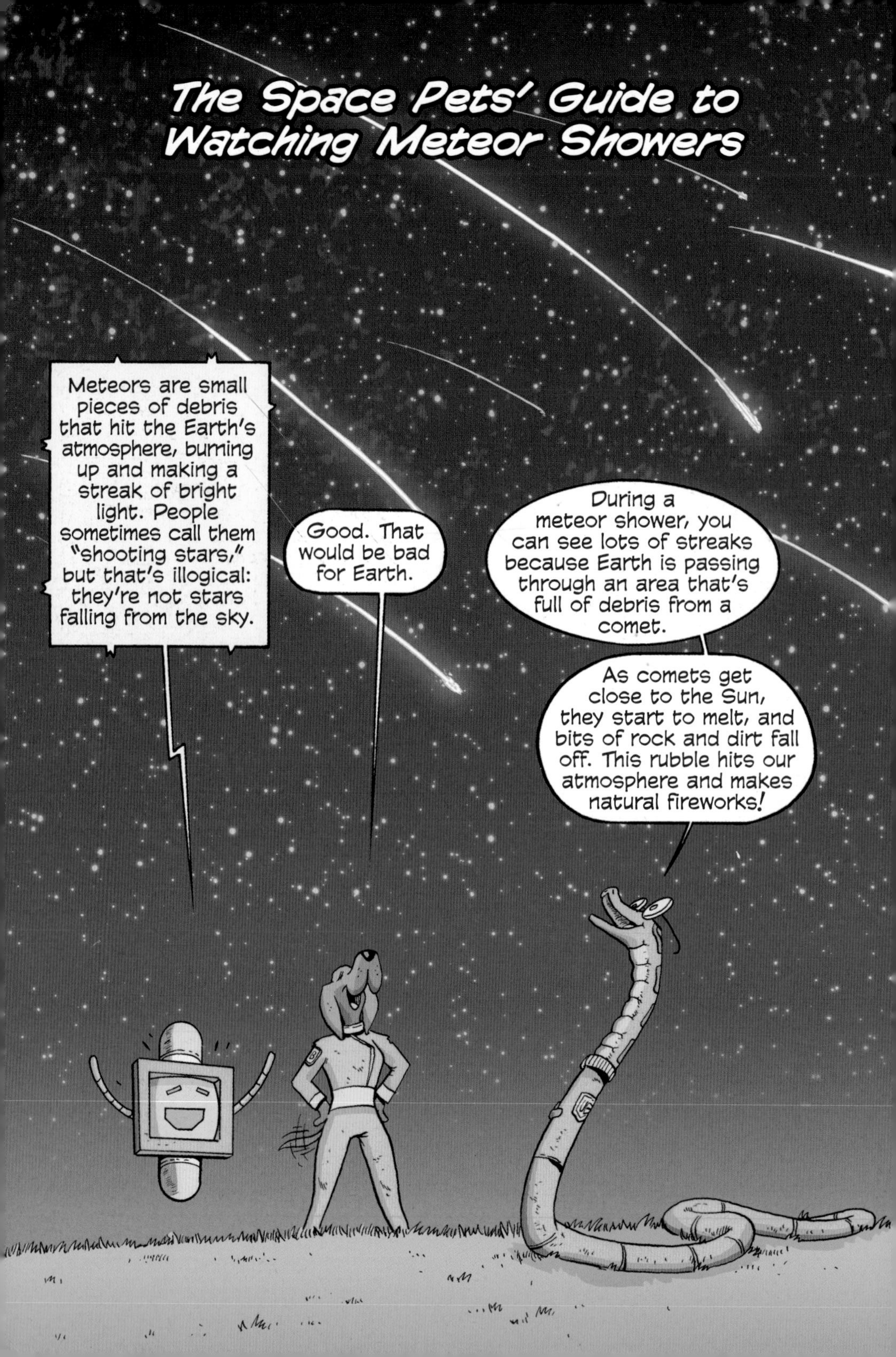
The Space Pets' Guide to Watching Meteor Showers
Meteors are small pieces of debris that hit the Earth's atmosphere, burning up and making a streak of bright light. People sometimes call them "shooting stars," but that's illogical: they're not stars falling from the sky.
Good. That would be bad for Earth.
During a meteor shower, you can see lots of streaks because Earth is passing through an area that's full of debris from a comet.
As comets get close to the Sun, they start to melt, and bits of rock and dirt fall off. This rubble hits our atmosphere and makes natural fireworks!

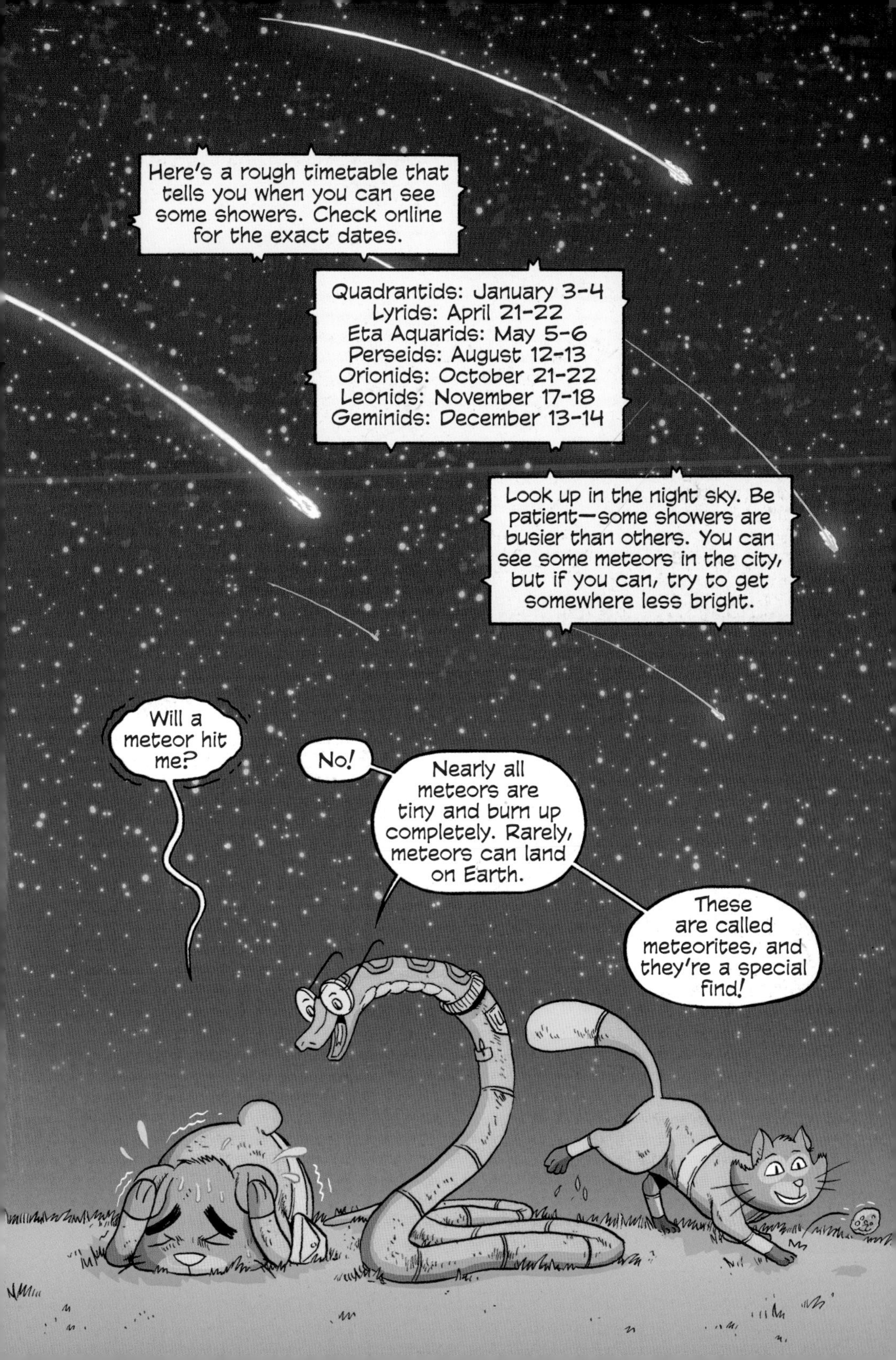
Here's a rough timetable that tells you when you can see some showers. Check online for the exact dates.
Quadrantids: January 3-4
Lyrids: April 21-22
Eta Aquarids: May 5-6
Perseids: August 12-13
Orionids: October 21-22
Leonids: November 17-18
Geminids: December 13-14
Look up in the night sky. Be patient—some showers are busier than others. You can see some meteors in the city, but if you can, try to get somewhere less bright.
Will a meteor hit me?
No!
Nearly all meteors are tiny and burn up completely. Rarely, meteors can land on Earth.
These are called meteorites, and they're a special find!

Glossary

Astronomical Unit
The average distance between the centers of the Earth and the Sun—about 93 million miles. Scientists use it to describe long distances.

Atmosphere
A layer of gases that wraps around a planet or other astronomical body.

Atom
A tiny unit of stuff that's made of smaller particles: protons, electrons, and neutrons. The number of small particles determines an atom's element.

Binary Stars
A system with two stars that orbit around a common central point in space.

Element
Substance made of one particular type of atom. Helium, carbon, and gold are all examples of elements.

Fusion
A reaction in which atoms of one element combine to form atoms of another, heavier element.

Galaxy
A huge collection of stars, gas, and dust that orbits a central point.

Impact Crater
A round hole made by a space rock that hits the surface of an astronomical body.

Kuiper Belt
A ring of icy chunks and dwarf planets (including Pluto).

Light-Year
The distance that light travels in a year—about 6 trillion miles.

Magnetic Field
An invisible envelope of magnetic force. It can move certain kinds of stuff, such as the charged particles streaming from the Sun.

Mass
The amount of material that's in an object. The weight of an object is its mass multiplied by the amount of gravity that's pulling on it.

Satellite
Any object that orbits around another object. It can be made by nature or humans.

Solar System
The Sun and all of the planets, moons, asteroids, dust, and other stuff that orbit around it.

Universe
An extremely large expanse that includes all of time, space, and everything else.